THE CHALKIES

EDUCATING AN ARMY FOR INDEPENDENCE

Darryl R Dymock is the author of *A sweet use of adversity: The Australian Army Education Service in World War II* and *Hustling Hinkler: The short tumultuous life of a trailblazing aviator.* In 1969, after a year's initial teaching in a Queensland high school, his marble came up for National Service, where he was selected for the Royal Australian Army Educational Corps, and posted to Papua New Guinea for 12 months as an Education Instructor, with the rank of Temporary Sergeant. His wife later joined him there, and the first of their four children was born in Port Moresby. After his discharge from the Army, Darryl returned to PNG to teach for a further three key years, 1973–75, before taking up a university career in Australia in the field of adult and vocational education. Currently he is an adjunct senior researcher and lecturer at Griffith University, Brisbane, as well as a published author.

Other books by Darryl R Dymock

Hustling Hinkler: The short tumultuous life of a trailblazing aviator

Extending your use-by date

'A special and distinctive role' in adult education: WEA Sydney 1953–2000

A sweet use of adversity: The Australian Army Education Service in World War II and its impact on Australian adult education

THE CHALKIES

EDUCATING AN ARMY FOR INDEPENDENCE

*How 300 conscripted Australian teachers survived
National Service and quietly helped educate an army in
Papua New Guinea while war raged in Vietnam*

DARRYL R DYMOCK

AUSTRALIAN SCHOLARLY

First published 2016 by
Australian Scholarly Publishing Pty Ltd

7 Lt Lothian St North, North Melbourne, Victoria 3051

www.scholarly.info / enquiries@scholarly.info / (61) (3) 93296963

ISBN 978-1-925333-77-0

Dedicated to Kenneth Allan Duffy, a National Service Private killed while serving with 6RAR in Phuoc Tuy Province, Vietnam, on 8 March 1970, one day before his 22nd birthday. Ken was a painter from Brisbane who went into the Army the same day I did, and shared a 16-man hut with me for ten weeks during recruit training at 3TB Singleton in 1969. Because of the proximity of our surnames, he often queued alongside me, and his Army number, 1735143, is only three digits away from mine. After recruit training, we were posted to different corps, and I never saw him again.

Contents

Foreword

Major General the Honourable Michael Jeffery, AC, AO (Mil), CVO, MC (Retd)

I would think that all we soldiers who served in Papua New Guinea would see that particular phase of our lives as a highlight of our military careers.

In part this was due to the grandeur and beauty of the country, but also to the loyalty, discipline and cultural magnificence of the many tribes comprising the Pacific Islands Regiment, and its supporting headquarters, training and logistic agencies.

An important contribution to this very positive state of affairs was the role played by over 300 Australian national service teachers who were posted to PNG to help educate its soldiers. And this, 'the Chalkies', as they were colloquially known, did magnificently.

In the dedication and professional teaching skills they displayed from 1966 to 1973, the Chalkies helped educate a substantial number of young Papua New Guineans to take on the heavy responsibility of Independence granted in 1975.

Dr Darryl Dymock's interviews with some 70 Chalkies have recorded their interesting, important and at times very challenging experiences.

In so doing, Dr Dymock – himself a Chalkie – has contributed substantially to Australia's proud history of military service to Papua New Guinea and its people.

As one who had the pleasure of twice serving with our Chalkies, may I add my thanks and congratulations for a job well and proudly done.

Michael Jeffery
Canberra
August 2016

To those who have neither art nor science, the world is a mere arrangement of colours, or a rough footway where they may very well break their shins.

El Dorado, R.L. Stevenson

Preface

A few years ago I wouldn't have written this book. What I had done as a National Serviceman decades earlier was something that had been swallowed up by the many happenings in my life since. I didn't particularly enjoy Army life, and was happy to let that memory lapse, although the experience of teaching in the Army in Papua New Guinea in 1969–70 had led me back to work in that country with my family for a further three years from 1973 and had helped shape my later career.

It all seemed a long time ago until one day a few years back I had a phone call from a Terry Edwinsmith, who told me he'd been a National Serviceman in Army Education 1968–69, and invited me to a get-together with a few others of similar background from around south-east Queensland. There was a small crowd there that day and as my wife and I listened to the stories from across the years, I not only identified with some of them, but I realised that my own 12-month term with the Army in Papua New Guinea had been part of a much bigger scheme.

I had never given it much thought in recent times, but I was surprised to learn that around 300 'Chalkies', as educators in the Army were widely known, had been sent to PNG between 1966 and 1973 in a concerted effort to raise the educational levels of the Army there. These were vital years in the lead-up to Papua New Guinea achieving self-government and independence, and our role in preparing the Army for that future was more significant than many of us realised at the time. What sort of impact we made was a matter for debate.

This information piqued my interest as an educator and historian and I began to delve further into the origins and dimensions of the scheme. Fortunately, another ex-Chalkie, Ian Ogston, had already begun to document some of the story and several former Chalkies had developed an active website where others had begun to tell their stories, and these resources provided an excellent basis for identifying some of the main themes and key issues. An Army History Research Grant then helped finance excursions to the Australian Archives in Canberra and Melbourne and the National Library.

The main sources of information for this book, however, are the Chalkies themselves – 73 of them responded willingly and generously to an online survey asking them for recollections of their time in National Service and in particular in PNG. The set of questions I sent triggered a flood of memories as if I'd swung a pick and discovered oil. We are all, as one of them pointed out, at a reflective time of our lives, and many of them took the opportunity, often for the first time, to reflect on their time in the Army and in PNG and to consider its significance for their careers and their lives. Some of the wives who joined their husbands in PNG all those years ago also generously sent their recollections.

What they provided is a kaleidoscope of memories that are not just personal recollections but an illumination of the human condition as they detail good, bad and unexpected experiences of the annual waves of young teachers the Army sent to live and work in Papua New Guinea. One of the wives said that when she arrived at Port Moresby airport, she was immediately aware that she was in 'someone else's country', and I have taken that phrase as a metaphor for the different 'countries' we Chalkies journeyed through – from the time we were 'balloted in' to National Service, though the rigours of recruit training, the anxiety of selection for Army Education, the distraction of Corps training, 'overnight' promotion, and our 'tour of duty' in Papua New Guinea, before we returned to take up the reins of civilian life after two years away from it.

We were always in 'someone else's country', trying to make sense of it. National Service for us was a series of personal and professional transitions and transformations within an often alien military environment, as well as a culturally different country, and it was inevitable that not everyone would take kindly to it, especially given that we'd been conscripted in the first place.

One of the advantages of hindsight is that it allows exploration of the political and military context within which we were operating, particularly when we were in Papua New Guinea. A particularly interesting finding from the research for this book is that senior Army leaders in PNG for most of the 60s appear to have been ahead of the Government in their preparation for independence, and that the educational scheme in which the Chalkies were involved was a key element of that plan. At the same time, for almost the whole period the Chalkies were in Papua New Guinea, the Australian Government was making decisions about the conflict in Vietnam – where some of the other young men we had trained with in Australia were fighting, and sometimes dying, in what many of the Chalkies regarded as someone else's war. From the beginning of the 1970s the Government also made decisions about the term of conscription itself, which inevitably affected not only the Chalkies but the capacity of the Educational Corps to continue to educate the Army in PNG.

A corporal at recruit training one year described a new intake of conscripted teachers as 'f***in' Nashos and educated to boot' because many of the regulars hadn't signed up to be saddled with training National Servicemen who mostly didn't want to be in the Army. In addition, we were considerably better educated than most of the NCOs, which some of them struggled with and sometimes reacted to. It was when we reached PNG that we really came into our own, because by then we had three stripes and were able to do what we had been trained for before we were called up, which is more than could be said of many of the poor sods who'd been posted elsewhere in Australia or shipped unwillingly to Vietnam.

This book tells the story of how more than 300 conscripted teachers survived recruit and other Army training, and of the experiences they had in educating the Army in Papua New Guinea between 1966 and 1973.

Darryl R Dymock
Griffith University
Chalkie, 1PIR, Taurama Barracks, PNG, 1969–70

Acknowledgements

I am very grateful for the input of the 73 ex-Chalkies who generously sent me their recollections of their time in National Service, and especially for the enthusiasm of the five who guided me along the way: Terry Edwinsmith, Greg Farr, Norm Hunter, Greg Ivey and Ian Ogston. I owe a special thank you to Terry for his efforts in establishing a database of ex-Chalkies over several years, and providing the list for Appendix 1, and to Greg Ivey, Ian Ogston and Frank Cordingley for the PNG Chalkie Nashos' active online presence.

Serving members of the Royal Australian Army Educational Corps also gave valuable support, particularly Major Mary-Lou Bates, who rightly promotes the value of the RAAEC Archives, and also the Head of Corps, Colonel Katrina Schildberger, and Major Gavin Sonsee, who arranged access to those archives. Others who contributed include Major-General Hori Howard and Lt. Col. Mauri Pears, former senior officers in PNG Command, Dan Winkel, formerly a Warrant Officer in the Educational Corps, and ex-RAAEC historian Shirley Crane. I am also appreciative of a small Army History Research Grant from the Department of Defence, which helped mainly with travel expenses from Brisbane to the National Archives in Melbourne and Canberra, and to the National Library.

For the photos in this book, I want to acknowledge the excellent PNG Nashos website (www.nashospng.com), whose contributors include: Colin Beszant, Rob Butcher, Peter Chard, Terry Edwinsmith, Martin Forbes, Neil Gibson, Ian Hodder, and Jenny Peters (on behalf of the late Geoff Peters), and thanks also to Merlyn Leader. The conscription marbles image is from the National Archives (http://vrroom.naa.gov.au/records/?ID=19537).

At Australian Scholarly Publishing, I am indebted to the Director, Nick Walker, for his willingness to publish this book, from the time the manuscript arrived on his desk, and to the assistance of Anastasia Buryak and Wayne Saunders in preparing the book for publication.

Finally, I thank my colleagues at Griffith University and in my writing group for their ongoing support, and my wife, Cheryl, who married me six weeks before I reported for National Service, joined me in PNG, and has remarkably stayed with me ever since.

Apart from the recollections of the ex-Chalkies and others reported here, however, the opinions, interpretations and errors in this book are entirely mine.

Abbreviations

1PIR	1st Battalion, Pacific Islands Regiment
2IC	Second-in-command
3TB	3rd Training Battalion
AAEC	Australian Army Education Corps
AAES	Australian Army Education Service
ABC	Australian Broadcasting Commission
ACE	Army Certificate of Education
ADAE	Assistant Director, Army Education
AHQ	Army Headquarters
AIF	Australian Imperial Force
ALP	Australian Labor Party
ANGAU	Australian New Guinea Administrative Unit
ARA	Australian Regular Army
AWOL	Absent without leave
CMF	Citizens' Military Forces
CO	Commanding Officer
DADAE	Deputy Assistant Director, Army Education
DLNS	Department of Labour and National Service
JSC	Joint Services College
MCS	Military Cadet School
NCO	Non-commissioned Officer
NGIB	New Guinea Infantry Battalion
OR	Other ranks
OTU	Officer Training Unit
PI	Pacific Islander
PIB	Papuan Infantry Battalion
PIR	Pacific Islands Regiment
PNG	Papua New Guinea
PNGDF	Papua New Guinea Defence Force
PNGVR	Papua New Guinea Volunteer Rifles
PM	Prime Minister
RAAEC	Royal Australian Army Educational Corps
RAAF	Royal Australian Air Force
RAEME	Royal Australian Electrical and Mechanical Engineers
RSL	Returned Services League
RSM	Regimental Sergeant Major
RTB	Recruit Training Battalion
TPNG	Territory of Papua and New Guinea

1

Conscription: An 'irresistible conclusion'

The year before, Frank Cordingley had sliced open frogs, combined chemical elements in glass jars and explained the intricacies of algebra and Euclidean geometry, in his first year as a maths/science teacher in the secondary department of Clermont State School in central Queensland. The summertime mercury sometimes nudged 40 degrees Celsius. Now he was shivering mid-winter in a tent in Healesville, 50 kilometres north-east of Melbourne, preparing for an uncertain and possibly short-lived future. All because he was born on 22 October 1946.

At 20 years of age, Cordingley might well have regarded himself as more endangered than the native fauna in the well-known animal sanctuary down the road. Those creatures were nurtured and mollycoddled, their every move monitored. Frank, on the other hand, had frequently been belittled and abused, and knew he would soon be shipped off to the frontline in Vietnam, where increasing numbers of Australian troops were fighting, and dying, alongside American soldiers, in the name of democracy.

Cordingley was one of tens of thousands of young Australian men whose birthday marble had been pulled out in the compulsory bi-annual lottery known as National Service, introduced by the Menzies Liberal-Country Party Government in 1964 to boost Army numbers. Since reluctantly signing on in February 1967, he'd already survived 'some bastardisation with a lot of nit-picking' during a rugged ten-week recruit training course at the Army's Singleton barracks in central New South Wales.

The 20-year-old didn't want to be in the Army. Cordingley Senior had been a conscientious objector in World War II, and although he

1

didn't follow his father's example, Frank had made it very clear that he had no intention of carrying a weapon in war, but was willing to serve as a non-combatant. The Army obliged by sending him to train as a medic at the School of Army Health at Healesville, where in winter the water in the fire buckets froze overnight in the tent-lines. Instead of a rifle, Private Cordingley would soon be carting a medical kit through a steamy Southeast Asian jungle, hoping to save lives instead of taking them, while at the same time dodging Viet Cong bullets that might well be meant for him.

So he was surprised when ordered in June 1967 to report for an interview at Watsonia Barracks, on the outskirts of Melbourne, about another possible posting. He grew increasingly nervous as he waited all day on a chair outside the interview room while a string of other conscripts was grilled at length. By the time he was called in, it was five o'clock. After sixteen weeks of saluting and 'Yes, sir', 'No, sir', he was surprised to find that the five men on the other side of the long table were in civilian clothes. He was even more surprised to be asked just one question: 'What would be your reaction if you were required to bunk in with native soldiers?' Clermont School, where he'd taught the previous year, had a sprinkling of Aboriginal children in its classes, and Cordingley had got on well with them. He looked across at the scrutinising faces of the Army panel. 'No problem,' he said.

'With that, the interview ended, and I thought that was the end of it,' he reported later. 'As it turned out, I was the only one selected – it must have been that I had had that year's experience teaching in the Queensland bush.' He never did find out why the interview panel was not in uniform.

A week later, Cordingley found himself in humid Port Moresby, with three stripes on his arm, teaching maths and science to a classroom of Pacific Islander soldiers. The Watsonia interview had been for selection in the Royal Australian Army Educational Corps, and Frank Cordingley was now a 'Chalkie'*, one of more than 300 conscripted teachers sent to boost the educational levels of the indigenous soldiers in the Army in Papua New Guinea† between 1966 and 1973.

---

* The term 'Chalkie' was (and is) colloquially used for all RAAEC members in the Australian Army; this book is particularly about National Service Chalkies – sergeants and officers – posted to PNG between 1966 and 1973.

† In this book, the name 'Papua New Guinea' and the abbreviation 'PNG' are often used for ease of reference, although post-WW2 until 1971 the country was officially known as the 'Territory of Papua and New Guinea' (TPNG).

He and his fellow Chalkies, some of whom had yet to experience their first year of teaching in an Australian classroom, found themselves at the forefront of a plan to rapidly educate a force of several thousand soldiers in a foreign land. Up to that time, most of them had never heard of Army Education, yet alone that it had a role in Papua New Guinea. Like Cordingley, they were there because their birth dates had been randomly pulled out of a barrel.

***

The first roll of the barrel had taken place early in 1965, and it happened because the Army Minister himself had been 'rolled', by his own Prime Minister, the long-serving Robert Menzies.

In the early 1960s, there had been concern for some time in the Liberal/Country Party Government about the strength of the Armed Forces, particularly the Army, in the face of increased military activity in Southeast Asia. Indonesia was on the prowl, forcing what it called a 'confrontation' with newly federated Malaysia through cross-border raids in 1963 and 1964, in an attempt to destabilise the fledgling country.

There was also tension between Indonesia and the Netherlands over the ownership of the area known as West New Guinea, which had been under the Netherlands' control since 1828. Following Indonesian paratrooper landings in the disputed territory in 1962, the United Nations became involved, and a subsequent negotiated settlement saw the Indonesians take over from the beginning of 1963. The new owners called the area West Irian (now West Papua). Since West Irian abutted the Territory of Papua and New Guinea, there was nervousness in Australia about possible Indonesian aspirations for eastward expansion, which would bring it within 150 kilometres of the Australian mainland.

Further north, the United States had been supporting South Vietnam (Republic of Vietnam) against North Vietnam (Democratic Republic of Vietnam) since the mid-1950s, and by the end of 1963 had committed 15,000 military 'advisors' to help the southerners in their fight against the communist Viet Cong. Australia had sent its own small team of advisors (Australian Army Training Team Vietnam) to South Vietnam in 1962, and marginally increased the number in 1964. In August of that year, US President Lyndon B. Johnson began to step up his country's involvement in the conflict, invoking the famous 'domino effect' metaphor of his predecessor ten years before, Dwight D. Eisenhower.

The Australian Army's strength at this time stood at around 22,500, whereas the government was aiming for 37,500. Improved pay and conditions in the first half of 1964 failed to attract sufficient suitable volunteer recruits to top up the existing force, although there was no lack of applicants. 11,000 men applied to join the Army in 1963, but only 2,900 were accepted. The Minister for the Army, Dr Forbes, said that up to 20% were rejected because they didn't have literacy skills equivalent to that of an average ten-year-old. 'The fact is that a large proportion of the flotsam and jetsam of Australian society find their way into the recruiting office,' Forbes said.[1] He blamed high employment for the poor quality of applicants.

Employment was high because the post-war economy was going gang-busters, bolstered by low inflation and impressive outputs in agriculture, mining and manufacturing and the strength of the services sector. The Government promoted home ownership, which one commentator said was in line with Menzies' vision of a 'patriotic, co-operative and cohesive society' that was also docile and compliant.[2] The population increased steadily, from just over 10 million in 1960 to more than 12 million by the end of the decade. This was partly due to assisted immigration, but until the later 1950s, the 'White Australia' policy had ensured these were only from the 'right' countries.

In the workplace, men were still the breadwinners, part-time work was difficult to come by, smoking was the norm, and tea ladies trundled their trolleys between the desks. Most people worked nine to five, Monday to Friday, and in 1963 annual leave for workers was extended to three weeks. Every census, almost 90% of the population indicated some sort of religious affiliation.

In this solid, stable world, the unsettling spectre of communist-backed rebel movements to Australia's north led to increasing calls for the introduction of conscription to boost Army numbers, including from Government backbenchers, the Australian Legion of Ex-Servicemen and Women, and even the Queensland Women's Electoral League. The RSL spokesman, Air Vice-Marshal F.M. Bladin, told an ABC *Four Corners* program in 1964 that such a scheme should not be called 'conscription' because 'this connotes in the public's mind something to do with compulsion.'[3] The Air Vice-Marshal rather liked the 'spiritual value' of the term 'national service'.

Up to this time, Australians were comfortable with the notion of conscription for military duty in Australia, but not for overseas service. The proposal had been defeated in two furiously debated referenda during World War I, under Prime Minister Billy Hughes. Like Air Vice-Marshal Bladin, in the first referendum (1916) Hughes preferred not to use the term 'conscription' on the ballot paper, but instead asked voters if they favoured the Government having 'compulsory powers over citizens in regard to requiring their military service, for the term of this war, outside the Commonwealth'.[4] The 'no' vote won with a slim majority. A second referendum the following year again avoided using 'conscription', but asked citizens if they were 'in favour of the proposal of the Commonwealth Government for reinforcing the Commonwealth Forces overseas?'[5]

After the narrow rejection of both those proposals, Labor Prime Minister John Curtin chose a more direct route in World War II. In 1943, as the Japanese moved rapidly and seemingly relentlessly southwards, Curtin pushed through legislation, against the wishes of his own party, for young men in the Militia (Army Reserve), originally conscripted to serve only within Australia, to also be sent beyond the mainland into the 'south-west Pacific'.

The next Government justification for conscription came just six years after the end of World War II, when Communism seemed to be encroaching on the democratic world: Mao Tse Tung had finished his long march to power in China, the USSR and the United States were frigidly confronting each other in the 'Cold War', the British were skirmishing with communist guerrillas in the rubber plantations of Malaya, insurgents were making their presence felt in seemingly every Southeast Asian country, and the North Koreans had decided to invade their southern neighbours. Robert Menzies, whose conservative government had come to power in 1949, decided two years later that it was time to bolster the Army through another compulsory scheme. This required all 18-year-old men to complete six months 'National Service' in one of the Armed Services, and to remain on call in the Citizens' Military Forces (CMF) for five years. Despite the country's involvement in the Korean War from 1950 to 1953, conscripts would remain on Australian soil, except for those who specifically requested the Navy or the Air Force. This six-month National Service scheme was wound back in 1957, and ended two years later.

The next bout of conscription crept up on the nation. It was one of those ideas that floated around because it seemed a way of rapidly increasing the size of the Army at a time when conventional recruiting practices had failed, and when the world was once again unsettled. Of course, the world has been more or less unsettled ever since Cain killed Abel in Biblical times, or since cave dwellers battled dinosaurs. In the early 1960s, however, the success of Ho Chi Minh's communist state in Vietnam and the subsequent commitment of United States troops to a war far from home, along with Indonesian belligerence to Australia's north, gave a credible edge to arguments for expanding the Army.

A major hurdle for the Government was that the Army didn't want conscription. In August 1964, the Army Minister, Dr Forbes, said the Government 'was ready to introduce national service, but its military advisors were unanimously opposed'.[6] On 27 October, Forbes told the national congress of the RSL in Hobart that the Government had an open mind on the matter, but reiterated that it had rejected conscription because the Army was against it. Among the reasons were that a two-year term would not only *not* provide the experienced officers, NCOs and specialists most needed, but would drag such personnel already in the Army away from their regular duties to train the newcomers. The Army also believed an 18-month period of service (after training) would be inadequate compared to the five-and-a-half years most regulars signed up for, and that the frequent turnover of conscripts would be disruptive to fighting units. The Army seemed to have a pretty good case.

But not good enough for the Prime Minister. Two weeks later, Menzies announced a new scheme of National Service. Apparently the needs of the nation were greater than the objections from the military. The PM said the Government had come to the 'irresistible conclusion' that the strategic position of Australia in the previous 12 months had deteriorated.[7]

On 10 November 1964, the eve of Remembrance Day, Menzies told a packed House of Representatives that from January the following year all 20-year-old men would be required to register for National Service and that a birthdate ballot would be used to select 4200 recruits to begin training in the second half of 1965, and 6900 annually thereafter. Those selected would undertake two years' full-time service, during which time they would be liable for 'special overseas service', followed by three years part-time in the Army Reserve.

According to Billy McMahon, who had held the post of Minister for Labour and National Service since 1958, the Government had received a 'new strategic appreciation' on 5 November, resulting in a decision to increase the size of the Army to 37,500 by the end of 1966.[8] 'It was immediately apparent that in order to do this, it was essential to introduce selective National Service training,' he said. It's amazing what one document can do to make the path ahead 'immediately apparent', when it wasn't quite as clear a fortnight before.

Meanwhile, the Army Minister, Dr Forbes, scrambling for credibility, could only echo his leader's words. He told Parliament that the Government had 'no alternative' to the introduction of National Service, and argued it was the only way that Australia could 'meet its defence commitments in the deteriorating situation in Southeast Asia'.[9]

Itself desperate for traction, the Labor Opposition argued that the move was a political device to improve the Government's chances in the half-Senate election due on 5 December rather than a military strategy. The party leader, Arthur Calwell, said Labor 'absolutely and utterly opposed conscription of young Australians for overseas service in peacetime'.[10]

The *Canberra Times*, which for months had been urging the Government to introduce conscription, was predictably delighted. 'It would seem very possible that the Military Board or the Chiefs of Staff Committee may have continued to recommend against National Service,' the newspaper's Defence Correspondent wrote. 'If they did, the Government was right to ignore or overrule them.'[11] The Associated Chamber of Manufactures was also pleased. Its Director, Mr R.W.C. Anderson, saw the decision as realistic and didn't think it would cause any serious disruption to Australian industry. He suggested that 'two years' military training will improve the character of many of these young men and make them better employees for the future'.[12]

The Government announced that the famous barrel used in Melbourne to choose winners of Tattersalls' lottery for more than 80 years, would be commandeered for selecting men for National Service. Minister McMahon claimed the new system had 'the great virtue of being simple, equitable and easily understood by those affected and it does not lend itself to any manipulation.'[13] However, the use of a lottery barrel, normally used to pick winners of massive fortunes, to choose birthdates that would potentially commit young Australian men to two years enforced service, and possibly to frontline action, had a curious air of game-playing about it. Calwell called it 'Russian roulette'.[14] Cartoonist Michael Leunig, whose number came up, said there was a joviality about the process that he found insulting. Other critics termed it the 'Unlucky Dip' and the 'Lottery of Death'.

***

Around the country, men born in 1945 and in the years immediately after (the first of the 'Baby Boomers') heard the news about 'National Service' with varying degrees of delight, horror, uncertainty and apathy. Most of us training for future careers at technical colleges and universities or undertaking apprenticeships were relieved to see there was provision for temporary deferments until we had completed our initial qualification. But we couldn't defer past age 26, unless we were in a longer university course, such as Medicine.

In any case, since the call-up age was 20, and some school leavers had already completed a two-year teacher training course, it was inevitable there would be teachers conscripted from the first intake onwards. Little did we know what was in store for us. What we soon did know was that at the end of April 1965, the Prime Minister committed the first Australian combat troops to Vietnam, a whole battalion of them, along with an armoured personnel carrier troop, a signals troop and a logistic support company. It was officially 'undeclared', but Australia was at war. And the first intake of 'Nashos' would conveniently begin training in June.

Those of us still doing teacher training hoped we didn't fail a course, since Billy McMahon told us our deferments depended on us being 'diligent' in our studies. Even when we finished training we knew that we still had to take our chances with the lottery; only a fraction of us actually wanted our birthdates pulled out. Graham Leader, a Western Australian who'd just finished training to be a high school teacher, waited anxiously to see if his number would come up. 'Two years isn't a long time in your life,' he said, 'but at age 20 it can be significant.'

2

Called up: Winning the lottery

Babies have a habit of coming into the world whenever they're ready to push their heads and shoulders through an impossibly small opening, often confounding the best predictions of doctors and parents alike. It's probably the only time in their lives that sort of wilfulness will be tolerated – children soon discover that their birthdates determine such critical events as when they can begin school, hold a driver's licence, and (legally) have their first glass of alcohol. In my case, it also decided whether or not I'd be conscripted into the Army for two years.

My father had enlisted as a regular soldier in the Australian Army before the Second World War, and served in the Artillery as a Gunner and Bombardier. Like many of his generation, he'd completed only primary schooling, but had good practical skills from working on his uncle's farm and as a sawmill hand. He might have stayed in the Army beyond the end of the war if he hadn't met my mother at a wartime Red Cross dance in Brisbane. They were married in 1943, and I arrived in April 1945, the month that American bombers sank the immense Imperial Japanese Navy battleship, *Yamato*, 300 kilometres north of Okinawa. Four months later, the Japanese surrendered, and the war in the Pacific was over.

With my birthdate, I was eligible for the first National Service intake: males born between 1 January and 30 June 1945. Across Australia we were required to register with the local office of Department of Labour and National Service (DLNS) over a two-week period. The first draw from Tattersall's barrel took place in Melbourne on 10 March 1965. There were 181 marbles in the barrel, each marked with two dates from the first half of the year. For every lottery, DLNS officers pre-determined the number of marbles to be drawn out, taking into account the total number of servicemen needed and estimates of the number likely to be exempted or deferred or declared medically unfit.

On this first occasion, Victorian Liberal MP Ewen Mackinnon drew 91 marbles, watched over by his Liberal colleague, Don Chipp, later to gain fame in another political party for his promise to 'keep the bastards honest'. One of the marbles Mackinnon pulled out that day with a pronged stick was marked '7 April', my birthday. Like the other 8,919 born on the dates drawn that day, I was now 'balloted in' – eligible for National Service. I had won the lottery. Ironically, our birthdates also prescribed what we couldn't do at that time: vote for or against the politicians who ran the country (and the lottery), or have a beer. We had to be 21 for that. 'No vote, no voice, no choice!' the protestors' banners read as they marched the streets.

Those whose birthdates were not drawn were 'balloted out' and could go on living their lives without the shadow of conscription hanging over them. The same procedure was used every six months for the next eight years.

I discovered later than my chances of being balloted in were higher for that first cohort (53%) than for any subsequent one, with the percentage dropping to 36% for those born in the second half of 1945, and to just 17% for men born in the first half of 1950. The chance of being selected for the Army over the eight years of the conscription lottery averaged around 26%. That equates to the chance of winning a mid-level prize in today's Tattslotto with 3 winning numbers plus 1 or 2 supplementary numbers over 12 games; the chance of winning the major prize with a single ticket is more than eight million to one.

Researchers Ville and Siminski suggested that the fluctuations in the percentages balloted in were due to the Government's anxiety to boost Army numbers quickly through the early ballots, coupled with inaccurate forecasting of the number of exemptions and deferments. They said this may have led to an oversupply of recruits for the initial intakes, and hence a deferment of their period of service until later intakes. Other anomalies, such as the return of eligible men who had been overseas at the time of their ballot, and the end of temporary deferment of apprentices and students as they completed their courses, saw those men fed into later intakes, thus reducing the likelihood of call-up of those born in later years.

I was among those granted a deferment – initially because I was undertaking university studies part-time, and subsequently because I was enrolled in a teacher training course. Most of the teachers who stories are told in this book were granted a similar deferment. So it was people like us who helped keep the numbers up in subsequent intakes and thus to reduce the number of those with later birthdates who were balloted in.

Ways of avoiding conscription included being married before your number came up, being a theological student or minister of religion, or having a more than minor criminal record. Another avenue was the Citizens' Military Forces which required six years' part-time service, to be served only in Australia. The catch was that you had to enlist in the CMF before your number came up in the ballot for your age group. There was also a fifth option, the one that Frank Cordingley's father had chosen in World War II: conscientious objection. A person whose conscientious beliefs did not permit him to engage in any form of military service could be exempted, but he had to convince a magistrate of the sincerity of those beliefs, and argue his case against that of a representative of the Minister for Labour and National Service.

In general, however, there was widespread public support for conscription; the two controversial aspects were selection by ballot and sending conscripts overseas, specifically to Vietnam. Historian Christina Twomey said that the language that dominated the conscription debate in the 1960s, at least until the end of the decade, 'was not about the heroic achievements of Australia's military forces in the past, but about the need to make boys into men and the considerable obligations people bore towards the state, within traditional and agreed upon limits'.[15]

Just 20 years after the end of World War II, and six years after the demise of the previous scheme, compulsory military training was generally seen as 'a good thing'. The war in Vietnam was just gathering momentum, and although there was opposition to Australia's involvement, it was not deafening.

In the early 60s, young people, including us Chalkies-to-be, were generally having a good time. Jobs weren't too hard to come by, and we were listening to Col Joye and the Joy Boys, the Bee Gees, the Seekers, and to Little Pattie singing 'My blonde-headed stompie-wompie real gone surfer boy'. In 1964, the Beatles hit Australia, part of the Mersey Beat invasion, and long hair, bell-bottom trousers, bright colours, and even tie-dye came into fashion for young men, bringing predictions of the end of civilisation as we know it. The mini-skirt raised hemlines and eyebrows, and the contraceptive pill revolutionised birth control.

11

Only 5% of the population went to university, but the demand for more places was growing.

The 60s were golden years for Australian sport, with tennis players such as Lew Hoad, Rod Laver and Margaret Court consistent winners at major international tournaments; tennis and Australian Rules football turned professional, and television coverage of sporting events began to attract big audiences. Test cricket retained its popularity, with Richie Benaud and Bob Simpson prominent players and captains of the time. 1961 was remembered for a dramatic tied cricket test in Brisbane between Australia and the West Indies, captained by Frank Worrell.

Another feature of the 1960s was the demand for teachers. With a rapid post-war increase in migration and the last surge of the baby boomers coming through, school numbers were swelling and more teachers were desperately needed. By 1964 there were twenty-nine teachers' colleges across Australia, compared with nine before World War II. To try to address the shortage of teachers, State education authorities lowered entry standards and shortened courses. Alongside the traditional courses in universities and teachers' colleges, in almost every state, education departments introduced fast-track programs intended to put teachers in front of classes as soon as possible.

Teachers called up for National Service from 1965 had generally completed either a two-year term at a teachers' college or a three-year degree and a Diploma of Education at a university; some had completed the first year of classroom teaching before we went into the Army, and a few had been teaching a year or two longer. As is the lot of our profession, those who had already been teaching had been dispersed across the country – high school teachers in cities and towns of reasonable size, primary teachers sometimes in communities just large enough to justify a one-teacher school, with parents taking it in turns to provide accommodation for the teacher.

Nevertheless, whatever path we had trod to this point, we were 'professionals'. We had a qualification to prove it. We'd learned a lot about teaching and learning and lesson-planning and classroom management (it was called 'discipline' in those days), and sharpened our understanding of our teaching subjects in high schools and broadened our knowledge of the primary school curriculum. Some of us had finished our training and accepted the responsibility of teaching a whole class *by ourselves*. So many new concepts crowded our brains that we might have wondered if we'd have time to put them all into practice.

Then along came another concept: conscription. We weren't trained to deal with that. Never seen it before. Not personally. How should we react? As Air Vice-Marshal Bladin had feared, the term did connote in our minds 'something to do with compulsion'. Of course, Prime Minister Menzies called it 'selective National Service', but most of us still thought it was conscription by lottery. And some of my teacher colleagues pointed out that though it might be called 'national service', it looked like 'military service', especially if you were sent to Vietnam. The opening lines of the 'Battle hymn of the compulsory crusaders', read out in the House of Representatives on 21 April 1966, put thoughts into words:

> Onward conscript soldiers,
> Marching as to war;
> The comrades you are leaving
> Were lucky in the draw! [16]

The Department of Veterans' Affairs website on the war in Vietnam says, 'Popular belief holds that the scheme was conceived specifically for Vietnam. Although untrue, the close timing of its introduction and Australia's growing commitment to the war made it seem so to many people.'[17] It certainly made it seem so to most of the conscripted teachers when we turned up for recruit training. Malaya and Indonesia were never mentioned; Vietnam was the focus, and it was predictable that platoon commanders, sometimes Nashos themselves, would argue the case for Australia's involvement, but perhaps surprising that Army chaplains were also recruited to the cause.

What did the teachers whose birthdates came out of the barrel and ended up in the Army think of the idea of conscription at the time?

When more than 70 of those then-young teachers were asked that question almost 50 years later, a quarter of them said that when they entered the Army they agreed with conscription, although not necessarily with random selection, one third described their attitude in ways that might be seen as neutral or ambivalent, and the rest, more than 40%, the largest group, were strongly opposed. Over half were aged 20 or 21 at the time they went into the Army; the oldest was 26.

Ian Lovell, a primary school teacher from New South Wales, had no qualms. 'Had to be done,' he said matter-of-factly. 'Father and Mother both Army personnel during WW2, and father was in PNG. I thought I would be sent to fight.' Another New South Welshman,

20-year-old John Herlihy, had already been contemplating joining the regular Army, so was not unhappy when his birthdate was drawn. On the other hand, Victorian Tom Derham wasn't happy when his marble *didn't* come out – so at age 23 he volunteered for National Service, something that would guarantee he was an object of mostly good-natured fun among the conscriptees during recruit training. 'I was generally positive about conscription and the reasons for Australia's involvement in Vietnam,' Derham said. He and Herlihy went on to become officers. Steven Hill also voluntarily became a Nasho – rather than eking out another four years part-time in the CMF in addition to the two he'd already served. 'I hadn't any negatives from those two years,' he said, 'and all male members of my family had been in service.'

Although they were only new to the profession, some young teachers, such as West Australian manual arts teacher John Fragomeni, already felt it tied them down, and saw National Service as a way of exploring the wider world. Similarly, John Morris was glad to escape from his first year of primary teaching – posted to a small New South Wales school in an isolated rural area, he'd found room and board at a local farm, but didn't much like the isolation or living on the homestead verandah. For these teachers, the ballot gave them a ticket to a sort of freedom, although their initial experience of recruit training may well have made them wonder if they should have been so pleased.

Others started out like 1966 Nasho, John Teggelove: 'accepting, open-minded and optimistic' about being balloted in, but changed their minds. 'I accepted conscription,' Ron Inglis said, 'for, as a very naïve young man, I thought that if the government said there was a threat to Australia, it must be true. Governments would not lie to you would they?' Inglis said that he was a very serious, sheltered young man at university. 'I paid very little attention to world affairs or student politics,' he said, 'even though there was much anti-Vietnam War agitation at Sydney University during my student years.'

Two years in the Army changed him. 'National Service radicalised me to a significant degree,' Inglis said. 'By the end, especially after some of the men I had completed infantry training with at Singleton were killed in Vietnam, I held that the Vietnam War was a terrible mistake, that politicians whipped up war fever just to win votes and that the whole National Service scheme was an expensive waste of time and money.'

Keith Werder came to a similar conclusion. He fully supported the need for conscription at the time he registered, 'to thwart the scourge of Communism in SE Asia', but had second thoughts in the three years that his call-up was deferred because of his university studies. In his final year, one of the courses included a topic on the current conscription process. 'It really opened my eyes to the unfairness of it and how it was "rigged" to include an inordinate number of teachers. … So I was bitterly opposed to being forced to leave behind my career for political purposes,' he said.

There has been considerable debate about whether the National Service scheme in the Vietnam War period was 'fixed' to exclude or include certain groups or individuals. Another Nasho teacher, Phil Adam said, 'I was not particularly happy with being conscripted, especially when people I knew with the same birthday were not selected.' The celebrated pop-star conscript Normie Rowe had similar suspicions. Author Mark Dapin was certain, however, that 'the ballot was not fixed, certain occupations were not favoured over others, and footballers were not exempt from war service'.[18] He did assert, however, that the very poorest families were under-represented because their sons couldn't pass the literacy or physical tests. Historian Paul Ham reported that 34% of the young men balloted in subsequently failed the Army's physical and/or psychological tests and were therefore excluded. Those of us who were there know that some of these were not detected until during recruit training. However, New South Wales high school teacher Ian Curtis recalled that '17 of us in October 1969 went to an afternoon medical and only three of us passed.'

Not all the teachers who went into 'Nasho' (a term used both for the National Service scheme and the individuals in it) would have regarded themselves as particularly fit, but apparently they were 'fit enough', and all passed the psychological tests, as well as being relatively literate. Whether these characteristics meant they were over-represented among the conscripts is hard to know without clear evidence for or against.

Some, like Bob Coppa, weren't persuaded by the Government's arguments. 'I was totally against conscription,' he said. 'I was aware of the history of conscription in Australia and I felt that to bring in conscription at the behest of the United States to fight in a "police action" in Vietnam was offensive in the extreme.' West Australian, John Ford, then aged 22, agreed: 'I was fiercely against NS before being called up. I considered the Vietnam War a huge mistake, Australia's involvement in the war entirely aimed at sucking up to the USA, and NS solely to supply gun fodder for the Vietnam War. I considered the war immoral and Communism not to be the threat to Australia and the West in general that the government of the day was spruiking.' Victorian Tom O'Meara took his protest to the streets, joining in Melbourne demonstrations against Lyndon B. Johnson, who had inherited the American presidency after the assassination of John F. Kennedy in 1963, and had taken the decision to significantly increase the US presence in Vietnam.

Despite their opposition, Coppa, Ford and O'Meara and others with similar views who had been called up could avoid National Service on the basis of their beliefs only if they were classified as conscientious objectors. Over the eight years of conscription, 1242 cases of conscientious objection reached the courts, of which 72% were successful. At least one of these was a teacher.

In a highly publicised case, a Sydney primary school teacher, William White, in 1966 refused to answer his call-up notice and sought conscientious objector status, on the grounds that he didn't want to kill another human being; he also opposed conscription and the Vietnam War. The New South Wales Education Department dismissed him from the service, and press photos of the day show the slightly-built protester being dragged from his house by three policemen who could only be described as 'burly'. White was initially unsuccessful in his court application, and sent to jail. The judge told him his position on conscription was a result of 'ignorance'. A short time later White's plea was granted, but there was only limited public sympathy for him.

None of the 73 ex-Chalkies whose stories are told in this book went down that road, although several mentioned that they thought about it at the time. 'I did talk about being a conscientious objector,' said Victorian secondary teacher, Glenn Hall, 'but in reality I was not committed enough to that cause.' Another Victorian, Les Rowe, who later became an Australian diplomat, said he was opposed to conscription and the Vietnam War but 'had no religious grounds to support a successful attempt to gain conscientious objection'. Denis Jenkins was frank: 'I had a half-baked anti-war stance – not strong enough to become a conscientious objector.' Yet another Victorian (were they more radical in that state?), Richard Boddington, said, 'A number of my friends at the time were quite opposed to conscription and the Vietnam War and encouraged me, unsuccessfully, to become a conscientious objector.'[19]

The dilemma for some was encapsulated by Andrew Remenyi, who said he had never been against National Service, but 'I was against conscription as it was devised, because of the unfairness of the ballot system, and because it was for military purposes to support the USA's war, of which we should have had no part.' Andrew Dalziel had a similar view. 'I didn't agree with the validity of the rationale for conscription (i.e. the Vietnam War) nor did I agree with the modus operandi (i.e. a random chance of approximately 1:12 of being conscripted and potentially sent to a war zone with all the danger that entailed, whilst the rest of the population my age and otherwise got on with their lives largely unaffected).' Despite his reservations, however, Dalziel accepted his fate. 'Notwithstanding all its flaws, I believe in our democratic system and therefore don't believe you can opt out when you feel like it. This would largely render the system unworkable.'

On the other hand, Bill Bailey was not opposed to conscription, but did agree the ballot system was 'a little unfair'. Peter Chard too believed it should have been 'one in, all in': 'It was totally wrong that life went on for the rest of Australia as normal while a few lost two years of their life or worse, their life,' he said.

This range of views shows that some of the teachers called up had definite views about conscription, for and against, before they went into the Army. Not all teachers had such clear opinions, sometimes because they found it difficult to decide if the political decisions made on behalf of the citizens of Australia were the right ones, and sometimes because they hadn't thought about it much. Even Ian Curtis, who was opposed to conscription and came from a strong Labor family, saw conscription as 'a far-off convenience' while he was still at university, until the North Vietnamese attacks known as the 'Tet offensive', in February 1968, suddenly made him realise 'we were not winning as we were being told'.

There was often a feeling of ambivalence about the call-up, as articulated by Queenslander Greg Farr, then a 21-year-old: 'A sense of national duty ingrained by the knowledge that two generations of our family had participated willingly in WW1 and WW2 when called upon (not up) was an influence, as was the situation that my brother at the time I received the notice was already a National Serviceman, and soon after that was to serve in Vietnam.' His brother's example weighed heavily upon him. 'I felt a personal leaning to participate willingly and without grievance.' On the other hand, Farr had 'a less than enthusiastic' attitude towards selective compulsory National Service, and was 'conflicted by the debate that raged over Vietnam, and more inclined towards the view that Vietnam was a civil war, not one to be messed with by foreign nations'.

Phil Adam too was uncomfortable with the Australian involvement in Vietnam, but said he also felt the pressure of the community and family 'to simply go along with the process without complaint'. He recalled that at the time of his call-up in January 1969 there was overwhelming community support for conscription and for Australian involvement in the Vietnam conflict. This position soon began to change, however, with opinion polls that year recording a majority against the war for the first time.

Perhaps it was an awareness of community support for conscription in those early years – despite the protests of organisations such as Save Our Sons and university students' opposition to Australia's participation in the Vietnam War – that saw some teachers resign themselves to the possibility of being balloted in. Queensland primary teacher Terry Edwinsmith said that since his birthday was drawn in the first ballot, he had little time to form an opinion one way or another. 'I believed that I was caught in the system and had no option other than to conform.'

Several teachers, being young and optimistic, thought the odds of being called up were pretty low. 'I had never considered that I would be called up,' Peter Darmody said. 'So I had fairly neutral views on conscription at the time I had to register, although I believed that if a person was conscripted he was obliged to serve as required.' There were other neutral views: 'I was ok with it', 'compliant and accepting', 'resignation to the fact'.

Rob Daniel was studying at the University of Western Australia, and thought seriously about joining the university's CMF unit for six years to fulfil his military obligations, but decided he'd take his chances in the lottery. He lost. 'I was disappointed to be required to do National Service,' he said, 'but was determined to make the best I could of it.'

Graham Lindsay, a 20-year-old primary school teacher in New South Wales, also had no objection to being called up, and would go wherever he was sent, with but one stipulation: like Frank Cordingley, he would not kill anyone. After recruit training, he was posted to 8 Field Ambulance at Puckapunyal, where his unit prepared to go

Vietnam. 'I had already informed my CO and others of my objection to killing people,' he said, 'but did not indicate unwillingness to go with the group.'

Some ex-Nashos who were in favour of conscription thought that there is still a place today for National Service. In 1969, 23-year-old Robbie Scott had just completed his Diploma of Education and been appointed as an agriculture teacher at Cooma High in southern New South Wales. 'Contrary to what [Federal Opposition Leader] Whitlam was saying, the government required me to register for conscription and I was glad to do so,' Scott said. 'My attitude has not changed and I believe conscription for all young people, including girls, should be re-introduced. Conscription does not necessarily mean military service.' Warren Ison was of a similar view, feeling that 'some sort of service would be valuable to most people'.

Ville and Siminski observed that the raising of armies for wartime military engagement had rarely been achieved 'without some degree of coercion'.[20] They pointed out that strategies such as patriotic appeals (as seen in Australia and elsewhere in both World Wars) and improving pay and conditions (as undertaken in the early 1960s in Australia) were usually unsuccessful in recruiting the numbers required to create a sufficient fighting force when danger loomed.

Of course, the circumstances were not as clear-cut in Australia when conscription was introduced in 1965. The populace was generally in favour of compulsory recruitment for the Army on a sort of 'good for the individual, good for the nation' basis, but there was no consensus, and sometimes violent opposition, about the random selection of only a proportion of eligible 20-year-olds, and about sending conscripts overseas to fight. Nor was there agreement, and often a degree of bafflement, about the reasons for Australia's involvement in the war in Vietnam.

The average of six national opinion polls, taken in Australia over the two years between late 1965 and late 1967, showed 65% in favour of conscription and 30% against, with 5% undecided. On the other hand, five polls conducted over the same period about sending conscripts to Vietnam saw just over 36% supportive and 52% opposed, with 11% unable to make up their minds. In 1972, as the last Australian troops pulled out of Vietnam, a *Sydney Morning Herald* poll showed almost two-thirds of respondents were still supportive of some sort of National Service scheme; less than a quarter were in favour of sending conscripts overseas.

In *The Nashos' war*, Dapin speculated that those born in the years immediately after World War II 'had no way to prove themselves as men beyond bare knuckles in the pub car park', and that 'the army meant freedom, and the chance of a bigger, more heroic life'.[21] He claimed that being conscripted gave these men 'an opportunity to measure up to the Anzacs, to march out of the bank and insurance offices and into history, and make their parents proud.' In the responses from the 73 teachers who contributed their views to the discussion in this book, while there are references to family traditions in the military and to escaping from the classroom in a few instances, even occasionally that 'Nasho', as it was popularly known, was an adventure, there is little to suggest they were keen to prove their manhood or 'march into history'. In fact, some came from families where militarism was not highly prized at all. The proportion of teachers in favour of what Ville and Simimski called 'enforced military enlistment'[22] was considerably less than that of the general population as shown in those early opinion polls. Dapin's characterisation of conscripts, particularly those in the first intake, may have been true for some men, but it didn't apply to the many teachers who saw themselves on the threshold of their new professional life and conscription as an unwanted intrusion.

Even some of those teachers who supported the idea of National Service, and Australia's involvement in Vietnam, were not happy with the randomness of the selection process. It seems that around two-thirds of those teachers, for and against, had considered the need for conscription, knew its history in Australia, evaluated the government's justification for committing troops in Vietnam, and developed their attitudes accordingly. None of those opposed sought to be officially designated as conscientious objectors, but not because, in Dapin's words, they were 'tamed and angry and desperately bored'.[23]

The other third 'went along' with registering for National Service and accepting the verdict of the lottery, in which they would take their chances, sometimes because they saw it as part of the democratic process, sometimes because they were generally apolitical and therefore had no strong opinions about conscription or the Vietnam War, and sometimes because they simply hadn't given much thought to it until their marble came out.

It's a matter for speculation whether any of those attitudes would have changed had we known how quickly and cynically the Australian

Government, and the Prime Minister in particular, had made the decision to introduce conscription, in the face of direct opposition from military leaders. Apart from those already through their teacher training, all we could do was continue with our studies and hope we didn't fail a course. We were not to know that the intellect, qualifications and skills so highly regarded in our profession and on which we individually prided ourselves, would be dashed into dust the minute we arrived for recruit training.

Life as we knew it was about to come to a screaming halt.

3

Recruit training: 'Yelling and abusing in the customary fashion'

A sound woke me and I rolled over groggily in bed, my eyes half closed in the darkness. I reached out to touch my new wife, thinking she may have called out in her sleep, but my outstretched fingers tickled only empty air. On the other side of me I felt a solid wall. Puzzled and still half-asleep, I lifted my head and immediately detected the steady drones of sleeping bodies. Male bodies! From somewhere close by came the regular buzzsaw of a man snoring. I groaned inwardly and lay my head back down on the pillow. This wasn't my love-nest; this was an Army hut, and I was sharing it with fifteen other men. My new bride was 800 kilometres away.

I'd just drifted back to sleep when the bright staccato tones of 'Reveille' bugle-ated in my head. A figure burst through the end door of the hut. 'Rise and shine, girls,' yelled a lanky corporal. 'Everyone on parade!' I would have groaned again but was too busy grabbing my sheet and heading for the parade ground before I copped a kitchen duty for being late. We stood shivering in rows in the cool morning air, our bedsheets draped around our heads and shoulders. 'A parade-ground of Caspers,' said fellow Nasho, Ian Curtis.

Welcome to recruit training.

***

I was in my first year of teaching, in the Secondary Department of Herberton State School on the Atherton Tableland in Far North Queensland, when the notice from the Department of Labour and National Service arrived in the latter half of 1968. Since I'd already been granted a deferral, I knew what it would say but still swore when I saw that it confirmed my call-up from early the next year. I'd completed the practical stage of my teacher training, and my deferment from the first intake, in 1965, was over.

The letter ordered me to report to a Commonwealth Medical Officer in the nearby coastal city of Cairns for a medical examination to ascertain my physical fitness. For the previous four years I'd been playing rugby union with Eastern Suburbs in Brisbane, and at the time of my medical I was coaching the Herberton State School rugby league team, so I didn't have any problem being classified as 'A': medically fit for all service duties. I'd half-hoped having to wear glasses might downgrade my classification, but since I played football without them, the result was predictable.

Shortly afterwards, my official call-up notice arrived, telling me that I had hereby been called up for 'national service with the Military Forces of the Commonwealth'. I was required to present myself to a certain officer at Enoggera Barracks in Brisbane on the morning of 29 January 1969. I rang my fiancée in Brisbane to tell her the date, and confirm our wedding plans. We were married on 16 December 1968; six weeks later my new wife drove me to Enoggera Barracks. For some reason she kept her sunglasses on all the time.

Although there were only two National Service ballots per year, there were four annual intakes, and I was in intake number 15, so by now the operation was as smooth as Army procedures can be. A bus transported me and my fellow conscripts almost 800 kilometres south to 3 Training Battalion (3TB) at Singleton, an historic Hunter Valley town 50 kilometres north-west of Newcastle. At that point I was less keen on the history and more interested in my possible future.

Singleton was the newest of the training battalions, built with some of the increased funding announced at the same time as conscription, which makes me wonder if it was given to the Army by the Government as a sort of softening-up gift for going against the wishes of the military leaders and making the Army Minister look foolish. Besides, the Government was sensitive about providing quality accommodation for its forced recruits.

The poet A.D. Hope once portrayed Australia's mainland capital cities as five teeming sores draining the country. A time-lapse camera poised over the continent like a spider-cam at the cricket might well have revealed a similar but more distorted pattern as the hundreds of teachers balloted in and subsequently deemed 'medically fit for all service duties' streamed from their homes across the nation to undertake their ten-week recruit training at one of the three designated centres.

By the time my intake arrived at Singleton in early 1969, 3rd Training Battalion was taking recruits from Queensland and northern NSW. All the other NSW and the ACT recruits went through 1st Recruit Training Battalion, Kapooka, just outside the rural city of Wagga Wagga in south-east New South Wales. The West Australians, South Australian, Tasmanians and Victorians went to 2nd Recruit Training Battalion at Puckapunyal ('Pucka'), 100 kilometres north of Melbourne. Geographically, the three locations lie in a temperate climate zone, but you could be forgiven for thinking the Army chose them on account of their sharp contrast between desiccating heat and brass-monkey cold. Another way of turning boys into men.

Teachers typically were required to report for National Service in late January or early February, having completed their teacher training or a full year of teaching at the end of the previous year. This meant that the first of the four intakes each year was top-heavy with teachers, and the staff of the recruit training centres seemed to brace themselves for the onslaught. Ian Colwell's busload from Brisbane was welcomed to Singleton barracks as 'f...ing Nashos, f...ing Queenslanders, and educated c...s to boot'.

Victorian primary teacher Phil Parker had a very strong memory of his first day in the Army, just three weeks short of his 21st birthday. 'The day we left Melbourne for Puckapunyal we drove past Pentridge Prison, the very day that Ronald Ryan was executed,'[24] Parker said. 'This was a very sobering beginning to a very emotional day. The feelings of uncertainty as to what lay ahead of us were obvious on most of our faces.'

***

There is nothing to compare to Army recruit training. It's a unique process devised to mould soft civilians into hardened fighting machines within a short timeframe. Apparently. There is no way to prepare for it, except to grit your teeth. And conscripts can't resign if they don't like it.

There was a certain sameness about the facilities. The inevitable parade ground took centre stage, it seemed ('Don't even bloody think of taking an f***in' short-cut across it or you'll cop a f***in' duty!'). There were four messes to eat in, reminding us that the Army is a hierarchy and that everyone knew his[25] place – recruits, other ranks (ORs), Sergeants, and Officers, along with lecture huts and administration buildings, all in pale green, as if the Army needed to camouflage everything it owned.

The huts in which we spent our nights (apart from when we might be ripped out for an urgent parade at 2 am by some crazed corporal) were also green – long weatherboard buildings on concrete stumps, with neat white-framed windows. There was a door at each end through which we belted on our way to a suddenly called parade, scuttling down the steps as if our lives depended on it (and sometimes it felt as if they did).

I felt overwhelmed. Even though I'd been in school cadets (rising to the dizzying rank of lance-corporal) and been to annual cadet camps for a few years, this was an entirely new military environment. My time was not my own, and blokes who didn't seem too bright but had one or two stripes on their sleeve kept shouting at me. My civilian clothes were stowed away in a trunk, and everything I owned now seemed to be green. I had a number instead of a name, I was living with a hut-full of blokes from all over Queensland and northern New South Wales and from all sorts of backgrounds, including one bloke who told me he was a dogger from Mount Isa. I wasn't sure if he rode cranes or shot dingoes, but I knew I was in a very different world from the safe one I'd come from. Every night in those first few weeks I lay awake after 'lights out' and thought about my previous life and my new wife, who'd gone back to live with her parents, while we waited to see what the Army had in store for me.

At Pucka, Richard Boddington remembered 'the spit polished boots; the beret to be two fingers' width above the eyebrow; the slouch hat chin strap buckle to be in line with one's mouth; the bed sheets to be turned down two bayonet lengths; hut windows to be opened a bayonet length; bayonets to be stored in one's cupboard; eyes front when officers inspected the hut'.[26] At Singleton, we were also required to set the hopper windows open at an angle exactly one bayonet-length from the sill. One hapless recruit caught out in a snap room inspection discovered that after checking the angle, he'd left his bayonet jammed in the window opening.

Inside, the huts were semi-divided into four cubicles, each with four beds and four two-door metal wardrobes with shelves and hanging space. In keeping with the adage, not only was there a place for everything, but everything had to be in its place. Russell Jenkin was given a guard duty for having an Army singlet folded the wrong way. One personal photo could be affixed inside the wardrobe doors, and since we wouldn't be allowed any leave for the first month, I tacked up a honeymoon photo of my wife, so I wouldn't forget what she looked like.

Many of the recruits had never lived away from home before. Even those who had were not always prepared for what awaited them.

'The first night we were shown how to make our beds,' John Morris said, 'and if the corporal couldn't bounce a 20c piece off your sheets in the morning he would throw our beds out the window (we were three storeys up!). In my room of four we all slept on the floor with our pillow that night and practiced with 20c pieces to ensure we passed the first test!'

The geography teachers among us would no doubt have described the gently undulating country and soft hills around the camps as woodland and open forest. A.D. Hope might well have been thinking of the same locations when he described Australia as 'a Nation of trees, drab green and desolate grey'.[27] It wasn't hard to feel drab and grey yourself sometimes when you were traipsing across the countryside during a map-reading exercise on a scorching day or crouching behind a shrub learning the rudiments of what Major-General T.S. Taylor called 'all the bloodiness and muck' of guerrilla fighting.[28] Sometimes on route marches we tramped along the roads that disappeared into the surrounding scrub, carrying our rifles and straining under the weight of our packs, serenaded by summer cicadas. If you want to get close to the Australian bush, join the Army. But don't expect to be allowed to stop and smell the roses.

'The first few weeks were a culture shock,' Russell Jenkin recalled of his time at Puckapunyal. The 22-year-old had already taught in two one-teacher schools in rural Victoria. 'I had been given authority, independence and responsibility,' he said 'and in one fell swoop, that was all taken away – and dramatically so, during the first days of recruit training.' What's more, 'it was February and hot and the physical and mental demands seemed relentless.' Jim Davidson was in the same 1967 intake at Pucka. 'Torrid' was his word for those early days of recruit training, 'because the weather was fiercely hot (declared heat-wave conditions prevailed)' and, like Jenkin, he found the pressure to conform 'relentless'. 'For some time we performed in the pre-dawn through until early afternoon before stand-down for the remainder of the day,' he said. '"Thank God for the Salvos", who wobbled out into the heat with loads of cold cordial.'

Queensland high school teacher Ian Ogston put pen to paper when he arrived at 3TB Singleton in January 1970:

> Drab rows of spartan huts
> Sprawled in military order
> Across the harsh, rounded Hunter hills.
> The dry summer heat shimmered the wheat-brown grassland.
> New soldiers marched.[29]

What else did these former recruits remember, apart from the searing summer heat? The camaraderie and challenges of close living; early morning 'fitness' runs; marching and rifle drill; weapons training with the SLR (self-loading rifle); target practice on the rifle range; being marched to the mess for meals (stepping it out across pace lines set 30 inches apart); two pots (schooners) per man at the boozer; marching until they were foot-sore; being dragged out of bed with little sleep; the relief of free time at night or when on leave; running a mile with rifle and full gear within a set time; 'lots of laughs and grizzles'; 'met a lot of great guys and some not so nice'; a recruit killed on the road while making the crazy quest to reach home during a weekend leave; peeling onions in the officers' mess kitchen; 'our sergeant ... who showed signs of being an alcoholic'; and graduation parade.' The loneliness,' one said, a reminder that even in the midst of hundreds of people we can still feel alone, and another recalled the death of a Nasho officer 'when grenade training went horribly wrong'.

Singleton and Puckapunyal took only Nashos; Kapooka also trained volunteers for the regular Army, alongside the conscripts. Since volunteers could enlist from age 17, they were often younger than the Nashos, and as the Minister for the Army had made clear to Parliament, many had limited schooling and therefore literacy skills. In the first National Service intake at 1RTB, only 31% of recruits had completed Intermediate level high school or above; in the same intake at 2RTB, the figure was 40%.

Secondary science teacher Steve Beveridge said that his platoon at Kapooka comprised almost half regular and half nasho recruits. 'I recall helping some of the "regs" with writing letters and spelling,' he said. 'It was a valuable experience for me, socialising with guys I'd never normally come across.'

Each batch of new arrivals was allocated to a platoon within a company, and then marched in as orderly fashion as we could manage to the Q Store for the issue of uniforms, bedding and the all-important mess gear. Each platoon was commanded by a lieutenant, in later years sometimes himself a Nasho graduate of the 22-week Officer Training course at Scheyville, near Sydney, but day-to-day training was the responsibility of the platoon sergeants and corporals. How comfortable the recruits' stay would be depended to a large extent on the attitude of the corporals, who, like the sergeants, were regular soldiers and had often served in Vietnam.

One of the Army's objections to conscription was that it would suck experienced personnel out of the fighting forces, and no doubt many of the 'regs' were as unhappy as most of the conscripts about being posted to a recruit training battalion. The corporals tended to train the recruits the way they themselves were probably trained – with abuse and humiliation. One boasted to an unappreciative audience of teachers how he had cheated in an exam while in Vietnam in order to obtain an Army Education certificate equivalent to junior high school level. 'They were a quite specific type of creature with quite marked characteristics,' Tom Derham said, 'different to all other humans I had encountered up to that stage in my life!'

The NCOs' treatment of the recruits didn't go down well with the teacher conscripts, who considered themselves worthy of respect. 'Initially it was a culture shock. I was totally unused to people yelling and abusing in the customary fashion at the time,' Richard Morgan said. Ten weeks later he regarded it as normal.

The strategy of cutting everyone down to size seems to have been inbred in some corporals. Sent to 2RTB Puckapunyal, Victorian primary school teacher Roger Grigg said, 'I remember wanting to do the right thing and being humiliated for trying, never rewarded for effort and often belittled.' Western Australian John Ford objected to the ways recruits at Pucka were individually singled out for iniquitous treatment: a recruit marching round the parade ground backwards chanting 'I am worthless'; another recruit scrubbing the concrete path in front of his hut with a tooth brush; still another crawling across the parade ground with a rifle slung round his neck, kissing the rifle and chanting 'I love my rifle'; on parade, corporals would indulge themselves by having a recruit put one foot forward, then further forward, then again, until he lost balance and fell over.

It's little wonder that in those times when we did have time to reflect on our circumstances – perhaps waiting listlessly on the side of a road for transport to take us back from the firing range, or lying under a gum tree on our backs against our loosened packs during a lunch break in the scrub – some of us wondered what the hell this was all about. Ian Curtis remembered watching a farmer's ute drive past his platoon as they trudged along a hot dusty road outside the Kapooka camp one summer afternoon, and longing to return to 'the real world'.

Just a few weeks earlier we'd been going about our 'normal' lives back home, teaching or training, fraternising with friends and family, playing sport, going to the pub; now we were running, marching, shooting, and climbing in a military environment that was as unfamiliar to most of us as a desert might be to a duck, yelled at by a bunch of corporals who generally seemed incensed that we had the hide to be educated. 'Basic training was very demeaning, particularly towards those recruits who had a university degree,' Graham Leader said. 'There was no scope for individuality.' On 8 March, 1970, when New South Wales high school teacher Ron Inglis was eight weeks into his ten-week recruit training at Kapooka, he wrote in his diary: 'Perhaps the hardest thing to put up with is the military monotony of the place. 'One is intellectually and spiritually deadened. "You are not paid to think, soldier. You are paid to do as you are told".'

When some corporals struck names they couldn't pronounce, such as that of Recruit Grozdanovski, they resorted to 'wheelbarrow with a G', or whatever the first letter of the surname was. Curtis observed that Grozdanovski 'wasn't a bad bloke, though the Army, and what he was doing in it, was a bit of a mystery to him'. Such was the legacy of conscription, and it was often the vulnerable recruits who suffered most from the humiliation the corporals dished out. One recruit at Kapooka was so uncoordinated he was discharged, making one wonder how he passed the medical. John Morris once asked a lance corporal why he swore so much when giving instructions. 'So the new Australians can understand me,' came the incongruous reply.

As might be expected when men of 20-something age were suddenly thrown into new and unknown surroundings, they reacted in different ways, including with initial bewilderment, trying to cope with the regimentation and the pressure to conform. Tom O'Meara said that even though Victoria was his home state, he unexpectedly found the

Army environment at Puckapunyal 'alien'. Secondary teacher Keith Bryant summed up his experience as a 20-year-old at Puckapunyal in 1966 in three words: 'tough, cold, boring'. His fellow West Australian, Rob Daniel, thought the sense of removal and isolation at Pucka was probably greater for Nashos from the west than that experienced by Victorians, who had more leave options.

Another West Australian, Graham Leader, thought the educated recruits suffered more than the others at the corporals' hands. On the other hand, teachers may have had more capacity to strike back. 'We did not enjoy being bastardised,' Graham Lindsay said, 'and responded accordingly in ways which went mostly undetected.' When they were found out, the reaction was swift: tasked with shining the barrack floors at Kapooka, 20-year-old Lindsay and his mates applied floor polish with brooms and proceeded to remove the polish with a 'pig in a blanket' — one recruit on a blanket towed by two others. An NCO caught them in the act, quickly grabbed a firehose and soaked the floor and the enterprising recruits. 'We then had to clean up again,' Lindsay lamented.

When Peter Shackleton, then a 22-year-old from South Australia, finished reading Tolstoy's *War and Peace*, he posted a derogatory quote from the book on the company noticeboard at Puckapunyal. Goodness only knows what the corporals made of that. Others wanted to take more direct action: John Morris said there were occasions when some recruits in his platoon had to be physically restrained from attacking the NCOs who dished out the abuse.

Many said they were surprised by the pettiness, including one instance at Singleton where personal mail was withheld as a platoon punishment. These were not the unquestioning recruits of the past, however, and a journalist in their midst warned that one of them would reach a telephone and that their treatment would soon be front-page news. The mail was immediately distributed, and after a meeting between the recruits and a senior officer, the officious corporal was replaced.

According to agriculture teacher Martin Forbes, it was just like the bastardisation he'd earlier experienced at boarding school, and he dealt with it the same way: 'putting up with it and pitying the idiots'. 23-year-old Ian Curtis arrived at Kapooka sporting a beard, and was derided by his platoon corporal as 'JB' (John the Baptist). 'He was always inviting me "around the back",' Curtis said. When the recruit continually refused the offer, he was often given the duty of cleaning the platoon urinals by hand. 'I delighted in driving him spare by smiling and whistling as I did the job.' Keith Werder, who said he was targeted by the NCOs because of his outspoken opposition to what he regarded as an unfair conscription scheme, adopted a strategy of yawning and looking out the window during lectures by the platoon sergeant, but making sure he knew the answer when inevitably asked a question. Ian Curtis took more direct action – while on kitchen duty in the sergeants' mess, he submerged a sneaker in a tub of jelly.

There were more extreme forms of bastardisation, however, not so easily deflected. As a 21-year-old, one conscripted teacher was affected by the abuse his platoon suffered under an alcoholic lance-corporal: 'After drinking heavily, he would sometimes come into our hut at 2 or 3 in the morning, the Nasho said. 'The training was physically tough and we couldn't afford to lose the sleep. But it was his outrageous behaviour that was most objectionable. One night, he sat with a towel over his head (pretending it was a judge's wig) and presided over "the court". He was brutal. Another night, he took three of us out in his clapped-out car on to the Puckapunyal airstrip. He raced with horrendous speed down the airstrip, trying to take off. He endangered all our lives.'

Andrew Remenyi, one of the older conscripts at age 24, said that there was a lot of bastardisation at Puckapunyal, and some vulnerable Nashos were badly treated. 'I know of one who just couldn't cope with commands and was, on three occasions, sent up "Tit Hill" (so called) to count the number of designated letters on a plaque there,' Remenyi said. 'One day he kept going over the hill to the Hume highway. The Military Provosts caught him and he came back badly beaten and bloodied. He was eventually given a "dishonourable discharge". I saw him years later as a hobo in the streets of Melbourne.'

There were other dark sides too. When one teacher recruit was training at Puckapunyal in 1969, another recruit apparently committed suicide by jumping off the roof of a building on to a concrete footpath below. 'No doubt he won't be recorded as a lost national serviceman,' the teacher said grimly. The same teacher also recalled an incident where another recruit had both wrists broken 'because we weren't supervised or shown how to flip over the top of a high rope net; we were just yelled at to do it.'

It's little wonder that several of the teacher conscripts said they 'hated' recruit training. John Dark described it as 'hard and merciless', and Norm Hunter couldn't think of much positive to say about it. Perhaps surprising, then, is that 10 of the 73 former Chalkies who gave their recollections had favourable memories of the experience. Steven Hill reckoned it was 'a cruise' and that he had to act dumb to avoid upsetting the platoon corporal. Despite the petty rules and regulations, Ed Diery found it 'interesting and enjoyable', and his fellow Queenslander, Terry Edwinsmith, said: 'I mixed with college peers and formed new friendships with other recruits. The physical activities were acceptable and mostly enjoyable. As Nashos, we were in it together. Help was at hand. The instructors were mainly "good blokes". It was an adventure!'

The then 21-year-old Edwinsmith's positive view of the instructors was shared by several of his fellow teachers. At Kapooka, Ron Inglis came across a number of officers and sergeants he thought were good leaders, Greg Ivey recalled the 'reasonableness' of his company commander and NCOs at Singleton, and another ex-Chalkie remembered a drill corporal at Puckapunyal who was good at his job 'and treated us as humans'. Phil Parker commented that at Puckapunyal, 'We were a bit fortunate in that our platoon NCOs weren't a bad lot. Our Sergeant was a decent bloke who I actually think felt sorry for us having been conscripted.' At Kapooka, Steve Beveridge was impressed by his platoon sergeant's ability as a leader. 'It was interesting to watch some of the (not-so-bright) recruits think they'd put one over Sergeant Binning, but he was always up to them,' Beveridge said. There were several other responses along similar lines, including praise for particular sergeants, but these are exceptions to the views generally expressed about the poor quality of the NCOs, especially the corporals the young teachers encountered during recruit training.

Nevertheless, between those who hated the experience and those who enjoyed it, was a large group who tolerated recruit training or found it initially tough but eventually regarded it as 'okay'. For them, the training was variously 'character-building', 'boring, but the novelty was interesting', 'I expected it to be what it was', 'helped me grow and mature', and 'tough, rigorous, but fair.'

'I understood that if you were going to be in the Army, you had to do these things,' Ian Ogston said. Bob Coppa reckoned his first five weeks at Puckapunyal were the worst: 'The weather (very hot) made it physically very difficult, and it took quite a time to adjust to the rules, expectations, shouted abuse, racism and seeming trivia of army discipline. Once you got this in perspective, it became easy to "roll with the punches".

Warren Ison, a primary school teacher from Queensland, had earlier experienced four years of Army Cadet training, and said that although the instructors at Singleton could be 'quite abusive', he knew what they were trying to achieve and didn't let it bother him. Hugh Wilkinson, who went on to become head of Army Education, agreed that the training was tough but that it was 'all about conditioning individuals into a disciplined group.' Another ex-Chalkie, Alex Thomson, had a different take on this from his time at Singleton: 'In general the instructors did a fairly good job of uniting us, even if it was only in detestation of them'.

'Conditioning individuals' was not only about moulding men into a team. Early morning runs in platoon formation, rope climbing, assault courses and route marches were all part of the agenda to get us fit. As a result, Warren Dunn described recruit training as 'horrible'. 'I was physically unfit,' he said, 'and being tall and thin with a weak upper body, I found the activities and exercises involving physical strength challenging.' On the other hand, some were surprised and often pleased by the level of fitness they acquired. 'Recruit training was a bit of a shock, in terms of my relatively poor level of fitness after a lazy four years at university,' Peter Darmody said, but by the end of the ten weeks, 'I appreciated feeling so fit'. Even Queenslander Tom Uil, who found recruit training 'dehumanising', admitted that 'it did get me fit'.

Steve Beveridge (NSW), Rob Daniel (WA), John Herlihy and Richard Morgan (both from NSW), regarded themselves as fit when they went into National Service, and relished the physical tasks. Morgan and Beveridge and I played rugby for the Army, which sometimes helped us avoid such energy-sapping activities as a route march, or brought us back early from an extended bivouac in the bush if a match was imminent. 'Playing rugby for Army while at Kapooka was a brilliant move,' Beveridge said. 'When the Colonel comes to watch training, you know it's all good!' For myself, selection in the Army rugby team restored a small sense of individuality.

Typically, the Army teams in the training battalions were composed of regulars and recruits – John Morris played in a cricket team that included his platoon commander, and the rugby team I played with included one of our physical fitness instructors and the sergeant cook from our mess (a definite bonus).

In addition to physical and military training, we were also subjected to political lectures which Victorian Senator John Gorton, a World War II RAAF pilot and Prime Minister from January 1968, hoped would reveal to us the 'vile nature of the Communists who are fighting in Vietnam.'[30] Greg Farr remembered that even as late as 1970, Army recruit training personnel insisted 'National Service is NOT preparing you for the Vietnam War'. When of course, it was,' he said. Fortunately for later Nashos, by 1971 Vietnam was no longer an option.

The recruit training curriculum also included 'character guidance' and talks by chaplains, 'aimed at inspiring a soldier with true national idealism and morality.'[31] Since a significant proportion of the conscripted teachers had already made their mind up about the morality of conscription and the Vietnam War, some did not take kindly to being lectured by padres. Nor does it seem reasonable to have co-opted Army chaplains essentially to argue the Government's position on Vietnam, and some of them understandably came under fire from conscripts who believed they should stick to their religious duties.

John Ford said he was repelled by what he saw as blatant Government propaganda advanced by Army chaplains as 'character guidance'. He said these 'men of God' stated as fact that 'the real enemy in Vietnam are the Chinese and they are using Vietnam as a puppet state ready for the launch of their invasion of Australia', and that 'the Vietcong soldier, referred in these sessions as "Charlie" and "Gooks" is brainwashed and high on drugs when in battle'. This 'indoctrination message' was the same in every denomination, he said. Phil Adam rejected it as 'political brainwashing', and Bob Coppa dismissed as 'weasel words' a padre's explanation that the commandment, 'Thou shalt not murder', did not apply to killing in a war situation.

Coppa was also confronted with compulsory 'church parades', when, on the first Sunday at Puckapunyal, his platoon was instructed to divide themselves into Catholics, Church of England and OPDs (other Protestant denominations). At the end of the division, Coppa was standing by himself. The corporal looked down at him and shouted, 'What are you! Are you a Jew or something?' Coppa replied that he was an agnostic. 'What's that?' the corporal asked.

'I started to tell him, when a major (padre) came out and took me into the building for a talk,' Coppa said. 'He tried to convince me that I was a Catholic because I had been to a Catholic primary school. We had a long discussion and I would not give ground. Ultimately he said, "If you don't go to church on Sunday, you will be doing KP [kitchen duty]." I immediately decided that being a Methodist was beneficial. We both nodded – we understood each other, and I went outside to join the OPDs.'

At Kapooka, Ian Curtis also found himself the odd man out at the church parade. The platoon corporal strode over. 'Don't you believe in God, Curtis? You'll f…ing believe in God when they come running over the hill, screaming, towards you …' Unable to convince the irreligious recruit, the corporal ordered him to spend the time on 'emu parade', picking up cigarette butts. The result? 'No supervision and wandering around out of sight and sitting down alone – first time not supervised and by myself in a week,' Curtis said. 'The following Sundays I was joined by many more.'

Despite their objections about 'propaganda' and 'brainwashing', there were signs that the 'relentless pressure' of recruit training was beginning to have some effect, much to the surprise of some of the recruits themselves.

Greg Farr was travelling by bus to Sydney with fellow Nashos for their first free weekend since their training at Singleton had begun. 'Our bus-load of recruits passed a couple of young fellas who had long hair and dressed accordingly,' he said. 'We hadn't seen anyone with long hair in a month or so. I found myself caught up in the cries of derision aimed at these two, who could have been any one of us a month before. Shock! Horror! That was me! The army had done its job well.' The revelation for Ron Inglis of the effect the system was having on him was even more significant: 'I remember once realizing to my horror that if someone had told me to go and kill a Viet Cong, I would most likely have obeyed the order.' Russell Jenkin, who initially opposed conscription and fighting in someone else's war, had a similar experience. 'Once I got used to things at Recruit Training, I saw this experience as significant, and I became mentally prepared for Vietnam,' he said. 'The Regs who trained us must have done a good job on that issue. I still didn't like the idea of fighting in a foreign war, but recruit training readied me for that possibility.'

Perhaps the one consistent theme about recruit training is a certain satisfaction, if not a sense of pride, that we lasted the distance. 'It sucked! But I endured,' Michael Lee said. In similar vein, Phil Doecke recalled that 'Militarisation and I didn't get on too well, but I'm a stayer.'

Even Ian Curtis, who had constant run-ins with authority, included in his long list of memories that his platoon won the graduation march-past. This sense of achievement is mostly implied rather than explicit, sometimes in the satisfaction of outsmarting the NCOs, sometimes in being 'the fittest I've ever been in my whole life', sometimes in learning new skills, sometimes in feeling that they knew how to play the game: 'coming to grips with it', 'working out the system'.

These were men who had been earlier trained to develop a lesson plan, to apply theory to practice. In the Army they were working backwards, catapulted into the practice and having to make sense of it for themselves. Russell Jenkin was one who analysed it later: 'Like most of my mates, I endured some pretty challenging experiences and in the end, managed quite well. It was one of life's lessons, learnt pretty early, i.e. one can find a way to manage even the most challenging circumstances, if one is prepared to persevere – although in this case, we had no choice!'

This is not to say that every Chalkie had a great time at recruit training. They were still in the Army, many of them still 'unwilling participants in the green machine', as Ian Colwell put it. Bastardisation was often pointed, personal and humiliating, both unwelcome and unwarranted. The training was mentally and physically demanding, and their time was not their own.

The randomness and basic unfairness of the lottery system was a constant irritation, if not despair at times. Called up in 1971, 20-year-old John Hain found himself thinking during recruit training that 'everyone went from school to uni and then to the Army because everyone around me did, but then suddenly realizing that this had not happened to any of my friends. They were free in civvy street.'

We all looked forward to going home on leave for a few days when that was allowed after a couple of months – at Singleton, the NSW recruits were able to go home for a weekend after four weeks' training, and bring their cars back with them if they wanted to, but the Army decided that was not enough time for the Queenslanders to get across the border and back in time, so took them for a day excursion by coach. I remember that the busload of Queenslanders in my intake travelled to the picturesque coastal town of Port Stephens, where there was some delay in our entering the RSL club en masse after lunch, apparently because some of our group had not yet reached the drinking age of 21. As the protesters said: 'Good enough to fight for Australia, but …'

By this time the Government had succumbed to public pressure and had legislated in 1966 to allow National Servicemen under 21 years of age on 'special duty' in Vietnam, Malaysia and Singapore to vote in national elections, but this had not been extended to all Nashos.

The possibility of being sent to Vietnam loomed like a grey shadow over all recruits' lives up to 1971. Occasionally they'd have us on our hands and knees and sometimes our stomachs, crawling under camouflage netting while live bullets whistled over our heads, just to get us used to the idea. Sweat trickled down our backs and dripped from our noses into the sand below, but no one was going to stick his head up to take a breath. 'I guess I understood what the Army was trying to achieve,' Glenn Hall said, 'that we there to become soldiers, that going to war was a real possibility.' A movie brought the truth home to Ian Curtis: 'We were taken to watch … a movie about the English civilian retreat and panic in Malaya (1942) as the Japanese swiftly outmanoeuvred and hunted them. Remember their lying in water, terrified and silent, soldiers wading through swamps looking for them. Realisation that this new life was not a game. Decision to become invisible.'

On the other hand, Steve Beveridge said, 'Interestingly, by the end of infantry training, I suspect I would have gone to Vietnam – which was far from my initial thoughts. This was probably a function of training with guys who were almost certainly going to Vietnam.' West Australian Ian Mackay never had any doubts – afterwards, he was glad he didn't go to Vietnam, but 'would have gone if asked to. I was a soldier in the Australian Army'.

One uniting force, which no doubt the Army was aiming for, was that the recruits generally recognised that they were in this boat together. In South Australian Bruce Nulty's hut at Puckapunyal in early 1967, a group of Nashos from NSW established a rule on the first day: 'We want to get through this experience with as little difficulty as possible. We do not stir up each other, nor the Corporals … etc.' 'It was a great rule,' Nulty said.

This sense of a shared experience came through strongly. 'I remember during the 20 km route match [at Kapooka] the platoon had to all 'cross the line' together before the expiry time – no good some forging ahead!!!' John Morris said. Teachers spoke of making new friends and learning to be part of a team, and 'the slow development of mateship'. The camaraderie that developed seems to have been partly the Army's doing and partly the result of the feeling that they needed to stick together to survive. Recruit training also gave Ron Inglis 'a glimpse of how my father, a World War Two veteran, had been severely damaged by involvement in real war'.

The conscripted teachers were also observers of other soldiers' lives. At Kapooka, Ian Curtis's platoon included a recruit from Tasmania, a Salvation Army member, who was officially a non-combatant and therefore not issued with a rifle. The well-respected platoon sergeant said this was not fair when the rest had to lug their rifles around on route marches and training patrols. So he issued the 'Sallie' with two bricks, about the equivalent of the weight of a rifle, to carry in his rucksack. 'We all thought this was fine,' Ian Curtis said, 'and the porter did too.'

Curtis also told of a Balmain wharfie ('a hard man') who one day told him he was going over the wall at Kapooka that night, where his girlfriend would be waiting to pick him up. 'Last we heard of him,' Curtis said. It was a similar story for the Italian boy who said he couldn't eat the food in the mess and disappeared after a week. Glenn Hall woke up in his hut at Puckapunyal one morning to find a recruit who'd shared his cubicle had gone AWOL during the night. At Kapooka, one recruit was taken away, never to return, after reportedly being caught smoking marijuana.

21-year-old Peter Darmody found himself on picket duty at Kapooka one night, 'keeping an eye on a couple of conscientious objectors'. Perhaps they were like Alwyn Henderson, whom Mark Dapin wrote about, who was already in the Army when he woke up one day and said, 'I'm not going to war anymore. I'm sorry, I'm staying in bed.'[32] At the other end of the conscription scale, there was a volunteer Nasho in Curtis's platoon. 'Every time a volunteer was requested for a duty, the entire platoon nominated him, as he was there by choice,' Curtis said. 'Much general stirring. He took it in good stead.'

Others were at pains to get out, however. Rostered on late night guard duty at Kapooka, John Morris met a dozen or so 'ex-recruits' waiting for the train to Sydney, where they were to be discharged. Several told him they'd gobbled down extra sugar to elevate their blood sugar levels, which meant they were found medically unfit for Army service. This story contrasted with the rumour (popular with army recruits around the world) that the Army was putting bromide in the tea to keep 'horniness' in check. 'The truth was,' Peter Chard commented, 'that we were all so tired with the consistent training, which included night training, no one could get horny!'

There were more serious issues, too. Les Rowe said he was amazed at the innocence and inexperience of many of the recruits at Puckapunyal. 'For a goodly number it was a bit of a lark,' he said, 'and there wasn't much comprehension of what going to Vietnam would entail.' Phil Adam also had reservations about the level of understanding of a couple of his fellow recruits at Singleton. 'I remember thinking that I would not be too happy if my life depended on their being able to carry out orders and procedures correctly.' Ogston wrote in the early months of 1970:

> Vietnam was another place,
> Another planet:
> Little did the green and savage shadows
> Of padi fields, bullets and bombs
> Cast themselves into the minds
> Of these innocent souls,
> Flung together by chance and political folly.
>
> And they were young –
> So very young.[33]

Rowe and Adam never found out what it was like to serve alongside those other recruits in Vietnam. After further training, the two high school teachers were posted to the Royal Australian Army Educational Corps. It was a path followed by more than 300 other conscripted teachers between 1966 and 1972. How these initially bewildered, often humiliated and increasingly fit recruits came to end up in Army Education was sometimes a mystery even to the men themselves.

Nevertheless, a whole new Army life opened up for us, which most of us had never envisaged nor could even have hoped for, one that would bring us face to face with new personal and professional challenges. It also required 'overseas service' – not in Vietnam, but Papua and New Guinea.

4

The Army in PNG: 'A good man, a good citizen – and then a good soldier'

When Australian Labor Prime Minister Paul Keating reached the Kokoda Track monument in Papua New Guinea in April 1992, he surprised onlookers by dropping to his knees to kiss the earth in front of it. Keating wanted to make a point: Australian troops' success in turning back the Japanese advance on Port Moresby, 50 years earlier, was significant for the nation, because it was 'the first time Australians fought alone on Australian territory'.[34] It was even more important than Gallipoli, he said, because the determined Australian fight-back looked forward to an independent nation, rather than back to ties with Britain. Keating was talking about an independent Australia, of course – in 1942, the thought of independence for Papua and New Guinea would have been laughable.

Australian interest in what is now Papua New Guinea began over a hundred years before Keating's visit. The western half of the main island had been part of the Dutch East Indies since 1848 and was known as Dutch New Guinea; the eastern portion was simply 'New Guinea', and not under any formal dominion for much of the 19th century. However, the Premier of the nearby British Colony of Queensland, Sir Thomas McIlwraith, was anxious about signs that German commercial interests in the north-east of New Guinea might lead to a political takeover, and in 1883 twice appealed to the British Colonial Office to annex the eastern half. McIlwraith even tried to claim the area for Queensland, pro-tem, but was rebuffed. 'Not on your Nelly,' replied the Colonial Office, or words to that effect. There is no evidence, said the Colonial Secretary, Lord Derby, that any foreign power is interested in New Guinea. Three months later, he had to wipe the egg off his face when Germany annexed the north-eastern part of the main island and some of the nearby islands, including New Ireland and the now ironically named New Britain.

The British rushed Commander J.E. Erskine and HMS *Nelson* to the scene and hastily arranged for him to annex whatever was left (although, of course, this is not how it was described in diplomatic terms). The outcome was that the south-east portion became the Protectorate of British New Guinea in 1884; the north-east and adjacent islands became known as German New Guinea.

Britain was forced to send a Special Commissioner to its new protectorate, Major General Sir Peter Scratchley, who established his headquarters at Port Moresby in 1885. The seeds of British administration had been sown. Despite some subsequent exploration and goldmining and Christian missionary activity, British New Guinea was described as 'still a poor country',[35] however, when it was (no doubt gladly) handed over to the newly independent Commonwealth of Australia in 1906. Australia changed the territory's name to 'Papua'.

In the north-eastern quarter, the Germans eventually established Rabaul as their administrative headquarters, and it was there that they surrendered to an Australian expeditionary force in September 1914, a month after the outbreak of World War I. An Australian military administration ruled German New Guinea for the next six years, and in 1920 the newly formed League of Nations handed administration of the now mandated territory over to Australia. For the next 20 years an Australian civil administrator operated out of Rabaul for what was now called 'New Guinea', and another one in Port Moresby was responsible for Papua. New Guinea did better economically as the result of gold discoveries and the copra trade, but Australian administration of both territories was relatively passive, with health and education left largely to missionary organisations. If this was 'benign neglect', the Australian government was very good at it.

There were around 1000 Europeans in Papua and over 4000 in New Guinea when Japanese forces landed on New Ireland and New Britain early in 1942, six weeks after Japan declared its expansionist intentions with a surprise attack on the US base at Pearl Harbour. In May 1942, US sea and air forces, with Australian support, inflicted significant damage on a Japanese fleet aiming to establish a strategic base at Port Moresby, in the Battle of the Coral Sea. As a result, Japan instead decided to use ground forces in an attempt to attack Port Moresby from the New Guinea side, across the rugged Owen Stanley Range, which bisected the eastern half of the island. Japanese troops were doing a pretty good job of it until they overstretched their supply lines and in late 1942 ran into the Australian forces on the Kokoda Track, from where they were eventually driven back. It was that success Paul Keating celebrated by kissing the earth 50 years later.

The Prime Minister was right about the connection – Hank Nelson noted that Papua and New Guinea were 'where Australians fought the battles of World War II closest to Australia, the theatre where most Australians went to war, and where over 8,000 Australians are named on the headstones and panels at the British Commonwealth war cemeteries at Rabaul, Lae and Port Moresby'.[36]

The so-called 'fuzzy wuzzy angels' are part of the folklore of World War II in Papua and New Guinea, but indigenous troops also served in Australian Army units in that conflict. Even before the Japanese invasion, the imminence of war in the Pacific had triggered the establishment of the Papuan Infantry Battalion (PIB) in June 1940, drawing on volunteers from the Royal Papuan Constabulary and various Papuan districts. The PIB consisted of Australian officers and indigenous privates and NCOs. Although they signed on for three years and were trained in Port Moresby by the Australian Instructional Corps, for the first 18 months the locals' work was restricted to 'prosaic tasks' such as roadmaking, wharf labouring, quarrying, and occasional guard duty at military installations. Once the Japanese had landed in New Guinea, however, the PIB moved into operational mode and proved themselves in actions against the enemy until the end of the war.

In 1944, with the Japanese now routed from Papua, two New Guinea Infantry Battalions (NGIB) were formed, one in May and the second in September. For some reason the Army decided at this point to segregate the Papuans into the PIB and the New Guineans into the NGIB, an unpopular decision with those in the original PIB, where integration had already occurred. The raising of the new battalions, as part of the Australian Army, led to the establishment in November 1944 of a new command to administer the PIB and NGIB: Headquarters, Pacific Islands Regiment (PIR), headed by Colonel W.M. Edwards, MBE. So the PIR was born, with a Depot Battalion to maintain the flow of partially trained reinforcements to the fighting battalions. By 1945, some indigenous PIR members had risen to the rank of Warrant Officer, and Pacific Islander members of the frontline battalions won three Distinguished Conduct Medals, a George Medal, and 12 Military Medals.

While PI soldiers may have earned the respect of Australian soldiers for their ability and tenacity as jungle and coastal fighters, however, many returning European settlers didn't think much of the idea of retaining a native military force in peacetime. The commander of the wartime administration in Papua and New Guinea, Major General Basil Morris, and the incoming head of the Department of District Services and Native Affairs, J.H. Jones, called for the disbandment of the Pacific Islands Regiment.

One of the justifications for the attitude of senior administrators was unrest within PIR battalions towards the end of the war and immediately afterwards. The first major unhappiness was among those New Guinean members of the original PIB who had been forced to leave that battalion to join 'New Guinean only' battalions – no one seemed to have a satisfactory reason for the lack of integration when there was a common wartime goal. Later, over-dispersal of the battalions into Australian units in mopping up operations against the Japanese also caused disaffection in the ranks. Indigenous troops were also disgruntled about the relativity of Army and police rates of pay – PI soldiers felt they'd done the main fighting and should be paid more. Challenges to NCOs' and officers' commands and to white authority increased among elements of the PIR, only exacerbating the concerns of many Europeans about the emerging cockiness. 'The worst misgivings of the critics seemed to have been justified,' Sinclair said.[37]

The lack of a clear role together with the opposition of senior military and civil personnel resulted in the disbandment of the PIR – after less than two years. 'The Pacific Islands Regiment simply ceased to exist,' Sinclair said.[38] PI soldiers were not only astounded, but bitter at this turn of events. After all their good work and commitment to the Allied cause during the war, and the deaths of the comrades they'd fought alongside, they were now forced to go back to their villages and old way of life. And it was the old way of life that prevailed across the two territories. 'Many of the pre-war European residents came back,' Sinclair said, 'seemingly determined to renew the old *master-boi* relationship that had been the standard of a world that had vanished.'

Among the main proponents for the status quo were members of the Australian New Guinea Administrative Unit (ANGAU), which the Australian Government had established in 1942 as a military administration to jointly govern both the Territory of Papua and the UN Mandated Territory of New Guinea. Its staff were mostly from the pre-war administrations of the two territories, and as Allied troops successively cleared enemy-held areas, ANGAU moved in to take administrative control. The success of this wartime administration led to an Australian decision to continue joint governance of the two territories after the war, an arrangement the newly formed United Nations Organization reluctantly agreed to as it handed over control to Australia of what was now called the Trusteeship Territory of New Guinea. Papua continued as an Australian possession.

The head of the Provisional Civilian Administration from 1945 to 1952, J.K. Murray, struggled to gain support from Europeans in the two territories and from his masters in Canberra. He was dubbed 'Kanaka Jack' for promoting the interests of the indigenous inhabitants. In addition, the Labor Government in Australia was reluctant to support large-scale 'white' investment in the region or extensively expand the employment of native labour to sustain it.

This attitude changed when Robert Menzies' Liberal-Country Party government came to power in 1949, sacked Murray in 1952, and announced a new three-pronged policy for Papua and New Guinea: development of the two territories as part of Australia's external defences, encouragement of private enterprise, and that 'the welfare and advancement of the natives should be a primary consideration'.[39] One outward sign of advancement was the establishment in 1951 of a Legislative Council, but the membership structure reveals that holding on to power remained an art form: of the 29 members, only three were indigenous, and all three were nominated not elected.

The justification of the Australian government's policy of 'gradualism' was that the local inhabitants could not be expected to be ready for self-government for another three generations. The Government's policy was 'to bring the Territory on, but by proper stages,' Menzies said during a visit to Port Moresby in 1957. 'And we are doing a much better job than any of those countries criticising us in the United Nations.'[40] Anti-colonial feeling was mounting across the world, and since Papua and New Guinea were the only significant external territories Australia was responsible for (apart from the Australian Antarctic Territory, unpopulated except for penguins), that's where the focus of criticism fell. As if to add fuel to the anti-colonial fire, the European population in PNG doubled to 20,000 in the decade to 1961.

One bright spot for former indigenous soldiers in the Government's new policy was a decision to revive the Pacific Islands Regiment. After the war, some ex-PIR men had returned to their villages disgruntled but prepared to use their new skills for the benefit of the community; others continued to harbour resentment and were restless and sometimes trouble-makers when they returned home. Their initial hope in the immediate post-war years that the PIR might still be re-formed soon evaporated as reconstruction of ravaged towns and villages took priority. However, in 1950, the Minister for Territories, Percy Spender, announced the raising of a locally-recruited battalion for Papua and New Guinea. It would be known as the Pacific Islands Regiment, as a tribute to the achievements of its predecessor in World War II.

'It would be idle to claim that the decision to re-raise a PNGuinean Battalion was welcomed by all the white population of PNG,' Sinclair said.[41] Some of the ANGAU officials had now become district officers and assistant district officers, and 'some retained their old prejudices'. There was considerable disquiet in the business and plantation communities about the move, whereas another decision about the same time, to establish a CMF-type organisation, the Papua New Guinea Volunteer Rifles, for whites only, apparently was not opposed in those quarters. The PNGVR did not become multi-racial until 1964.

The new PIR came into being on 11 March 1951 as a unit of the Australian Army, and Lt. Col. H.L. Sabin took command in October. The battalion had Australian officers, warrant officers and some sergeants, and in the Army structure was attached to Northern Command, based in Brisbane. Land for the new battalion was set aside on the outskirts of Port Moresby at the site of a wartime military hospital and given the name 'Taurama Barracks'. Many of those in the initial intake had been members of the first PIR.

From the start, attempts were made to enlist men equally from across Papua, the New Guinea mainland and the New Guinea islands, and recruits were deliberately allocated to sections to avoid concentrations of any particular tribal grouping. It was a deliberate policy, first followed in the original PIB, to have soldiers from different parts of the country train and work together and so minimise traditional hostilities. By 1952 there were sufficient numbers for four rifle companies and a Battalion HQ. One of the companies was posted to an outstation established late that year at Vanimo, a small town on the north-west coast of New

Guinea, close to the Dutch New Guinea border. In 1954 a second PIR outstation was established on Los Negros, an island off Manus Island in the Bismarck Sea, but in 1960 this was moved to Moem Point near Wewak. The battalion's Area Command was subsequently set up at Murray Barracks, Port Moresby.

The PIR was probably the only national organisation in the 1950s with a significant indigenous workforce, and even then the officers and senior NCOs were white. In 1960, the Minister for Territories, Paul Hasluck, was quoted by the *New York Times* as saying that 'Papuans would not be ready for self-determination for 30 years'.[42] The following year, when the Menzies Government was returned to power by a single seat, Australia initiated a reconstituted Legislative Council for Papua and New Guinea, with 47 members, of whom six were elected native members and six were nominated native members. There was no chance an indigenous majority might vote against an Administration measure, and a visiting UN mission in 1962 was unimpressed with the rate of progress, and called for an elected parliament by 1964, a pathway to higher education for local inhabitants, and a World Bank economic survey of the two territories.

The Australian Government bristled at the critical tenor of the report, and Hasluck scathingly described the chairman of the visiting mission, Sir Hugh Foot, as 'primarily an actor – the sort of actor who always tried to upstage other members of the cast'.[43] After the dust had settled, the Australian Government implemented most of the recommendations, with some modifications. In preparation for likely changes, from 1963 the Administration introduced political education of the local population and focused more on developing local government. 'There is no doubt,' Sinclair said, 'that this was the beginning of PNG's march to nationhood.'[44] For a while, however, it was a very slow march, with the Australian Government controlling the tempo.

A more pressing issue was possible encroachment from Indonesia. President Sukarno had led his country's independence from the Netherlands in 1949, except for the western half of New Guinea. From the mid-1950s, the Netherlands resisted his calls for what was now called West New Guinea to be returned to Indonesia, so in 1958, Sukarno nationalised Dutch interests, and in 1962 took direct action by first sending motor torpedo boats against the Dutch navy, then dropping paratroops into the disputed territory. After more military skirmishes and diplomatic to-ing and fro-ing, the United Nations became involved in mediation. Subsequent negotiations resulted in Indonesia taking over West New Guinea early in 1963, at which time it was given the name West Irian.

Concerns in the early 1960s about Indonesian incursions led to Australian attempts to better map the border of West Irian with Papua and New Guinea. While an aerial survey was under discussion, Paul Hasluck, the Minister for Territories, approved the erections of signs at the main crossing points along the border, indicating that 'somewhere within the next few hundred yards the track crossed from Australia into Indonesian territory'.[45] In other words, (except for a bend of the Fly River) no one knew exactly where the border was. Territory police and the PIR undertook regular border patrols.

Around the same time, Sukarno instituted a policy of 'confrontation' with the soon-to-be Federation of Malaysia – comprising Malaya and Singapore, along with Sarawak and Sabah on the island of Borneo – claiming the proposed amalgamation was a device by Britain to maintain its colonial power in the region. An Indonesian-supported insurrection in the independent state of Brunei in December 1962 was put down by British troops, but from early the next year trained Indonesian infiltrators regularly crossed borders in Borneo on propaganda and sabotage missions, and were dropped into Malaya.

This sabre-rattling and minor military action by its heavily populated northern neighbour alarmed the Australian Government, which not only administered two territories that had a common border with West New Guinea, but also had treaty obligations to assist Britain. The Australian External Affairs Minister, Sir Garfield Barwick, initiated talks in Jakarta in July 1962 about the 'serious danger of large-scale hostilities developing near Australia through miscalculations or misunderstanding.'[46]

Nevertheless, Australia initially rejected requests from the British and the Malaysian Governments for military aid because of fears the 'konfrontasi' might escalate to include the border with Papua and New Guinea. In fact, although Australia finally did commit a battalion and other Army units, along with elements of the Navy and Air Force, to active service in Malaysia, and 17 servicemen died there (including a National Serviceman in a truck accident in Borneo in 1966), the country maintained diplomatic relations with Indonesia throughout this period, and Indonesian officers continued to train at Australian military colleges.

All of this militarism gave the Pacific Islands Regiment, still led by white officers, an increased importance in Papua New Guinea, not for the good of the Territory but for the defence of Australia. In September 1963, as the Federation of Malaysia came into being and the Indonesian confrontation began to ramp up, the Menzies Government announced a major expansion of the Army in Papua and New Guinea – another battalion for the PIR, upgrading of the airstrip at Wewak, the building of new barracks, and the consolidation of the Training Depot at Goldie River, near Port Moresby. This was part of Australia's northern defence strategy, relying on mobile forces stationed at strategic bases, including the PIR, to move quickly to counter any sudden military attack. 'We must prepare for all eventualities, including the control and, if necessary, defence of the frontier between West New Guinea and the Territory of Papua and New Guinea,' Menzies told Parliament.[47] A third battalion was mooted.

Over the next few years, against the background of a Territory-wide election in 1964 for a new House of Assembly, the Army spread its handprint across the mainland – a new HQ at Murray Barracks, upgrading of the key facility of Goldie River Training Depot for recruits, extension of Taurama Barracks for 1PIR, and then a stretch across to the north-west where Moem Barracks was built at Wewak to house the new battalion, 2PIR, which was finally raised after an extended recruiting campaign. In 1968, the Army established a Military Cadet School at Igam Barracks, Lae, which had been designated for the proposed third battalion. 3PIR never eventuated, however, mostly due to the winding down of tensions with Indonesia as the 'confrontation' ended in 1966, followed shortly after by the deposal of President Sukarno and replacement with the more politically moderate Suharto.

Nevertheless, a company of 2PIR was stationed on a three-month rotation at Vanimo, and units of both battalions patrolled the Papua and New Guinea border with West Irian (these days known as West Papua). Border incursions were a topic of constant discussion between the Administration and the Australian Department of External Affairs throughout the 1960s, and the PNG Police Commissioner, Ray Whitrod, complained in 1969 that Territory police, who were not allowed to fire back, 'were taunted as "women"' and that 'Indonesian patrols well over the [PNG] side of the border are quite common.'[48] The situation was complicated by alleged border crossings back and forth by 'dissidents' opposed to the Indonesian presence in West Irian.

A company from 1PIR also did a twelve-month tour of duty at Igam Barracks on rotation, which Chalkie Ron Inglis later noted was a welcome posting for the PI troops because Lae was considered a much more pleasant environment than Port Moresby and their families could accompany them. Igam Barracks also housed other military units, including the headquarters of the PNGVR and of the high school Cadet Units.

When the Australian Government introduced conscription from 1965, there were rumours that National Servicemen might be sent to the Territory and based at Igam Barracks as part of their training. 'Surely,' said the Editor of the *South Pacific Post*, 'there is something to be said for giving National Service trainees a "finishing course" of say six months in PNG ...'[49]

During a visit to the Territory in April 1965, before the first intake of Nashos had entered the gates of Kapooka or Puckapunyal, the Army's Chief of General Staff, Lt. Gen. Sir John Wilton, quickly scotched the rumour. No Australian troops would be based at Igam Barracks or train in PNG, he said. At this stage, the idea of using conscript teachers wasn't even a whisper in the wind.

Although the full quiver of defence arrows announced by Menzies in 1963 was never released, the consequential Army build-up in Papua and New Guinea led to the establishment in 1965 of a separate command structure: PNG Command. The Pacific Islands Regiment, with two battalions of trained soldiers, and bases in and around Moresby and on the northern coast, was now a significant organised force in Papua New Guinea. There was enough evidence from newly independent nations elsewhere for some people to be concerned about the potential for the PIR to become an instrument to overthrow an elected government rather than to support it, when Papua New Guinea eventually became an independent country (whenever that might be).

In April 1966 the Army appointed Brigadier Ian Murray Hunter as head of PNG Command. Hunter had seen what had happened in some other developing countries and had very clear ideas about how to stabilise the Army to make it a servant of the government rather than for it to *become* the government. Education played a big part in Hunter's vision for the PIR and, since the Army already had an Educational Corps, all he needed to do was make sure there were enough teachers for the task. He just happened to have an idea about where those teachers might come from ...

5

Army Education: An act of faith

When my teacher colleagues and I were dragged mostly reluctantly into the Army by courtesy of Robert Menzies' lottery barrel, few of us had ever heard of Army Education. Even when we were invited to apply for the Royal Australian Army Educational Corps during recruit training, most of us didn't know too much about it. Those who were drafted in the early days from other Corps probably knew even less.

We certainly weren't aware that Army Education had been a part of the Australian Army as far back as 1918. It turned out that its existence was partly down to Charles Bean, Australia's Official Historian for World War I. As a war correspondent on the Western Front, Bean had seen the success of the short-lived AIF Education Service in keeping Australian troops occupied at the end of World War I while they waited for ships to transport them back to their native land. He described the Service as 'the godsend of the repatriation period',[50] and within days of Australia's declaration of its involvement in World War II in 1939, wrote to the Minister for the Army, urging an immediate start on 'a scheme of physical and mental recreation' for the troops.[51] There was initial scepticism and opposition, however, and it wasn't until early 1941 that Army Minister Percy Spender announced the establishment of the Australian Army Education Service (AAES). Its purpose was to 'give the soldier a chance to revert to civil life equipped mentally and vocationally to his own advantage and to the advantage of the society to which he must return'.[52] This was seen as especially important for a volunteer army.

When I asked my father about Army Education in World War II, in which he'd been in the regular army, he remembered the Service's regular magazine, 'Salt', but not much else. Yet the Service at its peak had 900 staff and a massive program of lectures, classes, libraries, publications and classical music concerts (rather different from the touring troupes that entertained Australian troops in Vietnam in the 1960s). Perhaps the volunteer soldiers made more use of the Service than regulars like my father ...

The first Army Education Officer sent to Papua and New Guinea, W.C. Groves, turned up in September 1941, just three months before Japan entered the war. He reported 'apathy common, antipathy here and there',[53] perhaps not unexpected responses, given that they expected war to land on their doorstep any minute.

Nevertheless, Groves's words could be a catch-cry for the Educational Corps down through the years, because it has had a roller coaster ride within the Army organisation. Major W.H. John, Director of Army Education 1952–55, observed: 'Not everyone believes in the need or even the desirability of a distinct Educational Corps in the Army. Its existence is, in some ways, an act of faith. Membership of such a Corps implies not only professional competence and personal integrity, but a faith in ends which are not altogether demonstrable and tangible'.[54]

Eventually Education Staff in PNG in World War II did produce demonstrable and tangible outcomes, particularly through the 'news-talk'. As the war moved back and forth across the island, the troops were starved of news of the progress of the war in the Pacific and Europe. Education officers and NCOs brought them up to date with regular briefings and then daily news-sheets churned out on portable duplicating machines. One officer estimated that he and a sergeant covered more than 2000 miles (3000 kilometres) on foot and borrowed horses, to give 65 news-talks inside a month.

Some of these talks were literally in the front line: 'On one occasion, I had just concluded the news-reading and commentary with map to about eight men,' wrote one education officer, 'when the Japs, who were in pillboxes about 25 yards away, started their morning hate session with a clatter of LMG [light machine gun] and MMG [medium machine gun] and rifle fire. We all ducked behind the big fallen tree trunk against which we were sitting, and the bullets went well over our heads. At the same time, a Jap sniper ... also opened up. He hit and killed one of the men in another of the foxholes just a few yards ahead.'[55]

By the time the war ended in August 1945, there were 65 Army Education Centres operating in the New Guinea-Solomons area, but the work of the Service wound down as troops were demobilised, and its main role post-war was supporting the British Commonwealth

Occupation Force in Japan. In 1948 Army Education was recognised as a full-blown Corps (AAEC) within the Army, and in 1960 received royal recognition and was designated the 'Royal Australian Army Educational Corps' (RAAEC).

Army Education came back to PNG in 1954, three years after the re-formation of the Pacific Islands Regiment, in the form of Warrant Officer Class 2 N.F. Clark. Up to this time, there was no basic educational level for indigenous recruits because most applicants had only a few years' primary education, most likely completed at a Mission school, the major providers of schooling at the time. Former members of the wartime PIR would have had even less, possibly none.

Warrant Officer Clark's job was to teach English to indigenous soldiers, the first time that students in Army Education classes were Papuans and New Guineans, since the wartime program had been only for Australian soldiers. Clark used what he called the 'situation system', then being used in Australia to teach 'New Australians' English. 'Only about 15 minutes of the hour's course comprises verbal instruction,' he said. 'The rest of the time is taken up with gestures. The first lesson the men received was on pronouns. I point to an illustration of a woman and say "she"; I point to myself and say "me". When pointing to a native soldier for 'he', I have to be careful that I don't look at him, because he may confuse it with you ...'[56]

Clark may also have confused his listeners, but whatever the method he used, his colleagues in other Corps were unimpressed, 'These English classes that Clark started didn't go down too well in the Sergeants' Mess,' Bill Guest said. 'Everything then was in Pidgin, orders and instructions. When they started to bring in English words, the troops were confused, and we found our happy little life as we had it in PIR started to go the other way. Like everything else, a little knowledge is a dangerous thing ...'[57]

Nevertheless, it was generally accepted that raising the standard of education in the PIR was essential if indigenous soldiers were to aspire to promotion beyond the lower levels. 'I suppose it had to come,' Guest said, 'but it seemed to me to be the turning-point in the degree of tranquillity of PIR.'

Perhaps education is always like that when it really makes an impact – a turning point, and perhaps that's what its role in PIR was from then on – to challenge the troops and give them confidence in communicating and problem-solving and understanding the world in preparation for a time when they themselves would need to make significant decisions in their own country. Times would not always be as tranquil as they were in 1954, although no one at that time would have been game to predict that within 20 years, a self-governing PNG would be on the brink of independence.

Clark was replaced by Captain Ian Bayles, who had the double-barrelled assignment of teaching English to the indigenous members of PIR and Pidgin to Australian troops. Although Bayles's work was applauded, predictably, given that he was the only teacher for a whole battalion, 'it was obvious throughout the year that the commitment was really beyond the capacity of one man, irrespective of his skill or energy.'[58] Even when Warrant Officer R.J. Williams arrived in 1958 to help Bayles, the going was tough: 'The task of teaching English as a foreign language even to literate people is always something of a challenge and to teach it to primitive natives requires great skill and patience.' Most of the soldiers in the lowest level class were from the highlands, and Bayles said 'the situations normally presented to elicit desired responses are so far removed from the experiences of these people that each new lesson has to be something of an experiment.'[59]

The early 60s was a time when 'Teaching English as a Second Language' was not a part of teacher preparation in Australia, so any teacher would have found the task in PIR an uphill battle. Bayles and his Army Education colleagues would have been through Australian teacher training programs, and clearly the educational theory they'd learned in those courses was under severe challenge when they tried to apply it in PNG.

At the recruit training depot, some newcomers couldn't speak any English at all. 'We tried to make sure the recruits could at least write their own names,' Henry Dachs, an AAEC Captain in PNG in 1959 said. 'Most could only make their mark (a thumb print using an ink pad) when they arrived at the Training Company, but it was seen as a very prestigious thing to be able to actually sign their names on the pay sheet when they collected their pay.'[60]

By 1962, before the expansion Menzies announced, PIR comprised 660 Pacific Islanders and 75 Australian officers and warrant officers. Its Commanding Officer, Brigadier J.W. Norrie, told the local *South Pacific Post* that education within the regiment was a key element of the soldiers' development. 'We want every Pacific Islander who leaves this regiment to be able to return to his main town or village and be capable of participating in local affairs.'[61] The picture Norrie painted was an indication of the emphasis the Army placed on education in the PIR as well as of the unique role the Brigadier saw for the Army in preparing soldiers to take more civic responsibility when they left the Army. It was a philosophy that Norrie's successors were to carry on.

Although Australia was moving slowly in handing over power, already the PIR was different from 'Territorial' armies in other colonised countries, because at this stage it was part of the defence strategy of the Australian Army, and even in these early years was being prepared for its part in an independent nation, considered to be a long time ahead.

In 1962 the RAAEC said that the 'educational spadework' of the past was producing results, but lamented once again that 'the task of developing real proficiency among native soldiers in both oral and written English is a formidable one and greater resources will be needed to carry out a really comprehensive educational programme.'[62] Within the next few years, those greater resources and a comprehensive educational program were to come about, initiated by two senior officers, neither of whom was in the Educational Corps: Brigadier Maurice Austin and Brigadier Ian Murray Hunter.

Austin was an experienced career soldier, having graduated from the Royal Military College, Duntroon in 1935 and served in the Middle East and New Guinea in World War II, and later in Korea. When the Military Board instituted a review of education in the Army in 1962, Colonel 'Bunny' Austin, then Director of Personnel Services at AHQ Canberra, was appointed to the committee, which was chaired by the Director of Military Training, Brigadier G.F. Larkin.

A major reason for the review was a concern about the level of education in the Australian Army, especially among the new recruits. Because of the solid state of the economy in the early 1960s, employment was high and those recruits who were accepted tended to be under-skilled and under-educated. They didn't deserve the epithets 'flotsam and jetsam' that the Minister for the Army inflicted on them, but many of them did need help with their literacy in particular and their education in general.

The Education Review Committee gave an expanded role to the RAAEC, which was a welcome acknowledgement for the Corps of its significance to the Army after some years of trying to find a clear place for itself.

It wasn't only Australian recruits who were deemed to be under-educated. A whole chapter of the Review Committee's 1963 report was devoted to the educational needs of the Pacific Islands Regiment, with the two most serious issues identified as the need to remedy 'the serious educational weaknesses of present members of PIR' and to 'superimpose higher education, as required, on the next generation of soldiers'.

The major specific educational weakness was seen as literacy in English, 'especially in relation to the ability to think in English', and the Education Review Committee recommended that 'in the interests of nationhood, English should be developed as soon as possible as the sole means of communication in the Regiment'.[63] This recommendation took into account a number of factors, including 'the imminence of self-government in Papua/New Guinea' and 'the role and responsibility of the PIR in the process of transition to self-government and administration in the territory'. The move towards using English was in line with Australian government policy for the Territory, but the mention of 'the imminence of self-government' in an Army document in 1963 is surprisingly ahead of Government thinking at the time. It shows how forward thinking Army leaders were in regard to PNG.

Although the Government's policy was no longer 'gradualism', it was certainly 'softly, softly'. In January 1964, just after he moved from the Territories portfolio to Defence, Paul Hasluck said: 'Self-government … means, in my book, government according to a form chosen by the people themselves, introduced at a time which they think appropriate and confided to a government which they themselves have entrusted with office. … They have to shape a government that can work in the circumstances in which they live.'[64] In other words, self-government in PNG was nowhere near 'imminent'. The next step, 'independence', was hardly in the Government's lexicon.

Hasluck later claimed to have made 'unremitting efforts' towards self-development for PNG but said he had failed to persuade others of the urgency. 'Unfortunately,' said Wolfers, 'his sense of urgency had been relative – to the complacent indifference of most Australians, to the lack of interest in political development on the part of the territorial administration, and to the contempt for, and at times the opposition to, government policy felt by much of the territory's expatriate community.'[65] If Wolfers is correct, this only makes the commitment of Army leaders and the Educational Corps to the development of PNG all the more remarkable.

The Review Committee noted that in the 1962 PIR recruit intake, only 11% were unable to speak in simple English, and that significant progress had been made in teaching English and Arithmetic at the basic level, but there was still much to be done. Indigenous soldiers were smart enough, but as Army educators had discovered, they were coming from a different baseline of knowledge to that required for a speedy assimilation of the subject matter in the Army certificates. What's more, once they'd finished basic training, it was hit or miss whether the PI soldiers ever had general education again once they were posted elsewhere – outside of Goldie River, only Taurama Barracks had Education staff, and then only one officer.

The committee saw this as an important and urgent problem, and proposed that from 1964 additional Education staff should be recruited for the Territory from 'young trained teachers' on secondment from Australian State Education Departments for two- or three-year periods. The National Service scheme was still 12 months away from being announced, but it was almost as if the committee had anticipated it with its recommendation that 'in view of the special nature of their duties, which combine those of soldier and teacher, those appointees should be given a military orientation and familiarisation course of some three months' duration before proceeding to their appointment'. The committee proposed an RAAEC complement of 10 officers and one warrant officer for PNG, headed by a Major, as against the existing establishment of two officers and one warrant officer. It went without saying that the new appointees would all be men, since the Educational Corps, along with most of the Army, had no women in its ranks in the 1960s.

In January 1965, about the same time as PNG Command was established, Major Henry Dachs returned to Moresby to take up the new position of Deputy Assistant Director, Army Education (DADAE). Dachs was grateful for the new Education officers and warrant officers, allocated to PNG Command, but still found himself short of support staff. 'When the new officers were due, I had to go out to the airstrip in a Moke, which was a very spartan, basic vehicle, to collect them,' he said. 'Needless to say, they were a bit taken aback that their driver was a Major, and they were even more startled when I showed them where they'd be sleeping. ... They hadn't visualised bunks in a tent when they'd embarked on the great adventure of serving in PNG.'[66]

1965 was also, of course, the year that the first intake of conscripts began training for National Service. Suddenly, the Educational Corps had another possible source of 'young trained teachers' who were obliged to undergo 'military orientation and familiarisation' as part of their training. It seemed that the stars were aligning, but a catalyst was needed to precipitate the recruitment of these 'soldiers and teachers' to the significant task of developing the indigenous Army in the Territory of Papua and New Guinea.

The spark appeared in the form of the re-institution early in 1966 of the AHQ Education Review Committee, with a broad brief 'to assess developing requirements and plan to meet them'.[67] This time 'Bunny' Austin, now a brigadier and Deputy Adjutant General in Canberra, chaired the committee. The exact chronology of events is not clear, but a second key player as far as PNG was concerned was Brigadier Ian M. Hunter, whose appointment as head of PNG Command in April 1966 coincided with the re-establishment of the Review Committee.

George Kearney, who was posted to PNG Command as a Major in Psychology Corps in 1966, believed Hunter took the initiative. 'Hunter had taken the view that if we could stabilise the Army and make it realise its civil and civic responsibilities, then we had a chance of that Army being useful when independence came,' Kearney said. '[He] went down to Canberra to the Chief of General Staff and they got an agreement that they would take as many Army educators as possible to PNG to become instructors. National Servicemen who were selected were guaranteed promotion to Sergeant and a teaching role in PNG.'[68] It seems likely that Hunter's visit to Canberra triggered the two-week visit by Austin to PNG Command in late May and early June 1966, with the intention of confirming the arrangement.

During that visit, Austin met with Mal Ashton, then an RAAEC officer at Goldie Barracks, later a Director of Army Education. 'I met him in the old Officers' Mess 'haus win' [open-air hut] overlooking the river,' Ashton recalled, 'and we talked education – what we were doing, what we planned/would like to do, and how we could do it. Bunny Austin, out of the blue, said that we had lots of National Servicemen in the system and asked what we could do if he gave us some.'[69]

This seems to have been the first time that the idea of utilising Nasho teachers in PNG had been proposed to serving members of the Corps, although a former RAAEC Warrant Officer 2, Dan Winkel, who was in PNG at that time, believed that Henry Dachs had a hand in it too. Ashton could hardly believe it. 'We thought it was Christmas,' he said. An RAAEC newsletter reported that 'important changes' for PNG Command were expected to follow the Army HQ Education Committee's review, with the first result being 'the attachment of 25 National Service teachers to this Command to give a much needed boost to the use of English'.[70] This number of appointments would triple the Education complement in the Command at the time.

'We suggested six at Goldie and that is what we got,' Ashton said.

The Director of Army Education in 1970, Brigadier Ernest Gould, agreed about the importance of Hunter's role in introducing the extensive use of conscripted teachers in PNG from 1966. 'The army scheme of education in Papua New Guinea owes an unpayable debt to its present Commander, Brigadier Ian Murray Hunter, CVO, MBE,' Gould said in 1970. 'It was he who, after analysing the problems of emergent nations in terms of the power groups inside them, came to the conclusion that emergent armies, no less than emergent nations, foundered because of the shallowness of their educational support. From this conviction, an educational scheme has been mounted which for magnitude, scope, intensity and enlightenment is without parallel in military history.'[71]

There was, however, a third person in this scenario: Malcolm Fraser, the Army Minister. Fraser was elected to parliament in 1955 and spent 10 years on the backbench in Robert Menzies' Government. When Menzies retired in January 1966, the new Prime Minister, Harold Holt, appointed Fraser as Minister for the Army, in what the PM regarded as his 'outer ministry'. Hunter took command in PNG in April that year, and as Army Minister, Fraser told the brigadier his role was 'first, to build an efficient national army capable of playing a vital part in the defence of the territory against aggression, and second, to provide for the future, an … army which is completely loyal to the Administration or established Government'.[72]

'That was the real turning point,' Hunter said later. 'In the past, military training had been considered as a purely repetitive procedure of teaching soldiers military skills. Now training was aimed at the most vital commodity – the man – to make him a good man and a good citizen, and then, and only then, a good soldier.'[73] It was a similar philosophy to the one the AAES had adopted in World War II, with its notion of the 'soldier-citizen', who would return to civilian life after the war.

So, in the first six months of 1966, key appointments brought together three men who had a similar outlook on the development of the Army in PNG: Malcom Fraser as Minister for the Army, Brigadier Ian Hunter as Head of PNG Command, and Brigadier Bunny Austin as Chair of the AHQ Education Committee. Fraser didn't tell Hunter how to achieve the outcome he wanted, of course, but this was the second year of the National Service scheme, and no doubt the two brigadiers quickly saw how they could utilise the training and capabilities of conscripted teachers to meet educational needs in PNG. The Army may have been opposed to conscription at the time Menzies introduced it, but here was an opportunity to exploit the consequences for the good of the individual, the Army and a nation-to-be.

'What I want is a young, virile army with just enough career men for experience and continuity,' Hunter said. 'The rest will be injected back into the community – better and more capable citizens for their years with us.'[74] With Hunter solidly behind the strategy, Austin had the clout as Deputy Adjutant General to redirect Nashos as required.

Back in Australia, a scattering of conscripted teachers, working on military bases as clerks, medics, artillerymen, signallers and numerous other Army occupations for which they had minimal training and often little interest, didn't know it, but they were about to help Brigadier Hunter achieve his vision.

6

Three stripes and you're in: Selection for Army Education

At age 20, Denis O'Rourke was in the first of the 'teacher cohorts' when he went into the Army on 2 January 1966, having completed his training the year before to be a New South Wales high school science teacher. He didn't want to be called up, but survived recruit training at Kapooka ('I expected it to be what it was'), and after that first ten weeks was sent to North Head in Sydney to train as a battery surveyor in the Artillery. O'Rourke was then posted to Wacol, on the outskirts of Brisbane, for more artillery training. Vietnam loomed.

Out of the blue, in July a mate in the office at 4 Field Regiment at Wacol asked him if he wanted to go to Sydney for the weekend. He said they wanted to interview schoolteachers.

'It wasn't until I got to Sydney that I found out what the interview was about,' O'Rourke said.

The Army was, of course, looking for teachers to send to PNG. Soon afterwards, O'Rourke was transferred to the Royal Australian Army Educational Corps, and on 12 August he and six other newly appointed Nasho teachers arrived in Port Moresby, with three stripes on their sleeves.

All of the 26 Education Sergeants posted to Papua and New Guinea in 1966 were appointed by inter-corps transfer, sometimes to their surprise, although most welcomed the opportunity. Presumably they were found by someone trawling though the records of the January intake, looking for suitable candidates. By the time I went into Nasho in 1969, the selection process was more organised, and in the later years most of us who ended up as sergeants in the RAAEC were invited to apply during recruit training. That invitation was the second one issued; the first was for officer training, which was available for all intakes from the beginning. Teachers, graduates and other recruits with at least a high school leaving certificate qualification were invited, sometimes even encouraged, to apply.

***

At the time National Service was reintroduced in 1965, the Australian Army trained its officers at the Royal Military College, Duntroon, Canberra, and at the Officer Cadet School at Portsea in coastal Victoria. The Duntroon course lasted for four years, and from 1967 included degree studies with the University of New South Wales; the Portsea program originally began as a six-month course, which was later extended to a year. Since Nashos were in the Army for 'only' two years, a 22-week 'fast-track' officer-training course was developed for them at the Officer Training Unit (OTU) at Scheyville, north-west of Sydney. Between 1965 and 1973, over 1600 of the almost 1900 Scheyville graduates were National Servicemen, the rest being regulars.

From the first year of Nasho, applications for officer training at Scheyville were called for in about the third week of recruit training, before requests for Corps posting were submitted. Teachers, graduates and other recruits with at least a leaving certificate qualification were invited, sometimes even encouraged, to apply.

A standard psychological test and an initial interview at the recruit training centre whittled down the numbers, and the survivors were then grouped in teams and tasked with an outdoor activity, such as finding their way across a pond using ropes and planks. An observer group watched the would-be officers for signs of problem-solving, ability to work with others, and leadership.

Tom Derham, a primary school teacher from Victoria, went through the full selection process at Puckapunyal in 1972. 'The final interview with a group of officers was harrowing,' he said, 'with the Psychology officer doing his best to try and destroy my confidence (in the reasons for my application) entirely.' Derham and the other recruits who made it through were sent straight to OTU.

The pressure-cooker course was designed to challenge, provoke and develop the trainees as leaders of men in battle, and all of them knew they could be doing just that in Vietnam within a very short time. Derham remembered the rigour of the program:

The first 30 days were full on, with no days off and 14-hour days of formal program activities, each hour (apart from meal breaks) included 55 minute sessions of drill, military lectures and training etc., and only 5 minutes to get from one session to another (always on the double), and sometimes a complete change of outfit/equipment was required in that time. Leaving of rooms in full inspection order at all times during the day was a requirement. All equipment care etc. to be maintained in full inspection order needed to be done in your own time.

If you were unlucky enough to be given a punishment of some kind for a minor infringement (extra drill or a charge), you then had to be on the parade ground at 6.30 am in full battle gear for inspections and a drill session. A charge also involved having to report on time to the Duty Officer at various times of the day for a uniform and equipment inspection. Your performance in every area was constantly being assessed by every officer and other training personnel in the Unit and you had a regular meeting with a guidance officer to assess your performance and progress.

It's little wonder that 30% of the trainees didn't finish the course. Tom Derham was not one of them. On graduation in mid-1972, he accepted a posting in the RAAEC to a position with 1PIR at Taurama Barracks, Port Moresby. He was one of possibly almost 20 Nasho officers posted with Army Education to PNG between 1966 and 1972.

Ian Hodder, whose call-up had been deferred from the first intake in 1965, also completed the OTU course, in 1967, but was told that he would not be one of two graduating officers to be posted to the RAAEC. He still had the option of going to Papua New Guinea, but as a sergeant. Hodder had enjoyed his time at Scheyville despite the bastardisation he said was ingrained into the system there, but decided he'd rather have three stripes on his sleeve as an Education Instructor. His decision not to become an officer was not well received by senior OTU staff. 'I was disappointed with my treatment when I decided to opt out,' he said, without enlargement.

John Herlihy had the opposite problem. When he entered National Service in early 1967, one month short of his 21st birthday, Herlihy had heard that recruits with a teaching qualification or degree were being selected for Army Education in PNG, but he was keen to go to Vietnam in one of the Arms Corps. 'With that in mind, I conveniently neglected to mention on my pre-entry NS paperwork that I had an Arts degree,' he said, 'listing my highest education qualification as the NSW Leaving Certificate.' He was selected for officer training at OTU and thought he had a high chance of going to Vietnam with the Armoured Corps.

'However, the system caught up with me,' he said, 'and a week before graduating from OTU Scheyville, I was paraded to the Commandant, reprimanded for the 'oversight' and told my graduation posting would be changed ... to RAAEC.' Herlihy subsequently spent 13 months as an officer in Army Education at Murray Barracks, Port Moresby, and then signed on for another 11 months to take a short service commission with the ARA. He was one of the few Nashos without a teacher qualification posted to Education Corps.

Some felt the icy wind of official disapproval earlier in the process. Rob Daniel's papers were stamped 'OFFICER POTENTIAL' during recruit training, and he duly applied. Prior to the interview, applicants were asked if they had any questions. 'At this time I revealed my opposition to the Vietnam War and withdrew from the process,' Daniel said. His attitude and decision rankled with senior staff, particularly as he had been an under-officer in his school cadet unit, and he said he was threatened with court martial. The threat was not carried through, but 'certainly made life for the next few weeks interesting and challenging, as I was painted as a stirrer,' the West Australian said.

Les Rowe was selected for officer training but withdrew when applications were called for Education Instructors in PNG. He'd already been to the Territory twice during his university years, and felt confident of being selected for the RAAEC, 'despite dire warnings from the Army psychologist that I could have shot myself in the foot by refusing to go to Scheyville'. A number of Rowe's fellow teacher conscripts told the OTU selection panel at their initial interview that their first preference was Army Education in PNG.

***

Those not eligible or rejected for OTU or who chose not to apply were able to nominate three preferences for the corps they would like to be posted to after recruit training. Some were anxious to make choices that would limit their chances of going to Vietnam; others were keen to go, or to make use of their skills developed in civilian life. However, there was a general belief among conscripts that the actual choices were Infantry, Infantry, or Infantry, since that was the largest corps, and specialist knowledge was not required. Teachers were hugely overqualified.

Even before the PNG scheme, a few conscripted teachers made it into Army Education. Private E. Taska from New South Wales,

Victorian Privates P. Rudnev and G. Wilding, and Private W.J. Lucas and Lieutenant L.J. Bruggeman, both from South Australia, all of whom were called up in the first intake in late June/early July 1965, were the first National Servicemen to be posted to the RAAEC. In September that year, after recruit training, the five participated in a five-day Corps familiarisation course at Puckapunyal where they learned what lay ahead for them in the next 21 months. Records are hard to come by, but it seems Wilding was later posted to PNG Training Depot at Goldie River, apparently the first Nasho Chalkie in PNG, but possibly without rank, and Lucas and Smith were promoted to Lance Corporal in Australian Education units early in 1966.

The fate of the other four is lost in Army files, but Lucas's first posting after the Puckapunyal orientation was Bandiana Ordnance Depot in Victoria, 'and here I was fortunate enough to be introduced to the delicate workings of an army RAAEC library,' he said.[75] Then the South Australian spent five months at the Education Section at Broadmeadows in Victoria, teaching Amy Education Certificate subjects, as well as 'learning every bend in the road between Melbourne and [hometown] Adelaide'. When Lucas was subsequently posted to the Education Section at Kapooka, which took both ARA and Nasho recruits, he was sure his final 17 months of Nasho would be an 'absolute misery'. Arriving at his new posting in January 1966 in the middle of a dust storm did nothing to change his feelings.

The dust bowl turned to green lawns and modern brick buildings appeared, however, and Lucas came to enjoy the experience of teaching in the Educational Corps. 'The benefits of teaching Social Studies, Arithmetic and English to recruits who have never excelled at school in any academic form before are untold,' the 21-year-old said on his return to a school in South Australia in 1967. 'The insight I gained into the problems existing in schools has been of considerable aid to me in my effectual return to civilian teaching.'[76]

When the PNG education scheme was introduced in mid-1966, Lucas and his colleagues had only six months of Nasho to go, so the Army turned to the likes of O'Rourke, Lindsay, and Teggelove, from the January intake that year, and simply transferred them to the Educational Corps. In later years, teachers were able to apply for the RAAEC during recruit training, which meant a PNG posting if successful. Occasional cross-corps transfers continued, however.

The possibility of a PNG posting had trickled through to a few teacher conscripts in later years, including John Humphrey, who was 25 when he entered National Service in 1970: 'I was quite happy to go into National Service, as I had heard about the Education Corps and possible postings to PNG,' Humphrey said. 'I had, for some time, dreamt of teaching in PNG, and I saw National Service as a means of achieving this.'

He was lucky. His optimism paid off, but not all conscripted teachers saw their wishes fulfilled so neatly. Some of those who nominated the RAAEC as one of their preferences were not selected for interview, and even for those who *were* chosen, on what basis they ended up in the Educational Corps was often a mystery. If you missed out on Education, your chances were high of scoring Infantry, and possibly of being sent to Vietnam.

Those interviewed for Education found themselves in front of a variety of panels, from the formal to the relaxed. One said his panel was chaired by a Brigadier; another said he had an interview with a single, 'unpleasant' Psych Corps officer. Andrew Dalziel was interviewed at Puckapunyal in 1971 by a 'panel of brass', and only later discovered that one of them was the CO of the Military Cadet School, Lae, where he was eventually posted. Reg Radford, then a 22-year-old high school teacher from Western Australia, said he hadn't given Army Education any thought until he was asked at the officer-training selection panel if he wanted to go to OTU or Education Corps in PNG. 'It was almost like I had already been earmarked for RAAEC,' he said.

Like Radford, many had no idea why they were finally selected for Army Education, apart from their teacher qualifications, and even then there were couple of 'interlopers': Herlihy's appointment to RAAEC in 1967 was based on the undergraduate degree he had tried to hide – on the pre-enlistment paperwork he had listed his employment as a 'labourer'. Strictly speaking it was true – in summer holidays whilst at university he had been a labourer on the Snowy Mountains scheme, in southern New South Wales; another non-teacher in the same intake, Jim Wells, had been a public servant in Victoria. As more teachers completed their training and became eligible for call-up, it seems likely that those two were the last Nashos appointed to the RAAEC who were not trained as teachers, apart from the agricultural specialists ('didimen') recruited for a sole position with 2PIR at Wewak, several of whom had ag qualifications but no teacher training.

Richard Boddington recalled that on his panel in 1971 there were at least five interviewers, including a psychologist, 'whose probes included suggesting/provoking that I seemed like a person who would not be able to tolerate the PNG heat. How he might deduce that went through to the keeper. I was subsequently told that the psychologist asked even more provocative questions of other applicants. Two of three questions I do remember came from [RAAEC] Captain Freeman: "Do you play back pocket or rover? Wicket keeper or spin bowler?" While I readily admitted I had no idea of the impact of Bougainville Copper on the PNG economy. Despite this admission, I was successful in my application for a posting to PNG with the Education Corps.'[77] Some teachers who had made their mark in sport, including hockey and rugby, felt that sporting ability also figured in the selection process.

Some of the successful ones guessed at why they were chosen over other applicants: 'my father had been on the Kokoda Track in 1942', 'my Christian faith and the global missionary view that goes with it', 'straight As in my primary teacher education course', 'my father had been a sergeant in the regular army', experience in teaching Aboriginal students, or, in Bill Larsen's case, 'sheer luck'. 'A number agreed with John Morris that the panel was looking for teachers 'who would demonstrate empathy and compassion towards the PNG soldiers', and Phil Adam recalled questions about his attitude to 'non-European' people.

In my own case, a sympathetic panel interviewed me at Singleton, including an officer who was involved with the rugby team. They too asked about my experience with teaching 'non-Europeans', and I was able to tell them that a couple of Papua New Guinean boys boarded at the local hostel in North Queensland and had been in my classes at Herberton Secondary Department the year before, and that one of them, Abe, was a key player in the rugby league team I coached. 'What would your wife think about your being posted to Papua New Guinea and possibly being away from her for twelve months or more?' the panel chairman asked me. I recall looking across at the three officers. 'She'd like it a lot more than if I was sent to Vietnam,' I said, wondering what sort of connotation they might put on that. I was relieved to see nods and smiles all round, but I still had an anxious wait until the final selections were announced. My wife was very pleased when the news came through, because not only did it mean I wasn't going to Vietnam, but also that she'd be able to join me in PNG.

Another Nasho teacher who ended up in Papua New Guinea,

Phil Parker, was originally sent after recruit training in 1967 to the Services Corps centre at Puckapunyal to do a clerical course. During the training, a number of teacher conscripts were invited to front up at Victoria Barracks for an interview for a teaching role in PNG. Two others made it through, but not Parker – he was given a role as assistant to the chief clerk at the Army Staff College, Fort Queenscliff, on the western entrance to Port Phillip Bay, Victoria. 'All the course members were Lt. Colonels or above, so whenever something moved you saluted,' he said.

'As the assistant to the chief clerk (a WO2), I got to open the half ton of correspondence each day, and the challenge was to work out who needed to read it,' Parker said. 'I never did get this completely under control, but had lots of fun trying.'

This not particularly taxing job had its own perks too. 'Staff College was pretty easy to cope with – my own room with balcony overlooking the entrance to Port Phillip Bay,' Parker said, 'every Friday afternoon off (for sport), fabulous food and a billiard room and bar just 20 metres away.' It seemed like an ideal way to see out his two years of Nasho. 'Imagine my surprise one morning while tackling the mail to see my name and the posting as T/Sgt to PNG as an Education Instructor,' he said. 'I'd forgotten all about the interview a couple of months earlier.' After a short period of leave, he was on his way north.

Another inter-corps transferee was Terry Edwinsmith, who didn't apply for Army Education when the call went out during his recruit training at Singleton in early 1967, and who was enjoying the subsequent Artillery course at North Head, Sydney when an RAAEC recruiting team visited the unit. 'As I only had to walk 150 metres from my room to the Admin building for this interview, I decided to go. … I went because I was there, rather than because I had a high desire to join RAAEC.'

Nothing happened immediately. At North Head he trained as a gunner, then as a radio operator. A posting to 105 Holding Battery at Wacol, Brisbane, followed. In July/August 1967, Edwinsmith undertook Jungle Warfare Training at Canungra in south Queensland, in preparation for Vietnam. A month later, a live firing exercise was held at Tin Can Bay prior to his deployment to Vietnam, and he was sent to Brisbane on pre-embarkation leave.

During that time, 'I was surprised to find the Wacol duty sergeant knock on my door at Kelvin Grove around 7 pm one evening, and hand me a ticket to board an aircraft, early next morning, for Port Moresby,' he said. Edwinsmith had been transferred to the RAAEC. Effective immediately. He phoned close mates to tell them of his departure, and that he was sorry he couldn't go with them to Vietnam. 'I did object at the time,' he said, 'but to no avail.' As 105 Holding Battery were off to Vietnam as replacements, he would have been at Wacol on his own. 'The easiest way to tie up loose ends,' he said, 'was to ship me out to PIR [i.e. PNG] Command, and become someone else's problem.'

Others too had finished their Corps training when their RAAEC posting came through. Queensland primary school teacher John Dark by mid-1970 had completed infantry training at Singleton and, like Edwinsmith three years before, was sent to Canungra prior to going to Vietnam. His company was on the parade ground when the names were read out of soldiers being sent to Papua New Guinea with Army Education. Dark was one of them.

After 22-year-old Russell Jenkin completed his recruit training in 1967, he was given an administrative appointment at RAEME workshops in Melbourne, first at Broadmeadows, and then Albert Park. He found the work monotonous. The only high point was playing AFL for Army against tough teams like the police and the firemen. 'The skill level was not so high, but the games could be brutal!' he said. At Albert Park, he was allowed to wear civilian clothes most days. 'And I could travel to work by tram!' he said. 'It didn't feel right, after the challenges of Recruit Training.' So he applied to do a training course at the Army base at Bandiana, in northern Victoria, with the intention of being selected to go to Vietnam. Before he was accepted for the course, however, he was invited to attend an interview at Victoria Barracks in St Kilda Road. Within a short time he was teaching at Moem Barracks, Wewak.

20-year-old NSW high school teacher Warren Dunn followed a different route when he was called up in 1971. His mother opposed conscription, and she initiated a letter-writing campaign to 'Letters-To-The-Editor' in the NSW print media, including the *Sydney Morning Herald* (which, incidentally, was a strong supporter of the war in Vietnam). At the time Billy McMahon was not only her local Federal Member of Parliament but also the Prime Minister, so he too received letters of opposition from Dunn's mother. Following his mother's example, Dunn picked up his pen when he was appointed to Infantry Corps after recruit training. 'Whilst still at Singleton, I sent a letter of complaint to Army Minister Malcolm Fraser,' he said, 'asking why he didn't send his sons to Vietnam, instead of me, if he liked the idea of killing! Needless to say within a very short period I was kicked out of Infantry and placed in a platoon of Chalkies at Singleton.'

Perhaps of all the Chalkies, the then-21-year-old Martin Forbes was the clearest on why he was chosen for Army Education in 1972, specifically for a specialist position teaching agriculture at Moem Barracks, Wewak: 'There were only two Ag trained people at 1RTB [Kapooka] at the time and the other bloke didn't volunteer!'

From 1968, many of the teachers selected for the RAAEC during recruit training were posted to 3TB at Singleton for three months' infantry training, alongside the Nashos and regulars who'd been appointed to Infantry Corps at the conclusion of their first ten weeks in the Army. For the Queenslanders and those for northern NSW who'd completed recruit training at Singleton, this meant a change of Company, platoon and hut; those who'd trained at 1RTB at Kapooka and 2RTB at Puckapunyal made the trip north-west for their next experience of the 'green machine'. For my own part, it meant I was able to continue playing rugby with the 3TB team.

The rationale for this posting after recruit training was vague, although John Humphrey recalled that 'We were told that we needed this as we would be working with infantry soldiers in PNG. I did not enjoy the training here at all – I can remember during a long march with full packs, all of us "chalkies" came in last by a long way.' Queenslander Keith Werder overheard an NCO say that the purpose of sending the teachers for infantry training was to 'make real men of them'. Often the Chalkies-to-be spent some of this time acting as the enemy in mock exercises in the lightly wooded hills around Singleton. It was a long way from the reality of what those Nashos posted to Vietnam as 'real' infantrymen would face.

All us Nasho Chalkies (except the few who went through officer training) were promoted from Private to Temporary Sergeant immediately before we left for the PNG. We were issued with the three chevrons of our new rank, which we self-consciously but proudly sewed on the sleeves of whatever uniform was required wearing at the time. Sergeants had been commonplace in the AAES at unit level in World War II, but at the time conscription was introduced in 1965, the RAAEC comprised mostly officers and warrant officers, with only a few sergeants.

Although we had no control over the Army's decision, regular Army sergeants who had taken years to reach that level through the ranks, and possibly also after a tour of duty in Vietnam, understandably sometimes resented what they saw as 'overnight' promotions of young soldiers with minimal military experience. The Army decision in 1968 to upgrade the Education Instructor's pay scale from level 6 to level 13 did nothing to ameliorate the tensions in some quarters. In fact, Dan Winkel, who was in PNG 1966 to 1969, said he believed Brigadier Ian Hunter and the DADAE, Major Henry Dachs, wanted National Service officer graduates from OTU Scheyville appointed to Army Education in PNG Command, but that the decision was made elsewhere to create temporary sergeants instead. Winkel said that Hunter was concerned about the potential for conflict in sergeants' messes when the newly promoted Nashos arrived.

In our naivety, most of us had no inkling as we sewed on our stripes that some of us might cop a bit of abuse in PNG about our rank. In fact, even those of us with interim postings to Education sections in Australia, where we worked with regular Army Education officers and warrant officers, some of whom had served in PNG, were unsure about exactly what to expect of our posting to the land to Australia's north.

7

Travelling north:
Political and personal transitions

'Australians have seen Papua New Guinea as a frontier of adventure, the beginning of the exotic, and where Australians have peculiar responsibilities,' historian Hank Nelson wrote. 'Australians wanting to go "overseas", searching for something more exciting than work in an insurance office or the daily milking of the cows and with an often unexpressed hope that they might make a name in national, church or commercial history, could get their fares to, and a job in, Papua New Guinea.'[78]

It's true that when the Army sent us to the Territory between 1966 and 1972 we had our fares paid and a job waiting for us, but as conscripts, when we first arrived we could hardly be regarded as typical Australian 'expats'. Before entering the Army, only a few of us knew that such a posting even existed. The transition from Army private in Australia to Education Sergeant in PNG was not only a geographical journey but also a cross-cultural experience and personal transition that few of us were fully prepared for.

Even the flight to Port Moresby was a significant event for most of the conscripted teachers because few had ever been on a plane before, and even fewer had travelled overseas. So there was a level of excitement about our new postings, as well as uncertainty about what the Army expected of us. In that sense the Territory *was* a 'frontier of adventure', but although we were young men engaged in a common task, our responses to it would inevitably vary. We'd already left behind the life we knew; now we were leaving behind the country we knew.

For most Australians, 'New Guinea', as it was commonly known, was an island probably as mysterious as anything Jules Verne invented, a mix of images we'd picked up from books, documentaries, newspaper reports, travellers' tales, and in some cases relatives who'd fought there in World War II. We knew it was a 'developing nation' and conjured up pictures of black mountains arching into tropical blue skies, dark green jungle so thick it needed a machete to hack a narrow path through it, fuzzy-wuzzy angels stretchering wounded Aussie soldiers with strips of white bandage around their heads and cigarettes gripped nonchalantly between their lips, romantic twin-hulled sailing craft with bamboo sails shaped like crabs' pincers, and the whole island peopled by a motley collection of gold-miners, coffee planters, missionaries, and possibly cannibals in the more remote parts, along with some sort of network of district commissioners whose word was law.

The Chalkies had already been advised that there was no TV and virtually only one radio station in PNG, and that Territorians of necessity were therefore used to making their own social life. Just in case we had thoughts of taking that notion to extreme, we were also warned: 'There is no doubt that you can have a pleasant, fruitful and enjoyable time here, but please remember that you are here in the Army to do a worthwhile job and not just to fill in your time or have a holiday at the Government's expense.'[79] This memo was sent in 1971, so perhaps there'd been Chalkies in the preceding years who hadn't been sufficiently focussed on their educational task!

Although few of us realised it at the time, the years the Chalkies were in PNG were vital years in the country's slow march to independence. As we made our own annual transitions from Australia to PNG and back again between 1966 and 1973, with hindsight it is evident that PNG was making its own transitions, against a background of Australian Government policy for the Territory as well as for the thousands of young men conscripted under the National Service scheme.

***

In 1966, the year of the first cohort of PNG Chalkies, a conservative government was still in power in Australia, but from January there was a new Prime Minister, Harold Holt, who'd taken over when the country's longest-serving leader, Robert Menzies, retired. In March that year, Holt announced a boost to troop numbers in Vietnam, adding another battalion and specialist units, including the first conscripts to be sent to the war zone. Two months later, the first National Servicemen was killed in action – 21-year-old South Australian, Errol Noack, only ten days after arriving in Vietnam. In August 1966, the Battle of Long

Tan resulted in the deaths of 245 of the enemy and 18 Australians, 11 of whom were National Servicemen. Later in the year, a Gallup Poll found that 63% of Australians were still in favour of conscription, but only 37% approved of sending National Servicemen to Vietnam.

The 1966 cohort of 26 Chalkies was the smallest of the seven annual groups to arrive. Precise figures are hard to come by, but it seems the number jumped to 40 in 1967 and 1968, to 42 in 1969 and to 44 in 1971. Former Chalkie, Terry Edwinsmith, for the past few years has been trying to compile a list of all Nasho Chalkies who served in PNG between 1966 and 1973, has found the names of more than 300 conscripted Chalkie sergeants and officers posted to PNG Command in that period (see Appendix 1). Because of the varied ways they reached their destinations, it was rare for Chalkies to know everyone else in their contingent, and they were most likely to appreciate the size of their group only when they met for an orientation in Moresby before being despatched to their postings.

There were five possible postings within PNG Command – Murray Barracks (PNG Command and Army Education HQ; Iduabada Technical College), Taurama Barracks (1st Battalion PIR), and Goldie River Training Depot (recruits), were in the Port Moresby area; the other two were at Wewak (2nd Battalion PIR, which had an outstation at Vanimo) and later at Lae (Lae Area units and Military Cadet School), on the northern coast.

When the initial seven Chalkies arrived in Moresby on 6 August 1966, an Army driver in a long-wheel-based jeep was waiting to transfer them to Murray Barracks. 'I vividly recall, en route, the multitude of locals sitting beside or strolling along the main road,' John Teggelove said later, 'and so early in the morning and seemingly aimless'. This would be the first of many memorable sights of 'someone else's country' for him and his colleagues over the next 15 months.

At the Headquarters of PNG Command at Murray Barracks, Brigadier Hunter and Major Henry Dachs welcomed the seven sergeants to the Command and briefed them on their roles. Hunter's presence was itself an indication of the importance he gave to the venture – brigadiers didn't usually turn up to welcome sergeants. Teggelove said the PNG Commander told them they were expected to 'assist the Australian Army in the development of an effective indigenous military force in and for the Territory of Papua New Guinea, with military discipline and education as key training components for all soldiers'.

Almost twelve months later, Hunter elaborated on this theme in a briefing in Canberra for the Chief of the General Staff. He said the Army's key task in PNG was to develop a national Army which would be 'efficient, well-disciplined, stable and reliable, and absolutely loyal to the Administration or elected government of the country'. The Brigadier suggested that the experience of other newly-emergent countries was that military training was not in itself sufficient 'to ensure that the Army's potential for power will not be used for undesirable ends'.

The 60s were a turbulent period for many countries in Africa and Asia that had shaken off their colonial masters, as they struggled to develop their economies and sometimes faced a new domination – from their own kind. In 1960 alone, 17 African countries gained their independence, 14 of them from France, mostly after extended anti-colonial protests and conflicts in the post-war period. 'The African winds of change scarcely touched Port Moresby,' Woolford wrote, 'and failed utterly to reach the Highlands.'[80] Some of the new African nations, such as Mali, Chad, Togo, and Benin, suffered internal instability almost from the start, and it was no doubt these sorts of examples that Brigadier Hunter had in mind in Canberra in 1967 when presenting his views on the future of Papua New Guinea.

To Australia's north, Asian politics in the late 60s was dominated by the Vietnam War, but that conflict came on top of a spate of successful post-war independence movements across the region, including India, Burma (Myanmar), Cambodia, and Ceylon (Sri Lanka), and Pakistan, as well as Indonesia. China and North Korea were following their own exclusive paths. In the southern hemisphere, Fidel Castro's Communist coup in Cuba in 1959 inspired an upsurge of often-violent guerrilla activity in Latin America over the years that followed, in response to what one commentator called 'the persistence of stark social inequality and political repression'.[81]

Political instability is not conducive to economic growth, and even in a democracy a colonial power handing over power does not guarantee good management by the incoming government. Many of the newly independent countries remained underdeveloped, and demanded economic and financial support from the developed countries of the world through international forums, such as the United Nations 1964 conference on trade development.[82]

Some speakers on such occasions included Australia's role in PNG in their criticism of colonial powers, and *The Australian* newspaper reported 'wild charges and fierce abuse' in a plenary session of the United Nations General Assembly in December 1966.[83] The Assembly reaffirmed the 'inalienable right of the people of Papua and New Guinea to self-determination and independence'. The UN body also 'deplored' Australia's failure to implement an earlier resolution that called for fixing 'an early date for independence in accordance with the freely expressed wishes of the people'.[84] Minister for Territories Barnes responded with the Australian government policy line that had applied since the beginning of the decade: 'In determining a its policy for Papua and New Guinea the Government will be influenced primarily by the wishes of the people of Papua and New Guinea.' He also said Australia had no obligation to follow a UN resolution that didn't recognise 'the situation in the Territory and everything that is known about its inhabitants'.[85]

Brigadier Hunter argued that the way to ensure an Army understood what its role was in an independent nation was to provide both training AND education. 'While in the Australian Army, Education activity tends to be seen as peripheral to the area of military training, in this [PNG] Command it is a vital and integral part of the military training programme,' Hunter told the Chief of the General Staff in July 1967. 'It does not concentrate exclusively on the 3Rs, as important as they are to the betterment of the soldier, nor does it aim to produce a narrowly oriented young intelligentsia.' He said these sorts of misconceptions had led to a fear in some quarters of the development of an 'Army elite' in PNG. 'The education programme is designed to develop the soldier's understanding, his reasoning powers and self-reliance, and to give him a firm, logical and reasoned basis for his behaviour in the potentially disturbed times ahead.'[86]

Hunter's belief in the need for such a program was not based entirely on the experiences of other countries. There had been disturbances over the years within the PIR, mainly over pay, and sometimes altercations with the police, whom the troops viewed as inferior to them in training and status. George Kearney, the Psychology Corps Major posted to PNG Command in 1966, related the story of a potentially serious incident: 'One of the worst and probably the most frightening occurred when the battalion at Taurama had two of its soldiers arrested by the police. To the PIR, this was an absolute affront. That these rubbish policemen would take two soldiers away and put them in Bomana Prison was absolutely unacceptable. The battalion as a whole marched through the gate, walking straight over the officers who tried to stop them. That was frightening as this had never happened before. They were all steamed up and they wanted to get their comrades back. They were able to get down to the Four Mile on the corner of Murray Barracks and the shops where they were eventually stopped by an old kiap [district officer] called Tom Ellis.[87] He managed to stop them and calm them down and get them back to the barracks. This was the first indication that the soldiers might not see themselves as being responsible to the civil authorities.'[88]

Hunter said that the educational program sought to show the soldier 'his duties and responsibilities as a member of a national Army in a developing nation, and to encourage him to develop positive attitudes which will improve him both as a soldier and a citizen'.

The Brigadier concluded his argument for the value of education with this comment: 'It is to this programme, original and far-sighted as it is, that we look for hope that we can convert a potential "Kanaka army" into one which can carry out its tasks under the most difficult circumstances.' Hunter's use of the term 'Kanaka army' might be seen as racist in some circles, and out of character for a senior officer who was passionate about the PIR's development, but he seems to have been trying to make the point that the Army had a task, even an obligation, to quickly develop mature attitudes and civic responsibility in men who mostly had not even completed primary school at the time of enlistment.

Kearney said that the role Hunter saw for Army Education was 'central to the concept that the Australian Government had for creating a stable and responsible military that would work cooperatively with the civil administration. This was critical to a successful, independent Papua New Guinea.'

Even though Hunter left PNG Command in 1969, his vison set the scene for the Chalkies' roles in PNG from 1966 to 1973, and their final year there coincided with the arrival of self-government.

***

Each contingent of Nashos was issued with the daytime uniform: short sleeved-shirts, shorts and long socks in juniper green (from the colour of the juniper berry), a three-inch black belt, shoes and beret, and once again we sewed our recently acquired three stripes on the sleeves. The night-time uniform comprised jungle-green long-sleeved shirts and trousers, worn with boots and puttees or gaiters. When off-duty at night, because of the danger of malaria-carrying mosquitoes, after 6.30 pm all Army personnel were required to change into long trousers, shirts with long sleeves rolled down and buttoned, and for mess wear, tie or cravat. As a result, we looked a lot more dapper in our leisure time in PNG than most of us ever did in Australia.

The first cohort of 25 conscripted teachers reached PNG in three batches in August 1966, the same month as the Battle of Long Tan. They would remain there until November 1967, a total of 15 months, when they would return to Australia in preparation for discharge at the end of their two-year term. Another Chalkie joined them on cross-corps transfer in December 1966.

Among the first to arrive was Graham Lindsay, with six others, all transferred to the RAAEC at short notice after Austin's visit to PNG Command in May and June. When called up, Lindsay had already spent three years in the Cadet Corps at Sydney Boys' High and two years with an Engineers unit in the CMF, so the 20-year-old primary school teacher found recruit training at Kapooka 'relatively enjoyable'. As a declared 'non-combatant', however, after the ten weeks of recruit training Lindsay was sent for medical corps training at the School of Army Health at Healesville, Victoria, and then posted to 8 Field Ambulance at Puckapunyal. The day before his unit was due to go to Vietnam, Lindsay was brought into the CO's office and told he was going to Watsonia Barracks and being transferred to the RAAEC. He was briefly interviewed at Watsonia Barracks by a panel who then assigned him to PNG, along with several others. 'Once accepted for the RAAEC we were instantly given three stripes to sew on our arms that day,' Lindsay said. 'We were introduced to the Sergeants' mess at Watsonia Barracks (you could feel the steely eyes piercing our winter uniforms).'

He was still wearing his serge winter uniform when he arrived on a commercial flight in Port Moresby a few days later, where the daily temperature ranges from the high 20s to the low 30s all year round. 'My first experience was exiting the plane's doorway and walking into a wall of heat that was thicker than anything I had ever known before,' Lindsay said. Welcome to Port Moresby.

Denis O'Rourke said that when he wore his new stripes in PNG Command in August 1966, he was welcomed in the Sergeants' Mess at both Murray and Taurama Barracks, but Keith Bryant reported that at Goldie River 'some of the regular Aussies in the sergeants' mess resented these young upstarts wearing stripes'.

Even within Army Education, there were misgivings about the sudden influx of Chalkie sergeants. Major Henry Dachs said later, 'The manner in which these people were injected into the system certainly alleviated the staff shortage, but created a whole new set of problems.' In Dachs's view, those problems stemmed from the novice sergeants' lack of understanding of the environment in which they were operating. 'The new arrivals had been sent to PNG with minimum military training and really had no idea what they were getting into,' he said.

Dachs thought the new sergeants lacked experience (which was true both of teaching and the Army), and also that they had unreasonable expectations about accommodation and catering. 'The native troops had their diet, which was unacceptable to the whites, and there were no permanent buildings [at Murray Barracks] to provide accommodation as a Sergeants' Mess – a bit of shock to some of the lads, that's for sure.'

While this was no doubt true in some cases, especially in 1966, it's also likely that the Army itself wasn't quite prepared for the arrival its new teaching workforce in PNG. After all, there'd been only two months between Bunny Austin floating the idea to Mal Ashton at Goldie River, and the arrival of the first Chalkies in Port Moresby. 'I really don't think that PNG Command were ready for us when we arrived,' said Graham Lindsay, a member of the first Chalkie cohort in August 1966.

Dachs clearly felt he was carrying the brunt of it. 'I had the task of working out a course that was needed to orientate officers who were newly commissioned and sent to PNG, total ignorant of the conditions,' he said. 'It was a case of trying to stop both officers and the sergeants from "putting their foot in it" when dealing with the native population.'

This was Dachs's second tour of Army duty in PNG, and prior to joining the RAAEC he'd been a school teacher in the Territory, so no doubt he felt he had experience and expertise to impart to the newcomers. 'For some of them, it required a whole new mindset,' he said. 'A lot of their attitudes really were quite inappropriate and had to be changed in a hurry.'

The new arrivals' induction included tours of Moresby and

surrounds, and visits to 1PIR at Taurama Barracks and to the recruit training depot at Goldie River. Teggelove said that at Goldie River, 'after my teacher-style interaction with a young army recruit, and pointing to a passage of text, the Education Corps OIC there suggested that I count the fingers on my hand, as the young recruit involved was from the Kukukuku tribe …, with a history of cannibalism.' It was a joke, but it also introduced the Chalkies to another aspect of PNG – the variety of tribes and the different ways they were perceived, both by Australian troops and by their fellow soldiers. In Australia, the only differentiation in Army classrooms was normally between Nashos and the regular Army recruits.

The Army in the Territory had a policy of integrating its soldiers from across all provinces, in a bid to break down the 'wantok' system, which is prevalent in some Pacific countries. 'Wantok' literally means 'person who speaks my language' and in a country with 700-800 languages, people of the same language group have built up a network of relationships and obligations that requires them to support each other in whatever situation they find themselves. This mutual obligation may work well in ensuring that tribal members who are not well off or are ill or old are looked after, but it can also result in the rise of cliques that defend their interests and concerns, sometimes irrationally, against any other group and often against the greater good. In earlier days it helped clans defend their gardens, villages and pigs against marauding tribes from the next valley. Clearly such parochialism is not desirable in a national army charged with defending and promoting unity, and from recruit training onwards the Army separated 'wantoks', and forced soldiers to sleep, eat and train with men from all across Papua and New Guinea, some of whom might have been traditional enemies. Each cohort of Chalkies had to find out about those aspects for themselves.

Dachs perceived that sometimes the new arrivals had trouble adjusting to their new environment. 'Some of them were in a state of shock,' he said.

This may have been true for a while, especially in the early days of the Education scheme, but as far as the Chalkie sergeants were concerned, they'd already survived recruit training, the mysteries of selection for RAAEC and the vagaries of Army-organised travel to Port Moresby, so their new roles and locations in PNG were simply another series of transitions, a progression of tastes, smells, sensations and experiences that each dealt with as best he could. Nevertheless, after the first contingent paved the way in 1966, there were some different experiences for each annual cohort, and sometimes a different political environment within PNG or in Australia.

***

Early in 1967, the year of the second Chalkie contingent to PNG, Arthur Calwell retired as Leader of the Australian Labor Party, and was replaced by Gough Whitlam, whose leadership was later to have a radical outcome for the people of Papua New Guinea. In March, the Minister for Territories, Ceb Barnes, told Federal Parliament that 'the people of the Territory [of P & NG] have the right to choose self-government or independence at any time'.[89] About the same time, the Assistant Administrator in Port Moresby, Les Johnson, predicted that the forthcoming report of the Select Committee on Constitutional Development for PNG would be conservative and that 'there will be no strongly supported suggestion for a move towards self-government', although Johnson thought that one committee member, John Guise MHA, was likely to favour 'a rapid advance'.[90]

Back in Australia, more than 60% of the adult population in 1967 continued to support the war in Vietnam, and not long after the September arrival in Moresby of the 1967–68 Chalkies, Prime Minister Holt announced Australia was sending 1700 more troops, including another battalion and a tank squadron, to the conflict zone.

The 1967 Chalkie cohort spent two days of orientation in Moresby. Some of us were told that we were going to 2PIR in Wewak, Jenkin said. 'I was quite keen on that idea, as Moresby had not impressed me during all of two days!'

Moresby as a tropical point of arrival was something of a disappointment for most of us. It could well have been the place Robert Louis Stevenson had in mind when he famously wrote that 'to travel hopefully is a better thing than to arrive'. Instead of lush jungles sweeping down to the sea, we were confronted by a semi-circle of brown hills that looked as if they'd been razed by a bushfire. Occasional thin columns of white smoke drifted up from scorched hills and hung lazily in the air. We discovered that the city has two distinct seasons, 'the wet' and 'the dry', and every year our arrival almost always coincided with the dry, late in the year. Hence the scorched earth. When the rains came, usually between January and March, they drenched the land; afternoon thunderstorms rumbled across as regularly as the raising and lowering of the flag at Murray Barracks. Even in the dry, Moresby's humidity sat at around 75%.

The city was clustered around a ragged harbour that further out featured the rusted wreck of the *Macdhui*, a cargo ship sunk by Japanese bombers in 1942, and seemingly preserved by neglect rather than historical intent. The town had expanded during the war as the major administrative centre for ANGAU and a vital logistical depot for the Army, with fuel and supply dumps and base hospitals. Twenty years later, Government-issue grey-white fibro houses, with banks of angled metal and glass louvres, clustered themselves neatly in the lower areas then straggled up the hills, gradually thinning out as if they'd climbed as far as they could and lay where they'd dropped. More picturesque was Ela Beach, a narrow strip of white sand not far from the city centre, where blue-green waters lapped enticingly. Further along the shoreline, Hanuabada, a village settled by the sea-faring Motu people, perched romantically above the water on stilts, but had a reputation as a place to avoid at night.

Some had memorable times even before they reached Moresby. When Frank Cordingley was dragged away from his medical training course at Healesville in Victoria in mid-1967, the Army sent him home to the Gold Coast for a few days leave so that they could complete the paperwork for his transfer to RAAEC. Since I'm now in Queensland, said 20-year-old Frank, and I'm heading north, how about I fly out of Brisbane? No go, said the Army. You're being posted from your training position in Victoria, so you have to leave from Melbourne. So back Cordingley went to Melbourne, boarded a plane at Essendon Airport for Sydney, and then flew over the top of Brisbane on his way to Port Moresby. It was 14 June, 1967, the same day his cousin sailed into Brisbane on HMAS *Sydney* with other troops returning from Vietnam. His cousin, also a Nasho, survived the Battle of Long Tan, and would later suffer from post-traumatic stress disorder (PTSD).

Ian Lovell flew from Sydney he flew to Moresby via Brisbane with TAA (Trans Australia Airlines). 'I had too much to drink,' he said. 'Couldn't relieve myself as the flight was descending, and learned not to repeat the drinking on future flights.' Phil Parker travelled with about a dozen other Chalkies and the 21-year-old Victorian marvelled that on his maiden aeroplane flight he was treated to a bird's eye view of the Great Barrier Reef. As with his colleagues, the heat and humidity of Moresby hit him hard. It was his first experience of tropical weather. 'We were transferred to Murray Barracks by truck, and were all keen to get a cool drink at the Sergeants' Mess,' he said. '"Get those bloody hats off!!!" was the greeting as we entered – [a photo of] the Queen was hanging on the wall. We learned quickly about that one and I'm sure none of us ever forgot.'

We all had to get used to Army protocols, and, like Parker, quickly discovered when we had stepped out of line, especially now that we were sergeants.

Some of the 1967 cohort may also have received more of an inkling about why they had been selected. One Chalkie recalled that the Port Moresby induction was heavily slanted towards what sport you played, and included time in the cricket nets and trials for AFL and rugby teams. Norm Hunter received a formal induction at Murray Barracks, followed by another one with the Adjutant at his posting at nearby Taurama Barracks, which was 'mainly about playing in the rugby team'.

They could not escape the fact that they were in a military environment, however. The new arrivals were given a refresher course on how to move a group of soldiers from one point to another. 'No doubt this was to prepare us for duty sergeant duties,' Phil Parker said. 'It was a whole new experience having to give the orders rather than just having to follow them.'

It was not an experience Frank Cordingley looked forward to for his first stint as Orderly Sergeant. 'I warned the adjutant of my lack of experience, especially having to drill the soldiers on charge,' he said. 'The adjutant said not to worry as there was a duty officer also. On all occasions, I don't think I ever met the duty officer – I was on my own. The first duty was over a weekend and someone was lost on the Kokoda Track, with Murray Barracks being the search co-ordination centre – quite a daunting prospect.'

The other novel experience for Cordingley was raising the flag outside the Brigadier's home in the morning and taking it down at night. 'I had never done that and was terrified I was going to raise the flag upside down,' he said. 'I was warned the Brigadier often supervised this activity.'

The thing is, of course, that Cordingley rose to the challenges and carried out the tasks allotted to him. Just as the other Chalkies did. We didn't know what to expect, or if we would be able to do what was asked of us, but we did. No doubt sometimes we could have done things better, but that's true of any job. Perhaps the Army did a better job of preparing us for our tasks than we realised, or were prepared to acknowledge, particularly as the PNG Education scheme bedded in after the first couple of years.

Jim Davidson's journey to PNG in 1967 began with an unexpected railway journey. After recruit training, he 'trained in blood and bandages at Healesville, in preparation for the RAAMC,' he said. Posted to Albert Park Barracks in Melbourne as a medical orderly, he spent much of the time filing medical records, 'held under archaic conditions in a maze of pigeon holes'. Davidson said it was very interesting when head office required all available documentation for the medical review of a long-serving regular soldier. 'Much dust was shifted,' he said.

On receiving his posting to PNG with Army Education, Davidson asked the Army Movements Officer in Melbourne where his flight departed from. Sydney, he was told (Melbourne didn't have international flights in those days). So the 21-year-old boarded a train and headed north. On the way, the train collected a large number of Nashos at Seymour, the station for Puckapunyal Army camp. As the train headed towards Sydney, 'the buffet was in full swing,' Davidson said, 'so most were largely anaesthetized for the onward journey'.

Unlike some Education Sergeants who had gone before him, after his flight from Sydney Davidson was met on arrival in Port Moresby, and soon found himself with the rest of the Chalkies from the 1967 intake, including those who were heading with him 'over the hills' to Moem Barracks at Wewak. Davidson recalled that the induction was 'all rather gentle and respectful of our professional standing'. It was a far cry from their recruit training days some months earlier.

Some of his colleagues had to find their own way from the airport. Russell Jenkin's prop-jet Vickers Viscount from Sydney (via Mackay, Rockhampton, Townsville and Cairns) landed at Jacksons Airport at 6 pm. 'When I walked to the front door of the plane to disembark, the tropical humidity hit me like a brick!' Jenkin said. 'There were no airport lights close-by. There was no-one at the terminal to meet me, so I had to beg a lift to the Army Barracks. When I got there, no-one knew I was coming, so I was sent off to a hut where some RAAF personnel were staying.'

In December 1967, just as the new cohort were settling into their PNG postings, and the previous cohort were back in Australia,

Prime Minister Holt disappeared while swimming off Cheviot Beach near Portsea, Victoria. Chalkie John Teggelove, back in Melbourne preparing for demobolisation at the end of his two-year term, said that a number of Nashos awaiting leave and discharge at Southern Command Personnel Depot had their plans delayed for a day or two when they were detailed to search for the missing Prime Minister. Holt's body was never found.

***

John Gorton became PM in January 1968, just in time for the series of North Vietnamese attacks known as the Tet Offensive. The attacks were eventually repelled, with severe enemy losses, but they demonstrated the vulnerability of the American forces and their allies, for the first time raising serious doubts in the US and Australia about whether the long-running war was winnable. A month later, Gorton announced there would be no increase in the Australian commitment in Vietnam. Throughout the year, the conflict continued, with no clear end in sight, and Australian casualties continued to rise. The defence of Fire Control Bases Coral and Balmoral in May and June was the largest single action of Australian troops in Vietnam – 26 of the country's soldiers died and over 100 were wounded.

Earlier in the year, a United Nations visiting mission had expressed concern 'that a sense of nationhood had not yet developed in Papua and New Guinea to any great degree'.[91] The Mission commended the Australian Government for advances made in education, particularly at the tertiary level, but said, 'While it appears that the people of the Territory do not yet feel ready for self-government or independence, the Mission feels that this attitude must not be used as an excuse for delaying progress towards self-determination.'[92] Gorton had renamed the Department of Territories as the Department of External Territories, in order to focus it on PNG, and Minister Barnes later circulated the UN report in Canberra and Port Moresby, noting that there had been 'a number of significant advances in the Territory' that were 'consistent with the Mission's findings'.[93] One of these advances was the establishment of the University of Papua New Guinea at Waigani in Port Moresby in 1965, after earlier Government protestations that there was insufficient schooling infrastructure in the Territory to produce enough enrolments for a university.

1968 also saw the second House of Assembly elections. 'There is no doubt that the black majority in the House, had it wished, could have forced the pace more quickly than Barnes and his advisers in External Territories wanted,' Woolford wrote. 'But the make-up of the House made this unlikely. Although there was a solid core of members with four years' parliamentary experience behind them, they and the bulk of their new colleagues remained uncertain about their own capacities, fearful of a changing future, and content largely to defer to the official view.'[94]

There had been ongoing debate between the Army Minister, Malcolm Fraser, and Ceb Barnes, about the appropriate size of the PIR, including a 'tense exchange of letters' in December 1967.[95] Barnes wanted to limit it; Fraser wanted to increase it. Doran noted that in a submission to the Joint Planning Committee in 1968, 'On the question of a military coup d'état [the Department of] Territories was initially disposed to argue that a three-battalion force constituted an inherently greater risk than a force of two battalions. ... In the same context, Territories tried to argue against having any or more than token Army forces stationed in the Port Moresby area.'[96]

Meanwhile, the 1968 batch of Nasho teachers prepared to take the place of the second cohort. One of that group, 21-year-old Victorian primary teacher, Roger Grigg, was no doubt looking forward to PNG – after recruit and infantry training, he'd spent much of his time with the Education Unit at Puckapunyal digging holes to plant trees for a car park.

Another of those waiting to go to Port Moresby, Peter Chard, was annoyed by the lack of detail about his departure. He'd spent a month's preparation at the Australian School of Pacific Administration at Middle Head, Sydney, and then another moth at Ingleburn/Holsworthy Education Centre in south-west Sydney, where he had his vaccination shots for PNG. At that stage the Army couldn't or wouldn't tell Chard and his fellow Sydney-based Chalkies exactly when they would depart, but gave them two weeks' leave and told them to report back to Victoria Barracks. When they fronted up on the Friday, as ordered, 'We were then told that we were to fly out to PNG the following morning!' Chard said. 'I told my parents that night, and it was then that they told me they'd arranged a farewell party on that Saturday night. The party went ahead but the main guest was spending his first night at Taurama Barracks!'

The 22-year-old was unimpressed. 'This was typical of the shitty way the Army treated us,' Chard said. 'Going to PNG wasn't a state secret. We could have been told at any time and we could have taken our leave in PNG rather than be given a day's notice of leave as we were.'

Not only did he miss the party, but Chard also had a memorable introduction to his new posting. On his first day in the Territory, the departing Chalkies they were about to replace invited them to go to an Aussie Rules match in the afternoon. 'I can't stand football in any shape or form,' said Chard, a keen squash player, 'but I went along not to be the odd one out. At the end of the match a fight broke out between some of the locals and next minute the Police Riot Squad went into action and dispelled the crowd.' Welcome to Port Moresby.

As Chard and his cohort began to become acculturated to the environment in which they would live and work for the next 12 months, the very experienced Secretary of the Department of Territories, Warwick Smith, provided an assessment of the state of the Territory's development. 'Papua and New Guinea is in very great degree a "least-developed" country,' he wrote. … The winds of change are under forced draught. High pressure change [is] the order of the day – change from a colonial traditional/subsistence society and economy towards a modern self-governing, educated, sophisticated society and economy. The pace of change is dramatic…'[97]

The 'forced draught' was created mainly by agitation in the United Nations. In 1968, Barnes said that his own view was that independence was 'another twenty to thirty years away' but added that 'the important thing is not what I say: it is what the people of the Territory say.'[98] In a lengthy confidential response, Government official C.E. McDonald argued that such a position was all very well, but that it failed to take account of the likely development of political leadership in PNG and 'international opinion about administering authorities having a duty to prepare and guide dependent people to accept responsibility for their own government'.[99] McDonald suggested that Australia's failure to set a date for independence despite mounting international pressure had made it a 'target of particular attention' from what he called 'rabid decolonisation forces' in the United Nations.[100]

Brigadier Hunter had made it clear that he saw an educated Army as part of the changes taking place in PNG, and that the Chalkies had a significant role to play in helping the Army be an active part of 'a modern self-governing, educated, sophisticated society and economy'.

In a newspaper interview at the time of his departure from PNG Command in February 1969, Hunter said, 'We are creating a national army here before there is a nation.'[101] When that nation was likely to evolve was very unclear, as Minister Barnes told the Australian Cabinet in May that year: 'There is no common mood in the House of Assembly. The members of the Highlands want no further political changes and seek economic development in which they feel they lag behind the earlier developed coastal areas of Papua and New Guinea. The Pangu Pati, which consists of 8 of the 84 elected members, seeks immediate "Home Rule" which it sees as something short of self-government. Two or three members have said self-government should come in 1972. Others have asked the Government to set target dates – 20 or 25 years being mentioned.'[102] Barnes indicated he would be amenable to a discussion about the criteria for self-government, if that was a recommendation of a Select Committee on constitutional development.

***

As they arrived in their new postings in late 1969, the fourth contingent of Chalkies had to come to grips with contemporary political sentiment in PNG so they could better help PI soldiers make sense of the changes occurring and likely to occur. By this time, most Chalkies were selected for the RAAEC during recruit training, but inter-corps transfers were still possible as Queenslander Steven Hill discovered during a rapid transition in the middle of that year from the School of Signals at Balcombe in Victoria to Army Education at Murray Barracks. 20 years old when he entered Nasho, Hill had decided to do the two-year training after time in the CMF – one year as a Q Store corporal and another at the Officer Cadet Training Unit (OCTU). 'I was told of the Corps transfer on the Wednesday,' he said. 'I was psyched on the Thursday for any racism. I flew to Brisbane on the Friday, and over the weekend mum sewed on the stripes. I flew to Port Moresby on the Monday.'

It seems that by 1969 the Army had also found more useful employment for other Chalkies before they went to PNG than digging holes for trees. Trained as a high school maths teacher, Alex Thomson taught the unlikely combination of maths and Australian history at Holsworthy Army camp, before being posted to Victoria Barracks in Sydney where he collated educational material and dispatched it and library books to RAAEC units. On the eve of Thomson's departure for Moresby, 20 September, 1969, the Army arranged a group booking for the Chalkies at the 1969 Rugby League Grand Final. With almost 59,000 others, they watched the Balmain Tigers beat the South Sydney Rabbitohs by 11 points to 2.

The Army was not so thoughtful about arrangements for Greg Ivey and Phil Adam, who had been posted after infantry training to Lavarack Barracks, Townsville. In November, when the rest of the 1969 intake were sent to Port Moresby from other points in Australia for a one-week orientation at Taurama Barracks, no one remembered to tell the two Chalkies in Townsville. It was not until the roll was called on day one at Taurama that the penny dropped, and a message was immediately sent to Lavarack Barracks.

'We were quickly given Sergeants' stripes for our uniforms,' Ivey said, 'and these were sewn in place by Q Store staff, including a Nasho mate from my Recruit Training course.' The pair were put aboard a RAAF Hercules aircraft transporting urgently needed medical supplies to combat a pneumonia outbreak in the PNG Highlands, and arrived late at night at Jacksons Aerodrome. As the tailgate on the Hercules was lowered, they were immediately struck by the same wall of hot and humid air that had assailed their colleagues. At least there was someone to meet them and smooth their path. 'We did not pass through Immigration or Customs,' Adam said. 'We went through a barbed wire fence and then off to Taurama.'

A fellow Chalkie posted to Lavarack Barracks, Keith Werder, had a more tumultuous time on his way to what became a last-minute change of posting. The weekends were the highlight of his time in Townsville, as the 23-year-old played A-grade rugby union on Saturdays and then lined up for A-grade rugby league on Sundays, always in the forwards. 'Usually I was so battered I'd crawl to work on Mondays,' he said. 'On one occasion, the CO warned me that if I turned up again so incapable of teaching, he'd put me on a charge. From then on, I just masked my injuries and bruisings until I could run them out at training during the next week.'

When his intake colleagues headed to Moresby in November 1969, around the time of his 24th birthday, Werder stayed back to do a university exam. It was a delay he came to regret. 'My original posting was Murray Barracks, but one of those lying bastards who claimed they were not married at the time of the [selection] interview assured a key decision-maker that Werder would not mind going to Goldie River and that he should assume Werder's place at Murray Barracks.'

As Werder saw it, the reason for the swap was that there was no married accommodation for that Chalkie and his wife at Goldie River. 'Of course, I was never consulted, and that decision-maker accepted that colleague's pleadings,' he said. 'I never did find out who managed the switch. I planned to give him an earful, when the time came.'

More was to come. Werder not only played rugby league and union, but was a talented cricketer. After being posted to Goldie River Training Depot, the new Chalkie sergeant accepted an invitation from a non-Army mate to join a Port Moresby civilian cricket side, and bought a VW Beetle to transport him the 50 kilometres from the Army base back and forth to Moresby. This mate happened to be a journalist, and soon afterwards a local newspaper carried the story of the top-notch cricketer from Army Education who had joined the town team.

When this news reached Brigadier Ralph Eldridge (1917–2001), who had taken over from Hunter, he immediately conveyed a message to Werder, strongly suggesting that the new arrival transfer to the Army cricket team rather than support a civilian one. Despite the fact that the Brigadier was the Officer Commanding PNG Command and more than a few levels higher in rank than a temporary sergeant, Werder chose to decline the proposal. According to the story, within days the Brigadier transferred the newly arrived sergeant to Wewak, with the words (conveyed via the Commanding Officer at Goldie River), 'Let's see how much bloody cricket he gets to play in Wewak.'

So, within two weeks of his arrival in Moresby, Werder was on his way to the other side of the country, in exchange for another Chalkie. His journo mate sold the VW Beetle on his behalf and sent him a cheque. Werder didn't play cricket in Wewak in the twelve or so months he spent there.

There were other shocks for new arrivals, as West Australian John Ford discovered. 'It was my first time out of my first world home of Australia, with its white Australia policy,'[103] he said, 'and arriving at Jacksons Airport I was very surprised, even shocked, to see all these black and even primitive looking people everywhere I looked.'

Presumably it was concern that Chalkies might be racist that led to the questions about 'non-Europeans' that some remembered from their interviews for RAAEC selection. 'I suppose it was an hour or two and I had adjusted to this alien sea of humanity,' Ford said, 'and I was quite relaxed dealing with the PI soldiers at Taurama, where we went straight from the airport.'

During 1969, the former Minister for Territories, Sir Paul Hasluck, who was responsible for PNG policy under Robert Menzies in the 1950s and early 1960s, was appointed Australian Governor-General. Around the same time, attitudes towards Australia's involvement in the Vietnam War began to change, with an August opinion poll finding that 55% wanted Australian troops brought home, the first time the balance had tipped in that direction. Despite the changing opinion, Australians didn't want to change their Government, and in October the Coalition was returned to power, defeating the ALP led by Gough Whitlam.

In December 1969, Opposition Leader Whitlam undertook a 15-day visit to Papua and New Guinea. He announced the ALP's plans for the Territory via Australian newspapers: full self-government as soon as Labor was elected, with independence to follow within the new government's first term of office. 'By urging rapid political change, irrespective of the wishes of the people of Papua New Guinea,' Woolford wrote, 'Whitlam challenged the central tenet of long-established Australian policy.' [104] His motivation, Woolford suggested, was that Australia was 'being corrupted by playing the role of colonial master and that it was urgent, for both ethical and foreign policy reasons, that this role be ended'. Woolford said that Whitlam had 'contempt' for most Australians in Papua New Guinea because they had a privileged elitist position that must corrupt them.

Had the 1969–70 Chalkies (including me), just settling into our new postings, been aware at the time of Whitlam's sentiments about Australians in PNG, we would all surely have been puzzled by them, and sure they didn't apply to us.

Around the same time that the spotlight was on Whitlam in PNG, Prime Minister Gorton announced that Australia would follow the US lead and shortly begin to decrease the number of troops in Vietnam. No doubt there was a collective sigh of relief from young men across the country whose birthdates had been drawn in the lottery, especially those about to go into the January 1970 intake, which included those teachers who would be selected to take our places in PNG after our tour of duty. There was no longer a chance that they would go to Vietnam.

Gorton visited PNG seven months after Whitlam, and promised advances along the road towards self-government. In the Highlands, however, local leader Tei Abal told him, 'Whitlam should never have come here. We hate him for it. We don't want self-government in 1972. We want to proceed slowly.'[105] The message was quite different when Gorton arrived in Rabaul, where for some time the local Mataungan Association had been resisting the Administration's attempt to establish a multi-racial council, which they believed would be dominated by Europeans and against their interests. 10,000 angry people turned out to meet (not greet) the Prime Minister, but his efforts to placate the crowd were unsuccessful, and behind the scenes there was concern for his safety. His six-day visit to PNG was a mixture of regional support for and opposition to Australia's policies, but the outcome was that Gorton's Government began to encourage Papua New Guineans to seek rapid change, although he refused to set target dates.[106]

Like their predecessors, Chalkies in the 1970 cohort spent their time after recruit and infantry training in various useful or otherwise pursuits before they headed to Moresby. Terry Clarke taught maths for four months at the Transportation Centre, Mosman, Sydney: 'Easy teaching and great views of Sydney Harbour!' he said. Science teacher John Humphrey was posted to Bandiana where his tasks included lecturing to officers on the chemistry of explosives and the physics of missile trajectories in artillery. In the several months he spent at Enoggera Barracks in Brisbane, Ian Ogston recalled 'not having to do very much', while Robbie Scott (who said he 'loved' infantry training) taught maths at Holsworthy Army camp during the day for three months, and every night went out 'to the wee hours' with a Nasho mate.

Some found their teaching more challenging. Queensland primary teacher John Dark and several other Chalkies were sent to Lavarack Barracks, Townsville, where Dark found himself teaching regular Army soldiers. 'This was a real trial,' he said. 'After being subjected to the demeaning treatment in basic training, as privates we found ourselves teaching captains, lieutenants and warrant officers.' Greg Farr, on the other hand, said he enjoyed teaching SGCE English and Logic to a mixed group of airmen from Garbutt Air Base in Townsville, along with soldiers from Lavarack with rankings from corporal to captain.

20-year-old John Morris, was posted in mid-1970 to the Army Education unit back at his former recruit training centre at Kapooka,

1RTB, where he taught mainly Australian history. The Services General Certificate in Education (SGCE) had by then become a promotion requirement, and one of Private Morris's tasks was to teach the course to the 1RTB Regimental Sergeant Major, WO1 'Tilly' Devine. 'This wasn't a pleasant experience, and I was always on edge teaching the RSM,' he said. 'But the experience was rewarding and I felt useful.'

Others took the opportunity of the relative freedom they now had as RAAEC privates. 'Recruit and infantry training did transform me from being a shy, reserved mummy's boy to being super fit and thinking I was ten-foot tall and bullet-proof,' Ron Inglis said. 'On leave I swaggered around Sydney in my uniform to impress the world at large and women in particular.' His strategy worked – he met the woman who later became his wife, and said that when he flew to PNG in November 1970, 'I was air-sick and love-sick all the way to Moresby.'

As the 1970 cohort took over from their predecessors, Australia's 8th battalion returned from Vietnam; Prime Minister Gorton had announced earlier in the year that it would not be replaced. Opposition in Australia to what was increasingly seen as an unwinnable the war was growing and a 'Don't register' campaign was gathering momentum. Two moratorium marches attracted hundreds of thousands of people in major cities. Another occasion that attracted a big crowd was the 1970 VFL grand finale at the MCG, when more than 120,000 saw Carlton defeat Collingwood after being 44 points down at half time.

In March 1971, William McMahon replaced Gorton as Prime Minister, and shortly afterwards announced another reduction in Australian numbers in Vietnam. Five months later, he told Parliament that all Australian troops except for a small advisory team would soon be withdrawn from the war-ravaged country. Even more pertinent for Nashos was the announcement that National Service was to be reduced from two years to 18 months. The decision, which was followed up with legislation in September 1971, caused a dilemma for Chalkies and the Education Corps alike.

Lynch said that men called up in January 1970 (which meant all of the Chalkies from that year), would be discharged in mid-November 1971, just two months after the legislation was introduced. Those called up in April 1970 would be discharged in early December 1971, and so on; new recruits from July 1972 would be committed to only an 18-month term.

In PNG, this meant immediate decisions for the Chalkies and a 'particularly hectic' period for the RAAEC in PNG Command.[107] For the 1970–71 cohort, a mid-November discharge meant an October departure from the Territory to allow for leave and processing before their shortened term ended; for PNG Command, it meant a hiatus of a month or two before the arrival of the 1971–72 cohort.

Most of the Education Sergeants at Murray Barracks decided to take the 'early' option; four decided to stay on for the two-year term. In farewelling the departing Chalkies, the Murray Barracks regulars Army Education staff hoped that they 'haven't forgotten completely the subtleties of civilian life.'[108] Lae Area reported that they had 'successfully survived the drama of the acceleration of NS discharge', and had only one 'escapee', Roger Stapleton: 'Roger leaves on 20 October, but as he is going South to be married, we can forgive his desertion.'[109] 'Almost all the chalkies in Lae elected to stay on for the full two years,' Ron Inglis said, 'especially those from New South Wales. We knew we were on a good wicket.'

Inglis was referring in particular to the NSW Government's policy of 'topping up' the pay of conscripted teachers from that state to the level their salaries would have been if they had not been called up. This generous action was not copied by the Queensland and Victorian governments, at least, and gave NSW Chalkies a financial boost, since their Army board and lodging were provided at modest cost.

At 1PIR Taurama, five sergeants, Russell Bates, Nev Corrie, Graham Leader, Peter Porteous and Wayne Wallace elected to take early discharge, and left at the end of October; Ray Bassett, Kev Horton and John Moore stayed on. The departures coincided with a scheduled company course, so two sergeants, John Speakman and Dave Van Pelt, were drafted from Wewak to cover the science teaching at Taurama in what was described as 'a difficult period'. Goldie River Education Section said the barracks was 'in a state of flux', with the "old" line of Education Instructors preparing for departure and the incoming group being 'tormented with tales, tall and true, telling the terrors of Territory teaching'.[110]

***

For some of those new arrivals, in late 1971, the preparation in Australia had been different to that of previous cohorts. In the fortnight before they left for Moresby, Andrew Dalziel, John Fragomeni, John Hain and others in the southern states were sent to Canberra on a RAAEC training course, which included corps orientation and an introduction to Pidgin. This latter inclusion was an acknowledgement that English was still not sufficiently the 'lingua franca' of the Army in PNG, despite the official policy and the ongoing efforts of educators. Education Sergeants at Goldie River had lamented during 1971 that 'there is still a tendency of some army personnel in PNG to regard Pidgin as the most suitable language for expressing a precise point during training or in the normal working situation, although this is gradually being de-emphasised'.[111]

While he waited to take up his PNG posting, John Fragomeni was kept busy, as he and several other teachers at Holsworthy Education not only taught classes of soldiers wanting to upgrade their educational qualifications, but also to rewrite various SGCE handbooks for use by students from all of the defence arms. 'I was surprised at the amount of teaching the conscripts, at the rank of Private had to do, as well as the study guides rewrites,' he said, 'considering the fact that there was a full complement of ARA education officers in the cell, almost all of whom did not appear to do much during work hours.'

When it was time for the 1971–72 cohort of Chalkies to head north, the first group undertaking the 18-month term of National Service, Andrew Dalziel was nursing a hangover, having spent the previous night in the Sergeant's Mess at South Head, Sydney, celebrating his new stripes and saying farewell to Australia. Warren Dunn, who had spent the intervening months at Puckapunyal Education section rewriting the Asian Social Studies correspondence course, arrived alone at Jacksons Airport on a different flight, and was convinced there were 10,000 locals there to greet him. A jungle-green Army Kombie ferried him to Murray Barracks. There he met up with the other Chalkies who were then introduced to the 'Wash-Iron Boys'.

'Wash-Iron Boys' were not boys at all, but Papuan and New Guinean men, sometimes of middle age, whom single Australian NCOs and Officers paid not very much to do as their designation suggests: wash and iron the soldiers' clothes, particularly their juniper green shirts and shorts, which were required to be starched. That this meeting took place on the day of arrival suggests the Army viewed this role as vital in keeping the soldiers looking sharp. It was an in-house laundry service, and often a subject of criticism from anti-colonialists.[112]

During the week-long induction program, the Education Sergeants slept in the OR barracks and ate with the PIR soldiers. It was an informal and close introduction to the sort of men they would soon be teaching. The program included lessons in Tok Pisin and intensive use of the language laboratory, as well as the usual sightseeing trips around town, this time in what Warren Dunn described as 'unroadworthy local buses' instead of the Army trucks their predecessors had scored.

A small group undertook a three-week introduction to language and teaching at Lae Institute of Technology and on 28 September they experienced a PNG specialty: an earthquake (known locally as a guria) which registered a newsworthy 5 on the Richter scale. Minor earth tremors are an ongoing feature of life in PNG, shaking the house gently and rattling the crockery on the shelves, and residents and expatriates alike soon become used to them, but they are disconcerting nevertheless.

The other encounter was not a geophysical one: during the 1971 Moresby orientation the group learned about the politics of PNG and met Michael Somare, who spent some time with them. At the time, Somare was leader of the Opposition Pangu Pati, which he had founded four years earlier. He would go on to become founding Prime Minister of an independent Papua New Guinea. The Army's involvement in setting up the meeting and Somare's willingness to meet the Chalkies, are indications of the significant place the Army and the PNG leader saw for the education program, as well as of the path that the country was then treading. At the time, however, there was no Australian Government timeline for self-government or independence for the Territory.

The contingent that undertook the three-week orientation at Lae Institute of Technology also met the sort of attitude that some Europeans had towards the indigenous population at the time: 'One lecturer at Lae led us to believe that there is boiling resentment towards Europeans amongst a great many local people, and this can be manifest in the students going to sleep in the course of a lesson to 'spite' the teacher,' Chalkies Bob Strachan and J. McPhee wrote after they had been teaching for a short time at Goldie River. 'Personally, we believe that cases of student sleeping sickness is [sic] more likely to be due to the strenuous programme of work they are required to handle outside the classroom. Mostly in conditions of oppressive heat and humidity. The tendency to "nod off" in the course of a lesson would appear to be their greatest problem, and the greatest challenge facing the teacher, i.e. to keep the students alert through interesting work rather than out of fear of the consequences.'[113]

In Australia, 1971 was politically noteworthy not only for the change of Prime Minister in March, but also for the first ever Australian political delegation to China, in July, led by Opposition Leader Gough Whitlam, and the withdrawal in November of Australian troops from Nui Dat, ending the country's combat role in Vietnam. Mid-year, a tour by the all-white South African rugby team attracted lively anti-apartheid demonstrations and interruptions to matches.

The 1971–72 Chalkies were the sixth cohort to arrive, and at Taurama Barracks, at least, there was by then apparent acceptance of their role in the battalion, according to one report: 'After the normal Sergeants' Mess greeting of 'Not another lot of b....y Chalkies', the new Chalkies settled in with the aid of Captain Mobbs and Lieutenant Slater and two of the 'old' Chalkies, Sergeants John Moore and Ray Bassett. Once the heat and Orientation Course 'shock' had worn off, the boys started to unbend a little.' [114]

By now the likelihood of an independent PNG in the near future was beginning to gather steam, although there was still opposition from within the country, from both Europeans and conservative Papua New Guineans, particularly those from the Highlands. In 1970, academic Ted Wolfers, who would later join the Select Committee deciding on the country's constitution, wrote, somewhat cynically: 'Self-government, followed soon after by independence, is now a comparatively short way off, if for no better reason than that neither the Liberal-Country Part government in Australia nor the Labor opposition, is prepared to make the economic and political sacrifices, nor to use the force that would be required, to maintain an Australian presence in Papua and New Guinea even to 1980, or to preserve the territory's fragile unity, until the majority of its reluctant leaders feel that they are "ready" to take over.'[115]

***

1972 turned out to be politically the most significant of the seven years the Chalkies had been in PNG. In July, at the third national House of Assembly elections, Michael Somare became Chief Minister and committed himself to leading the country to self-government and independence. At the same time, the name of the Territory was

96

changed to Papua New Guinea. In December that year, one result of a national election in Australia was that the 1972–73 Chalkies would be the last Nasho teachers to be sent to PNG.

Nevertheless, the cohort wasn't aware of that as they flew into Jacksons Airport late in 1972, and their reaction was no different to the one that their predecessors had experienced annually since 1966: 'Seeing Port Moresby from the air was quite a shock, as it was the middle of the dry season and fires were burning on the brown and blackened hills around the airport,' said Victorian Tom Derham, newly graduated as an RAAEC officer from OTU. 'There was no tropical paradise to be seen anywhere! Getting out of the plane and being enveloped in smoke and hot humid air was an experience! The airport at that time was little more than a glorified warehouse and was pretty basic.'

The personal transitions the Chalkies made in the period between 1966 and 1973 as they arrived in and engaged with 'someone else's country' were intertwined with PNG's own journey towards nationhood and the upgrading of education in the Army for that purpose. Despite lacklustre Australian Government policy for the Territory in the 1960s, and uncertainty within the country about the rate of change, Army leaders in PNG had a vision they thought these particular National Servicemen could help with. How they went about implementing that vision is as varied as the number of Chalkies who told their stories about it.

8

Teaching in PNG:
Taim bilong tisas bilong armi

When the first Chalkies arrived in PNG in 1966, it was 25 years since Army Education staff had first been posted there. Like their predecessors, they were always operating within two cultures, the military culture into which most of them had been conscripted, and the culture of a foreign land, the split-level Territory of Papua and New Guinea, not yet a country in its own right. Depending on their individual circumstances and year of call-up, they'd been in the Army for between four and twelve months before their northern posting, and many of them were still feeling their military way, especially since most of them had been sergeants only from the time they stepped on to the plane in Australia. They were also feeling their way professionally, being new to teaching as well as to teaching in the Army, and most discovered they had a lot to learn.

The Army had to work out how best to use them, too. Denis O'Rourke said that when he and his fellow sergeants arrived at Taurama Barracks in August 1966, 'Nobody was entirely sure what to do with us. I was assigned to A Coy as their Education Sergeant. We wore the PIR insignia on out green berets and we thought we were more PIR than RAAEC. It was resolved that the six of us would teach each Company when it was the Company's turn for education.'

At that stage, Education staff in the two infantry regiments also wore the red lanyard of Infantry Corps looped through their right epaulette, but later Chalkies reverted to the RAAEC's traditional blue lanyard. Those in the two regiments wore green berets with the Education badge (which changed over the period of the Education scheme), while on other bases the Chalkies wore black berets, in keeping with local usage.

Acculturating to PNG was a work in progress, as they tussled with teaching in situations where English was a second language and grappled with the beliefs, values and practices of people in two jointly administered but legally different regions, some 20 provinces and an estimated 700 local languages, that were slowly emerging from colonial rule – 'taim bilong masta', as Hank Nelson called it – into the modern world. The PIR was changing too: 'It used to be enough for recruits to be so many inches high and physically fit,' Brigadier Hunter said. 'We now choose those with the best capacity to absorb training.'[116]

Warren Dunn discovered that training wasn't the only thing Pacific Islander soldiers were able to absorb. In late 1971 Dunn was teaching at Igam Barracks, Lae, about the Industrial Revolution, as part of the Social Studies curriculum, and had trouble conveying the concept of a 'production line'. He decided he needed to take the troops to see a production line in action. The only business enterprise in Lae that had such a facility was the South Pacific Brewery, home of the locally famous Green SP and Brown SP beer, so he organised a visit.

'The students were loaded onto the Army bus and we eventually were welcomed by the Brewery Manager,' Dunn said. 'The party, including the Lance-Corporal Driver, was then invited to sample the local product at the conclusion of the tour. Returning, the bus was involved in what could not be called a serious accident, but the journey back to base with a group of paralytic passengers did not earn me any "Brownie" points from the CO.'

Social Studies was one of the subjects taught in the Army's suite of PNG Certificates of Education, which also included English, Mathematics and General Science, which supposedly equated with Territory high school Forms 1, 2 and 3, although most of us wouldn't have known what the high school curriculum looked like. There was an additional and compulsory 'Civics' requirement, which helped in 'the promotion of those characteristics, beliefs and attitudes of mind considered essential to the development of a loyal and disciplined Army'.[117] Some of us also taught the Australian versions of these courses, as well as the Services General Certificate of Education, initially only to regular Australian troops in PNG, later to Pacific Islanders as their general level of education increased.

Our basic task was simple: 'We were made aware of what we were expected to do in PNG,' John Meyer said. We were to help educate indigenous soldiers. Our role was to help raise the general level of education of soldiers sent to do our courses.'

As Warren Dunn discovered, one of the challenges was finding a foundation on which to build new learning. It's a major tenet of the notion of constructivism in educational theory, but the transition for student and teacher alike was often demanding, as Sergeants Bassett, Leader and Wallace learned in 1971: 'When teaching Science, the instructor will find that cognitive skills are lacking; the strangeness of Science is a direct cause of this problem, which is related to their ancestral background. The natives had no need to understand why things happened; events were taken for granted. The cargo cult influence in this area is very strong. Folklore and traditions are deep-rooted and a definite obstacle to teaching. Abstract phenomena such as electricity, magnetism, refraction and energy, which have observable effects but no observable causes, are explained by magic or spirits. ... Science is only a new explanation and has to compete with these beliefs.'[118] These are generalisations, of course, because there were also soldiers with high school education, who had a more sophisticated understanding of science than this, but it showed the need just four years before independence to keep educating all the troops if they were to play their part in a modern PNG.

In terms of numbers alone, the impact of the Chalkies in PNG Command was impressive. When the second contingent of Nashos arrived in 1967, the RAAEC establishment in PNG was set at 62: 17 regular officers, four regular warrant officers, a PI corporal as librarian, and 40 National Service sergeants (Taurama: 10, Wewak: 11, Goldie River Training Depot: 8, Murray Barracks: 11; Lae area was not yet operational).[119] Included in these were a specialist agricultural teacher (didiman) position at Moem Barracks, Wewak, and two trade teachers appointed to Iduabada Technical College in Moresby. 'The appointment of two chalkies to Iduabada Tech College was a quid pro quo,' Peter Shackleford explained, 'whereby the College/PNG Education department provided the equivalent of secondary and initial trade training for army apprentices, and the army supplied some instructors to the College in return.'

In 1967, these educators were part of a total force of some 2200 Pacific Islanders and just over 550 Australians. In other words, more than 10% of the Australian Army workforce in PNG Command at that time were with Education. No wonder sergeants in other Corps noted the Chalkie presence and the privilege of rapid promotion. A contributor to the RAAEC Newsletter of October 1967 commented tongue-in-cheek: 'There is believed to be no truth in the rumour that the raising of 1st Pacific Islands Education Regiment is imminent; it is, however, becoming increasingly difficult to persuade the members of other, minor Corps in this Command that it is only a rumour.'[120]

All of the Nasho 'teaching task-force' in PNG between 1966 and 1973 primarily taught classes, mostly with small numbers, not always within their areas of expertise; a few had a purely administrative role at Education HQ, Murray Barracks. On occasions Chalkies took on other teaching tasks on request or as volunteers.

In general, the classes the Chalkies taught were not large – around 15-20 was the norm, with figures as high as 30 and as low as five. Resources were mostly adequate, occasionally plentiful and sometimes non-existent. There were green chalkboards, 'butcher's paper' (flip charts), and a variety of teaching materials, sometimes left behind by the previous intake of education sergeants, sometimes self-developed. In the days before the ubiquitous photocopier, each Education unit also usually had a spirit ink duplicator ('Gestetner') that required nurturing and gave a purple tinge to the multiple copies of reproduced handouts and exercises, and often to the operator's hands.

Peter Chard taught science at Taurama in 1968–69, where resources were limited. 'I remember killing cane toads for dissection, using of all things hydrogen sulphide to kill them. Excursions to Sogeri and Taurama Beach were a lurk for teaching science!' Less than 50 kilometres from Moresby, Sogeri is a complete contrast to the rain-shadow dryness of the country's capital, with gorges, waterfalls and jungle-clad ridges offering a cool highland retreat from the heat of the coastal plain. As its name suggests, Taurama Beach is not far from the Barracks and, with its narrow strip of grey-white gravelly sand and gently-lapping waves, a popular family swimming spot. It was usually possible to order a couple of four-wheel drive Landrovers or an Army truck at short notice to transport the eager students.

At Goldie River, Ian Ogston was impressed in 1970–71 by the quality of the teaching facilities and resources, including a well-stocked library with a librarian, which he reckoned were better than in the school where he'd taught before being drafted. 'Even an epidiascope, for goodness sake!!!' he said.[121] Ogston also featured in a note in the Army Education newsletter, which reported in August 1971 that he had returned from compassionate leave in Australia 'with a light heart and heavy debt', as a result of becoming engaged while on leave, with plans to marry on his return to Australia.[122] Life beyond the Army always beckoned for most conscripts.

The different purposes of the barracks determined the nature and timetabling of the classes, and the sorts of students they found in their classrooms. Goldie River was probably the most demanding because it took the recruits, making their first contact with the Army, just as the Chalkies had not all that long before. Writing in the RAAEC Newsletter in late 1966, regular Army lieutenant Adrien Sandery explained that education at Goldie had four aims: to teach the recruits English, to inculcate a 'civilised and sophisticated' way of life (including ironing clothes, making beds and using a knife and fork), to develop an understanding of the democratic way of life, and to upgrade their formal educational standards. 'Since Papua and New Guinea is a Colonial dependency progressing towards a democratic nation,' Sandery said, 'it is hoped that recruits will apply the principles learnt, in discussion with the rest of the nation, as the movement towards democratic independence is made.'[123]

When John Teggelove arrived at the Training Depot in 1966, '[the recruits] were truly representative of the wide diversity of languages, cultures and religions manifested throughout Papua New Guinea. … There was supposedly a 17 years' minimum age for recruits although awareness of birthdates was often vague. Some recruits spoke only 'tok ples' (tribal language) although most could converse in 'tok pisin' (Pidgin), the most widespread and common language of the Territory. The majority had attended a few years of elementary schooling and developed basic or better English literacy, as well as numeracy.'

At that stage education courses ran through 18 of the 22-week training course and there were two intakes a year, each with a slightly different profile, as Keith Bryant explained: 'The mid-year intake of new recruits at Goldie were mostly at about middle to lower primary level with some having had very limited exposure to any formal schooling and consequently poor English speaking skills. Recruits in the intake at the start of the year were mostly school-leavers from around mid-primary to some from lower secondary. They were generally quite young and more academically able. A big range of ability and level of prior schooling meant the teaching was quite demanding at times, although many recruits were quite keen.'

Recruits attended, in their platoon sections, for several classes a week, focusing on Literacy and Numeracy skills development. Night classes were held for Social Studies (including history and geography of the Territory, Civics and Citizenship) lessons. 'How can one forget the class chants of the mantra, "Democracy is Government OF the people, FOR the people and BY the people"!' Teggelove said.

When John Morris arrived three year later, new recruits had 32 weeks of basic training, 16 of which were for education. 'Of the five Education Sergeants posted to the PNG Training Depot at Goldie River, I was the only primary school teacher and thus was allocated classes where the recruits spoke liklik [little] or no English,' he said. 'Teaching English as a second language was our major approach. For me I used 'textbooks' already prepared with PNG content (I got to know the main character in the material – Ruka, very well!!!!).'

English was the major focus for those five Chalkies, but they also taught Mathematics, Social Studies and Science. Projector (OHP) was the main teaching aid used. 'There was much repetition in my classes – almost rote learning, but it achieved results,' Morris said. 'The education day worked like a high school timetable, 50 minutes teaching English with a 10-minute break (where we all tried to learn as much Pidgin as possible!!!!).'

'At Goldie River, we were into cultural development too,' Keith Werder said, following his short-lived stint there. 'For example, we introduced the recruits to the use of tooth brush and paste as part of their induction process.' At the other end of the scale, in 1970, Education staff were required to assist candidates on an Officer Qualifying Course at Goldie River with essay writing, lecturettes, debating, public speaking and military history. During the break between recruit intakes that year, four of the Education Sergeants tramped to Menari, on the Kokoda Track, and back.

In 1970, when I was based at Tuarama Barracks, 1PIR soldiers were attending education courses for nine weeks a year at the double-storeyed dedicated education centre, and sometimes a company was available for an extra two-week block. A report at the time said that 'with some 220 soldiers in the centre, the place is really swinging and RAAEC instructors are tearing their hair out.'

With the luxury of having ten 'supernumerary' National Service sergeants, the OIC, Captain Wolf Fladun (who said he once belonged to Hitler Youth), didn't need to teach a class, but his 2IC, Lieutenant Chris Burgin, taught current affairs year-round. That year Burgin introduced the 'situational method' to his classes: 'the situation being the position of PNG as a developing, not yet independent nation'. The following year, 1971, the current affairs course focussed on local politics, a timely topic ahead of the national House of Assembly elections to be held in 1972.

The Education Section at Taurama also developed several courses in addition to the PNG ACE quartet of English, Maths, Social Studies and Science, to meet particular educational needs of the 1st Battalion: health and hygiene, map reading, basic accounts and one called 'General Studies', which I was responsible for writing. From this distance, I don't recall the content of that particular course, but a report of the time said that I 'fathered the general studies course through the initial difficulties'. Those additional courses are another example of the responsibility Chalkies were given for developing new curricula, which we would never have had back in schools in Australia at that stage of our professional lives.

In addition, that same year Sergeants John Ford and Barry Nunn coached a number of 1PIR soldiers undertaking PNG Form IV studies by correspondence, with the Section acting as a Registered Secondary School for the purpose. 'It is a pity,' Captain Fladun said, 'that the two NS sergeants will not see the results of their work as they will have returned to Australia by then.' As it happened, Ford, a West Australian, extended his stay in PNG by three months for personal reasons.

In the year before his call-up, Ian Curtis had been teaching 28 forty-minute periods a week in a New South Wales high school. At the Military Cadet School (MCS) in Lae in 1970–71, he was teaching classes of 12 cadets for 12 hours a week. Nevertheless, he said, the teaching had different demands, and he was also responsible for writing the English curriculum for the classes he taught. He also established a writing magazine, *Poroman* ('friend/companion' in Pidgin), as an outlet for the students' creative writing. By 1971, the Military Cadet School at Igam Barracks, Lae, comprised a total of 63 cadets and staff, with three concurrent classes. Curtis also helped organise a two-week Social Studies excursion to Sydney of the Intermediate and Senior classes, which were accompanied by the School's OC, Major Underwood, and two sergeants in addition to Curtis – Terry Clarke and Wolf Iwanowitsch. 'A big job,' Curtis said.

When Peter Darmody arrived at Murray Barracks in 1967, an Education building was still under construction, so for some months they taught classes of about ten students of greatly varying abilities in tiny LEP (Locally Employed Personnel) married quarters, in rooms the size of a small modern-day unit. 'They were poorly ventilated and hot as the hobs of hell – even for the local soldiers,' John Herlihy said. 'On a really hot day we let them sit at their desks just in shorts and sandals.' Their predecessors were worse off, however – when he arrived with the first batch of Chalkies in 1966, Peter Wedgwood was teaching under canvas. 'Explaining doors and windows in a tent was interesting,' he said. There were also constant reminders that this wasn't like teaching in Australia. 'There were the occasional personal issues,' Darmody said, 'e.g. one student who was under great psychological pressure because he had a curse put on him for marrying a girl from another region.'

Peter Shackleford, who was based at Murray Barracks in 1972–73 but taught at Iduabada Technical College, received a set of instructions for soldiers at the College when he was duty NCO, which included calling the roll and issuing Paludrine tablets, 'inspect troops daily at 0700 hrs for shaves, hair-cuts, clean footwear and clean serviceable work dress', and enforcing discipline at all times – 'Remember Apprentices are soldiers'. The Education Sergeants at Iduabada Tech wore civilian dress, since they were also teaching non-Army apprentices.

Greg Farr oragnised visits to SP Brewery's Port Moresby facility, with classes from Murray Barracks in 1970–71, apparently without the sort of incident that Dunn had to contend with in Lae, although the other Chalkies always competed to accompany the 'expedition' in order to take advantage of the manager's post-tour hospitality.

Terry Edwinsmith, took his Civics class from 1PIR to the House of Assembly to see 'democracy in action'. The PNG parliament was created as the House of Assembly of Papua and New Guinea after the first national elections in 1964, and the building, in downtown Port Moresby, had previously been used as a hospital. On one occasion, in 1968, the year of the second national elections, Sir John Guise, the Speaker of the House, and later the country's Governor-General, interrupted parliamentary proceedings to speak to Edwinsmith about the group of soldiers he had brought to the public gallery. 'He wished that we could stay longer,' Edwinsmith said, 'but I told him that we were required back at the battalion … A small incident, but one that all present would remember for the rest of their lives.'

At Taurama Barracks in 1972–73, Tom Derham said that the most important thing he had to learn in class management as a junior

Education Officer was 'to conduct classes in such a way that you would not put yourself in a situation where you might have to say publicly that someone was "wrong" or "incorrect". If you did do this, causing loss of face, then the whole class would just seem to shut down on you, and any learning would be over for the day.' When Derham was subsequently posted to Goldie River, he was given the task of teaching the equivalent of Year 10/11 mathematics to a small class of specially selected soldiers who were to be the first PNG group to be sent to Point Cook in Victoria for pilot training.

The enthusiasm of the troops for education is a common theme, and in a military environment, discipline was rarely an issue, something many of the Chalkies no doubt remembered nostalgically later in their teaching careers, when they had returned to classrooms in Australia. Ron Inglis said, 'It was not until I returned to Australia and began regular high school teaching that I realized how easy we had it in the military in PNG. Teaching duties were nowhere near as demanding as those on a first-year-out teacher at Fort Street Boys High [Sydney].' Steven Hill, who was a 20-year-old primary school teacher from Queensland when he went into National Service, said that he came to realise 'the students were intelligent [which] removed for ever any racism I held, which was good for me in the new era of understanding our indigenous fellow citizens.'

There were also educational activities outside the Army classroom, such as a program conducted in 1971 by Murray Barracks RAAEC staff for children from the nearby seaside village of Hanuabada. Once a week, the Education Unit transported to the barracks a group of children aged 6 to 15, many of whom had been expelled from school, for a morning of educational movies and games, followed by lunch. Greg Farr said that attendance was boosted once or twice with the promise of a trip into the bush where the boys could gather firewood from the roadside to take home for their families. Also at Murray Barracks, in 1968 one of the Chalkies taught English literacy every Monday morning to a group of haus bois from the base's married quarters. At Taurama Barracks, Chalkie sergeants filled teaching positions in the local primary school, and in 1970 Greg Ivey was seconded for three months from Moem Barracks to run a pilot program in English as a second language for recruits at Bomana Police College in Port Moresby.

When Tom O'Meara, a Victorian-trained high school teacher, arrived at Taurama in 1971, he may have been the first to claim actual expertise in teaching English as a second language. He developed his own materials and, with the aid of an Australian regular soldier who hung out with the Chalkies, installed a language laboratory at the barracks in 1972.

Despite such innovations as language laboratories, however, there was sometimes a lack of overlap with basic resources, as Strachan and McPhee found to their annoyance when they arrived in 1971: 'The greatest resources with which to work must lie with the experiences and proven methods of past instructors. We have found that there has been no recording of old instructors' ideas. Old lesson plans, programmes of work with added comments on success or failure would be invaluable for the new line of instructors. An Education Sgt has one year of teaching experience in PNG. At the end of that time he must have learnt something to hand on. It is up to them to hand on this knowledge.'[124]

One of the Moem 'didimen', Robbie Scott, reckoned he had the best job at those barracks in 1970–71, alternating his teaching between the classroom and the specially developed agriculture plot. Agricultural courses were conducted over a three-month period and were intended for those soldiers, often older ones, who struggled with the PNG ACE subjects. Originally introduced to the curriculum by a Chalkie with a farming background, they had been carried on by a succession of individual sergeants with agricultural qualifications, and according to Scott, its influence was beginning to spread throughout the 'agriculturally backward' Sepik District. 'Already many soldiers in the unit are constructing fowl pens, are raising their own animals along modern lines, and are seeing tangible rewards for their labour', he said.[125]

'The emphasis of my teaching was to show not only the importance of protein in the diets of village people', Scott said, 'but that the protein should come in small packages such as eggs, chickens and fish.' To introduce the soldiers to fish-farming, Scott arranged for Army engineers to supervise the exploding of 'bee-hive mines' (turned upside down) to create large craters that could then be filled with water.

In addition to basic aspects of agriculture such as burning bush materials and returning the ash to the garden, Scott purchased about a thousand chickens from Brisbane, in several batches, which the soldiers tended and then took back to their villages when they retired from the army. One on occasion shipping delays resulted in a batch of 200 chickens arriving in Wewak 'as close to dead as it is possible to get'.[126] Fortunately, some 190 survived, proving company for the five pigs already ensconced at the farm.

'We built pig pens (concrete and metal) and started to look at the difference in growth of the pigs when fed local bush foods as opposed to slops from the army kitchens,' Scott said. In addition to this introduction to modern pig husbandry, the pigs potentially were a source of quality animals for soldiers to buy and take back to their villages (as well as providing an immediate cheap food source for company barbecues, of course).

John Fragomeni, a manual arts teacher from Western Australia, had a supplementary task when he arrived at Moem the following year: teaching the soldiers who were involved in agriculture how to construct the necessary infrastructure – fences, concrete floors, sheds and storage huts using local materials. Another didiman, Greg Smith, arranged visits during his term in 1969–70 around the East Sepik district to agricultural research and education facilities.

The furthermost Army posting for Chalkies in PNG was to Vanimo, a small north-western coastal town 50 kilometres from the border with Indonesia, and 100 kilometres from the town of Jayapura in the north-west of the Indonesian province now called West Papua. Vanimo's proximity to the Indonesian border, along one of the few roads in the west of Papua New Guinea, has meant that it has had a strategic significance for first the Australian and then the Papua New Guinean Government since the time of Indonesian independence in 1945.

In the 1960s, one company of PIR's Second Battalion, based at Moem Barracks, Wewak, was sent to Vanimo for three months at a time, on a rotating basis. Army Education staff accompanied them, teaching the same sorts of courses as they did in the main centres. Conditions were quite different, however. Initially, the classroom was a basic tin shed, unlined, with no windows as such, but it did have shutters that could be propped open to get a little fresh air. Greg Ivey recalled that education space and the resources were more limited, but 'the rapport with Servicemen on course was closer' for the two Chalkies sent there for three months at a time in 1970. Ivey said that an additional fortnightly duty was the distribution of newspapers to the men who cut the grass and shrubs around the Barracks. The gardeners didn't want to keep up with the news, just make sure their 'roll-your-own' cigarettes were well-wrapped.

When John Humphrey was posted to Moem Barracks the following year, each of the Chalkies took it turns to go to Vanimo for only two months at a time. A new Education building was constructed there that same year. A big after-hours attraction for the Chalkies at Vanimo was the haus win – the thatch-roofed open-air 'beer garden' in the shadow of tall coconut palms set alongside a glistening white beach and the rolling blue waves of the Bismarck Sea. These days there's a surfing lodge at Vanimo that promotes 'a wave mecca on Australia's doorstep'. In addition to 'quality waves', the area offers 'tropical remote wilderness, thousands of coconut palms, occasional village huts and pristine jungle.'[127] Just as it did when the Chalkies were there back in the 60s.

If these young men posted to PNG had been back in Australia teaching, most of them would have been in their first or second year in a classroom and, if they were not required for extra-curricular activities, would have knocked off about 4 pm and gone home, to cricket or footy training or the pub, seen their girlfriends later, or otherwise lived their lives until they turned up at school the next morning. The Army claimed their lives 24/7, however, and many of them had other tasks to perform.

9

'A responsibility thrust upon us': Other military tasks and duties

Orderly Sergeant was the most frequent of the additional duties required of Chalkies in PNG, and rarely welcomed. Orderly Sergeant meant being responsible, in conjunction with the Duty Officer, for maintaining order around the whole barracks and dealing with 'incidents' for a period of 24 hours, beginning at 6 pm. It also meant raising and lowering the Australian flag on the base, and sleeping in the duty room overnight. To make sure everyone knew who was on duty that day, the Orderly Sergeant wore a diagonal red sash across his starched juniper green uniform. No doubt the sash has historical significance, but when I had to go off base while on duty, I felt very conspicuous in public places in my 'beauty queen' ribbon.

One of the required duties of the Orderly Sergeant was to do a parade-ground 'changing of the guard' – 'which I was no good at,' John Ford said, 'and we also had to spend the night at Battalion Headquarters and got little or no sleep and attend to after-hours irregularities and problems'. It would have been good training for a boarding school housemaster.

Another task of the Orderly Sergeant was to raise the Australian flag every morning and ensure it was lowered at night. At Murray Barracks, 'I got into trouble for getting the soldiers on duty with me to allow the flag, when raised, to get caught in the pulley at the top, leaving about 2 cm free at the top,' Graham Lindsay said. 'The flag pole was situated outside the Brigadier's office window. On previous days, sergeants on duty had reported having to "send one of the boys shinnying up the pole" to release the flag. I achieved the status of 'reprobate' for this heinous act.' Such were the incidents that could make a sergeant's life a challenge in PNG Command.

There were other inconveniences, as John Ford recalled. 'Being "Chalkie" sergeants, the PI soldiers recognized we were out of our comfort zone and often niggled us, given the opportunity,' he said.

One weekend at Taurama, Ford and I shared the weekend duties – I had the Saturday, followed by Ford on the Sunday. One of my jobs as duty sergeant (apart from picking up the Battalion newspapers in town) was to organise a team of soldiers to clean up the outdoor area of the detritus in the Sergeants' Mess after the Friday-night movies. The PI Corporal in charge of this group advised me that the soldiers were not available until the following morning, so I passed this information on to Ford when he took over as Orderly Sergeant on the Sunday. Ford contacted the Corporal and was told the soldiers were still not available, firstly on Sunday morning, later Sunday afternoon and then not on Sunday evening either. Next day, the Regimental Sergeant Major, Warrant Officer Osi, was furious that the Mess was left in an absolute mess for such a period, and blamed us two for not getting it cleaned up. He dragged us before the Adjutant. Once told the circumstances, the Adjutant said he understood the problem and suggested that there should not be consecutive "Chalkie" Orderly Sergeants in the future. We were babes in the wood. No wonder the regulars scoffed.

Sometimes the duty sergeant had to supervise soldiers who'd been charged with minor infringements of Army regulations or Camp Standing Orders. At Goldie River Training Depot, John Teggelove suspected that there was an unwritten practice that all recruits would, sometime during their training, be 'charged' for some infringement or other, in order to experience 'extra duties'.

The recruits weren't the only ones. As punishment for not saluting the Administration Officer at Goldie River, Chalkie John Morris was charged and given two extra duties – Orderly Sergeant on Christmas Day and New Year's Day. 'Duty on New Year's Eve was something to remember!!!!' Morris said. 'And I was glad when 8 am the following morning arrived. Many of the soldiers had been to the Wet Canteen, consuming either South Pacific green or brown beer, and at closing time they made as much noise as possible with garbage lids, long into the night. It was frightening.'

Lindy Horton, whose husband Kevin was posted 1970–71 to Taurama Barracks, where they were eventually given an Army married quarter, said she never got used to the nights alone when Kev was Duty Sergeant. 'On one particular night there had been a major problem with the 'Labour Line' men involving 'payback' for an axe murder near the Boroko Hotel,' she said. 'I knew Kev would have to assist in checking the Labour Line accommodation area outside the army compound during the night. I guess there had to be some drawbacks for a fairly idyllic existence.'[128]

Other Chalkies commented on the challenge of closing the wet canteen on pay nights, and Andrew Remenyi said that checking on the behaviour of soldiers in the ORs' Mess at Igam Barracks was sometimes dangerous because of the level of intoxication and the proximity of the soldiers' married quarters. 'One night I had to supervise a soldier to hospital,' Remenyi said, 'because he had gotten into an argument with another soldier concerning his wife's extra-marital activities.'

Education sergeants also had more mundane duties – treasurer of the sergeants' mess, librarian, movie projectionist (requiring an Army certificate of competency), which they carried out with varying degrees of enthusiasm. Ron Inglis said they put him behind the bar at Moem and Igam Barracks on dining-in nights (when all sergeants were required to be in the Mess) because he didn't drink. 'Before too long, I was the only one sober enough to serve drinks,' he said. Some Chalkie officers also were posted into non-RAAEC positions on PNG Army units. For example, John Herlihy was appointed as Assistant Adjutant at Murray Barracks after a stint of teaching.

Positions in the mess generally brought respect from fellow sergeants as well as helped some Chalkies avoid morning parades. In some instances, this respect was hard won – regular sergeants who had worked their way up through the ranks sometimes resented the 'overnight' promotion of Nasho privates to temporary sergeants, even though this was an Army decision. The resentment, which was not uniform across PNG bases, was expressed verbally rather than physically, and the first cohort probably felt the initial brunt, as John Teggelove explained: 'We were the first batch of Nasho Chalkies and of "professional promotions" that many of the antagonists had come across, and with familiarisation and the realisation that we posed no threat to their military expertise, the resentment mostly soon dissipated.' One Chalkie reported that the strongest animosity came from regular sergeants' wives, who didn't feel constrained by Army discipline.

It may have been concern about the reaction from regulars that led the Brigadier to refuse to allow Steven Hill to be granted permanent sergeant's rank at Murray Barracks in 1970, despite Hill having completed all the Army exams for promotion to that rank.

Perhaps the best opportunity for Chalkies to show that they were 'real' soldiers came when they went out on patrol. 'The MCS was a fairly full-on military training establishment and when your class "went bush" so did you,' Andrew Dalziel said.' This meant training exercises in the mountains behind Lae and outside Madang and a five day forced march from the old gold-mining town of Wau across the mountains to the village of Salamaua, on the south coast of the Huon Gulf were for everyone. On the latter trek they followed the 'Black Cat Track', described by Lonely Planet as 'suitable only for masochists and Israeli Paratroopers'.[129] And Chalkies, apparently. More recently it was the scene of an ambush of tourists by local 'rascals', which resulted in the deaths of two indigenous helpers.

At Igam Barracks, Education Sergeants accompanied students on their patrols at the end of each term. Ian Curtis went to the Fly River, trekked from Telefomin to Olsobip over the Star Mountains, and did a military history excursion to Finschhafen to check out Japanese World War II fortifications and allied invasion sites. One week he sailed as 'crew' aboard an AB boat on an extended trip through the islands of the Bismarck Sea to Rabaul, rather different from what he would have been doing as school teacher in Australia.

John Teggelove also managed to wangle a sea voyage. Towards the end of 1966 and between recruit intakes at Goldie River, he won a ballot for the position of ration clerk on an Army Landing Barge, a 78-foot vessel transporting supplies from Port Moresby around the PNG coastline to Vanimo. 'It was a truly amazing and wonderful experience seeing the mainland's rugged and tropical coastline; fishing, reading and generally relaxing whilst basking in perfect weather; calling into major ports including Lae, Madang and Wewak; and piecing together some of Australia's WW2 history on New Guinea's northern shores in the Morobe and Oro Districts,' Teggelove said.

His 'swanning around' came to a painful and disappointing end after one week: when the boat reached Vanimo, the turnaround point, and was about to nose into shore, the skipper asked Teggelove to let himself over the side to determine the depth of water below us. 'I'd barely eased my feet into the water when the water bloodied up,' he said, 'and I realized I'd stood on some sharp metal and gashed my right foot.' An Orderly at the Medical Outpost cleaned up the wound and inserted 22 stitches, but because of the high risk of infection in the tropics, he was compelled to forego the return trip by boat and fly back to Moresby.

As if in punishment for his having had such a good time, on Teggelove's arrival back at Goldie River, still mastering his crutches, it was decided that since he was going to be camp-bound, and just about everyone else was off doing other things over the holiday period, he could pick up some extra Orderly Sergeant shifts, including Christmas Day.

A week later, Teggelove had to go to the Medical Centre at Taurama Barracks to have the stitches removed. The doctor removed the first 10 stitches and then allowed six medical corps novices, fresh from Goldie River Recruit Training, to remove two stitches each. 'Despite assurances that it wasn't retribution,' Teggelove said, 'I swear each of the novices tried to remove the cut stitches by pulling through the knotted ends whilst I gripped the metal bed-head for dear life and sweated profusely.'

Other Chalkies accompanied 'civic action' patrols, intended to promote the role of the Army in supporting the Territory's development as well as contribute to community projects for the benefit of local villagers. John Meyer went to the Gulf District to help build a medical aid post, and Phil Parker accompanied a patrol into the Western District, up the Bensbach and Fly Rivers 'and many places in between', which he said was one of the highlights of his time in the Territory. Taurama-based Sergeant, Ray Bassett in 1971 accompanied B Company on a patrol to Angoram in the Sepik District, and reportedly returned with a deep dislike of kau-kau, the ubiquitous locally grown sweet potato – during the patrol there was a problem with a food resupply, and his platoon had to live on native foods for 10 days. One Chalkie also had a memorable excursion into the Highlands – the patrol carried sub-machine guns with live ammunition because they were in 'cannibal' areas.

Tom O'Meara, who was based at Taurama Barracks in 1972, accompanied a 1PIR company to the island of Buka, in the Solomon Sea, east of the Papua and New Guinea mainland. 'My job was to update the military maps (ironic given I basically failed map reading at "Pucka"), and to explain the role of the modern army to tribesmen who emerged from the bush in ceremonial garb. This of course had to be done in pidgin, and apart from possibly declaring war on one tribe, I think I did quite well.' There was another challenge, too, for the

Victorian school teacher: 'One night a young, well-educated Corporal said the men wanted me to explain all about the moon landing a few years previously. In pidgin!!!'

Prior to PNG, everything Max Quanchi had learned about jungles came from years of reading Phantom comics and watching Jungle Jim movies. On a one-month patrol with a rifle company from 2PIR in 1968, he found himself deep within the real thing. 'The jungle is never dry,' he said (which itself almost sounds like an old Phantom saying). 'We were there in the wet season, and it was drenched. It was nothing strange to see streams rise and fall four feet and to have this happen three times a week in that season. The sun rarely shines through to the ground, and the traveller does not feel its direct rays except when he encounters the odd kunai grass patch or native garden area.'

Once he became used to his new environment, Quanchi found that the green surroundings brought their own sense of peace and a new appreciation of the country and its people. 'As a tourist, I was impressed by the untouched natural scenery, by the peaceful quietness of the jungle, by the natural charm of many of the people and their homes and way of life,' he said. 'As a soldier and an educator, I welcomed the opportunity to get to know the PI soldier well, to see more deeply into his personality and to asses more fully the effect on him of his environment.' No doubt the PI soldiers were similarly making their assessment of their Education Sergeant.

Quanchi could see how his new-found knowledge would benefit his teaching: 'I consider I am better fitted to take him as a pidgin speaker, to teach him English to the point where he gains his English Speaking Badge, to take him further to the stage where he gains his Army Certificates of Education, and, in the end, through education, to make him a better citizen of this, his country.'

While not all Chalkies expressed those sentiments so elegantly, and they saw the aims of education in the Army in a variety of ways, from short-term to long-term, it seems that most were able to identify a sense of purpose in their teaching in the way that Quanchi did.

In September 1972, Education Sergeant P.J. Semmens, from the Examinations and Methods Cell at Education HQ at Murray Barracks, took part in a ten-day 'adventure training exercise' from Wau, an old gold mining town in the valleys south-west of Lae, across the Owen Stanley Range to Malalaua, on the Papuan Coast north of Port Moresby. The journey brought him into touch not only with the culture and topography of that part of PNG, but also its relatively recent wartime history. The first part of the trip was across the Bulldog Track, built between Wau and the village of Bulldog in the Gulf District by Australian Army Engineers in 1943 as a supply route from the south. By the time it was finished, however, the war had moved on, and Semmens said it was fairly certain the PI troops he was with were the first to cross the complete 70 miles of road since the one and only inaugural jeep convoy 29 years earlier.

The final part of the journey was by canoe. Semmens provided a picture of the level of development of some of the Territory's citizens immediately prior to self-government as the patrol passed through a valley not far from Bulldog: 'The three villages we passed through in this valley ... were all peopled by Kukukukus. They were poor people and had an entirely subsistence economy. Nearly all the people still wore as everyday dress the traditional sporrans and bark cloaks of the Kukukuku. Although our carriers were the same people as the villagers, they were too frightened of being alone (unaccompanied by Europeans) on their return to come any further south with us. They insisted we pay them off at ... the first village we encountered, and returned to Wau after buying a few essential foodstuffs from the villagers.'[130]

Not all Chalkies went on patrol, and there was a variety of individual tasks they were required to do or volunteered for in the Army. These included escorting a group of soldiers to the Highland Show in Goroka, and providing driver instruction when there was not enough for the Education staff to do. John Teggelove and another Chalkie helped with the National Census in 1966, collecting information from families in the Goldie River Married Quarters. 'This proved to be a very challenging but insightful task, with most of the Army wives very shy, reluctant to communicate and vague about the information required,' he said.

John Ford took on a particular task at Taurama Barracks in 1971, curator of the Battalion Scrap Book, mainly because he had little else to do for four months. He'd extended his time in PNG for that period solely to ensure that his ownership of a Jaguar saloon he'd purchased in Moresby on arrival extended beyond 15 months and therefore would not incur heavy customs duties when imported into Australia. He parked the Jaguar in the car park outside the sergeants' accommodation, to the envy of other soldiers on the base. The Army granted Ford the extension he wanted but 'really had no role for me, so I became the curator of this book and got it into quite a tidy piece of Battalion historical record,' he said.

Steven Hill went with the engineers to Lake Kopiago to 'show the movies and sell beer', Tom Uil was involved in a search and rescue mission for a missing plane, and Michael Turnbull went on several Army recruiting drives into rural areas. Phil Adam was coach (and player) for the Murray Barracks soccer team in the first division, and Steve Beveridge was Secretary of the Papuan Amateur Boxing Association during most of his stay in PNG. He went to Rabaul with groups of boxers, generally in the Caribous of 38 Squadron RAAF. 'There was a strong connection between the Police and Army in the Association,' he said, one of the more positive links between two groups that suspicion, animosity and pay differences often divided. South Australian Ian Hodder coached the 1PIR women's softball team to victory in 1968, and with other Chalkies acted as the enemy for the infantry companies' 'search and destroy' mission.

Teggelove also performed a role as enemy for the recruits' final exercises at Goldie River, in mountainous terrain in the foothills of the Owen Stanley Ranges. He commanded a platoon of camp administrative staff ('Dad's Army') whose task was to harass the patrols, engage them in skirmishes and generally frustrate their operations. 'Thank goodness for blank bullets!' Teggelove said. He also observed how soldiers from the various areas of PNG were 'built' for their tribal terrain: 'Highlanders were stocky, with massive legs/calves, and they 'raced' up the hills, whilst those from flatter Provinces, like Milne Bay, New Ireland and New Britain, were taller and leaner, and found the hill-climbing as challenging as we Europeans did!'

There were other challenges in the jungle for Teggelove's 'enemy' platoon besides harassing the patrolling recruits: 'One time we came across the scary sight of a huge python, well over six metres long, that had a huge lump down its throat, having seemingly just recently swallowed a whole magani (wallaby).'

Sometimes the 'exercises' were almost real. While stationed at Vanimo outpost in 1969, Roger Grigg, a Victorian primary school teacher, went on a 'border patrol' where the PIR troops carried live ammunition ('we were never told why'), and their purpose was 'waving the flag at Indonesia'. Two weeks later, the Indonesian Army came through the same border village, Grigg said, 'firing machine guns and mortar bombs'. There were no casualties, but it seems the cross-border incursions that had worried the Menzies Government back in 1963 had not dissipated by the end of the decade.

***

We were never just teachers in the Army. We were always soldiers and teachers. Had we been at schools in Australia, as first- or second-year teachers we would have taught what was in the syllabus, coached school sporting teams, and helped out with social events like the school dance and the annual concert. That's what I did in my first year of teaching in North Queensland. In PNG the Army expected more of us, partly because we were in a military organisation and so had to obey orders, but also because we were intimately involved in the educational and personal development of soldiers that was part of a plan to give some substance to the indigenous Army, to boost its standards and the troops' understanding of its role. It was a responsibility thrust upon us, young men in our early 20s who mostly had never wanted or imagined this role for ourselves.

Not all of us recognised that self-government and independence were close at hand, but we generally accepted the tasks allocated to us and carried them out to the best of our ability; and some of us extended our role to civic action patrols and other travel. Yet even while we fulfilled our teaching and military responsibilities, and even experienced the 'frontier of adventure' that Hank Nelson referred to, most of us were conscious that we were still conscripts, not in the Army or PNG by choice, and that when our two-year terms were up, most of us would return to Australia, glad to leave the Army behind. Yet, although we didn't always realise it at the time, the 'forced' experience of another culture, would stay with most of us all our lives, to a greater or lesser extent.

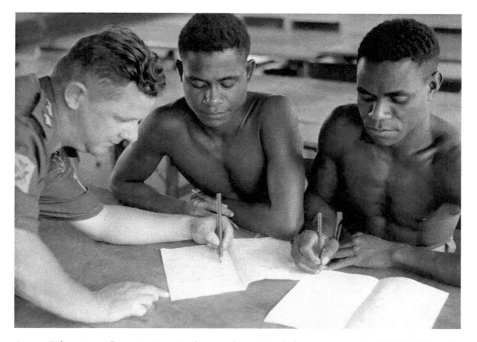

Army Education Captain Ian Bayles teaching English to recruits in PNG 1959–60, before the Nasho Education scheme

The ballot balls used in the lottery to select Australian 20-year-olds for National Service 1965–72

Nasho recruits outside accommodation hut, 3rd Training Battalion, Singleton, early 1969

Nasho Chalkie-to-be, Brian Haines (2nd from right), recruit training

New Chalkie privates, Geoff Peters (left rear) & Andrew Remenyi (right front) with other Nashos during Corps training, Singleton, 1969

New Chalkie privates, at Education Unit, Holsworthy Army Camp, 1971, pre-PNG. L–R: Bob Strachan, Andy Dalziel, John Hain, Ross Yates; front: John Fragomeni

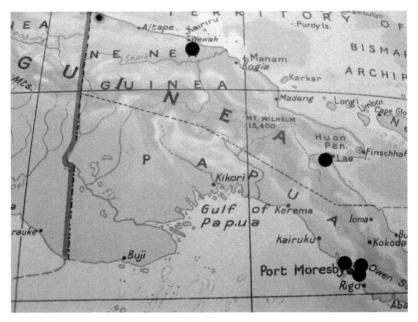

Chalkie postings PNG 1966–73: Murray Barracks, Taurama Barracks, Goldie River Training Depot (Port Moresby area), Moem Barracks (Wewak) & outstation, Vanimo, Igam Barracks (Lae)

Brigadier Ian Hunter with Chalkie sergeants – Sgt. Peter Darmody in centre

Brigadier Ernest Gould, RAAEC Director, with PIR soldier and Sgt. Neil Gibson, 1966

Sgt. Ian Bowen with science class, Murray Barracks, September 1968

First Nasho Chalkie wedding in PNG: Peter and Pam Wedgwood, Port Moresby, May 1967

Murray Barracks' Chalkies on Kokoda Track, 1968: Sgts Neil Gibson in front, Don Benson (R), Frank Cordingley (L), and Ken Morcom

Murray Barracks Chalkies 1970: Anti-clockwise from Sgt. Robert Coppa (second from left corner): Sgts Phil Adam, Mick Lee, Capt. John (Tich) Freeman, Lt. Jim Murray, Sgts John Meyer, Brendan Nolan, Randy Wittwer, unknown young woman, Bridie Freeman

Iduabada Technical College, where some Murray Barracks Chalkies taught

John Harris in his tent home for first months, Taurama Barracks, 1966

1PIR troops in Sgt. Ian Hodder's Education classroom, Taurama Barracks, 1968

Sgts Bruce Boxall (L), Bob Foster (R), Norm Hunter (back to the camera) in Taurama Library, 1968

Dining-in night, Sergeants' Mess, Taurama. L–R: Sgts John Gibson, Bob Green & Roger Howard, 1967–68

Sgt. Peter Karake (L) & Cpl. Atisi in Sgt. Peter Chard's science class, Taurama, 1969

Sgt. Phil Parker, Battalion Orderly Sergeant, Changing of the Guard, Taurama

1PIR troops boarding Caribou for Civic Action patrol, 1969

Sgt. Peter Chard with Peter Driwa, 1PIR Civic Action patrol, 1969

Chalkies, Taurama Barracks, 1969–70. Rear (L–R): Sgts Barry Nunn, Darryl Dymock, Lt. Chris Burgin (2IC), Sgt. Mick Mulligan, Capt. Wolf Fladun (OC), Pte. John Gaira (Education Assistant), Sgts Tom Uil, Ian Mackay; Front: Sgts John Ford, Darryl Stewart & PI soldiers

Merlyn Leader (wife of Sgt. Graham Leader), Taurama Barracks Primary School, 1971

Warrant Officer Class 1 Osi Ivaraoa BEM, Regimental Sergeant Major, 1PIR Taurama Barracks, 1968–1973, on recruiting poster

Taurama Chalkies 1971. Rear (L–R): Sgts Ray Bassett, Graham Leader, Russell Bates, Kev Horton; Front: Sgts Wayne Wallace, Neville Corrie, John Moore

Sgt. Bill Bailey at chalkboard,
Goldie River, 1968–69

Goldie River Chalkies 1969–70.
L–R: Sgts Paul Johnson, Alex
Thomson, Rod Wilbers, Ray
Nicol, with popular cleaner
George Tolata

Sgt. Alex Thomson on duty as Orderly
Sergeant, with Sgt. Rod Wilbers,
Goldie River, 1969–70

Goldie River Army Education staff 1970: Back (L–R): L/Cpl.Michael
Irima (Library Assistant), Sgts Paul Taylor, Bernard Neeson, Wayne
Dark, George Tolata (Cleaner); Front (L–R): Sgt. Bill Bailey, Lt. Michael
Forster, Capt. Richard (Dick) Robinson (CO), Lt. Jim Pyle, Sgt. Arthur
Mousamas

Colourful in 'civvies', Goldie River Chalkies, May 1972. L–R: Sgts Jim Connolly, Bruce Hartshorn, Guy Bodizsky, Frank Nolan, Gunter Schmidt, Ron Lynch and Phil Shea

Sgt. Greg Ivey with 2PIR soldiers, Moem Barracks, 1969

Moem Chalkies at iconic haus tambaran, Maprik, 1970. L–R: Sgts Phil Imison, Boyd Robertson, Greg Smith

Self-described 'Moem Synchronised Riding Team', Sepik River 1968. L–R: Chalkie Sgts Jim Davidson, Peter Tymoc, Geoff O'Reilly, John Todd, Bruce Richter, Ray Deane & Russell Jenkin

Pond and piggery ('haus pig'), 2PIR farm, Moem Barracks, managed by the Nasho Chalkie agriculturalist specialist ('didiman')

Sgt. Kevin Smith, Vanimo outstation, 2PIR, 1967

2PIR buildings at Vanimo outstation. L–R: Officers' quarters, dining building, sergeants' accommodation; haus win in front

Sgt. Rob Duff & 2PIR soldiers on fishing trip west of Vanimo, 1970

2PIR students in Classroom, Vanimo

A DC3 on one of Chalkie Warrant Officer Dan Winkel's popular charter tours, Popondetta airstrip, 1967

Sgt. Andy Dalziel and Military Cadet School students, Lae, 1970–71

Chalkie Sergeants, Igam Barracks, Lae, 1968. L–R: Sgts Rusty Morris, Graham 'Knobby' Carnes, Peter Darmody, Alan Calder, [unidentified], Bruce Nulty, Jim Wells

Chalkies Igam Barracks, 1970. L–R: Sgts Andrew Remenyi, Geoff Peters, Capt. Dick Robinson, Sgts David Pollock, [unidentified], Bob Humphries, Lt. Tom Hall, Sgt. Les Rowe

10

PNG: Land of the unexpected

Papua New Guinea is sometimes called the 'Land of the unexpected', which sounds like a marketing cliche, but is remarkably true for those coming from a Western culture. The Territory hit most Chalkies in the face the day they flew into Port Moresby, and their experiences over the rest of their time in the country served only to underline the unpredictability of their temporary home. Living and working in a developing country was a whole lot different to what they would have faced teaching in schools back in Australia.

Asked to recall particularly significant incidents or events in their time in PNG, the Chalkies responded with a raft of different sorts of occasions they remembered with joy, bemusement, distaste, satisfaction or straight-out awe after almost 50 years.

Denis O'Rourke will never forget his encounter with the 'real' PNG when he flew into Tarpini in the southern Highlands on a RAAF Caribou in 1967, as part of a 1PIR Company undertaking a civic action patrol. One of the platoons had arrived a couple of days earlier and had gone off exploring while they waited for the rest of the Company, and had come back with a wooden box they were guarding.

'I asked what was in the box,' O'Rourke said, 'and they replied that they were the bones of a 14-year-old male who had recently been eaten.'

The young science teacher from New South Wales was stunned to learn that cannibalism was still being practised. He asked who was responsible. 'The soldiers pointed to the natives that were there at the scene armed with their bows and arrows,' he said. 'They saw my expression of shock and reassured me that I was too skinny to eat, but added a rider that I would make good soup.'

O'Rourke said that he didn't sleep well that night. 'I imagined every sound was these cannibals stalking me,' he said.

Other events, incidents and sights that struck the fancy of these young Education Sergeants in the time they spent with the Army in PNG included: living in thatched huts in the old camp for most of the time at Goldie River 1966–67; establishing strong friendships with PIR soldiers; having a good insight into another culture; visiting Rabaul and walking the rim of the volcano; several World War II aircraft remains in the area between Cape Hoskins and Talasea in New Britain, seen while on a civic action patrol; the Lae Show with the marvellous tribal costumes and makeup of the participants, and the many deceased family members brought along for the show; getting shipwrecked (boat sprang a serious leak) and being saved after the sun had gone down; seeing Michael Somare [future Prime Minister] in real native dress walking along the road near his village; little girls coming up to my wife in a remote village and touching her hair as they'd never seen straight hair before; rainforest de-afforestation near Vanimo; diving in areas probably never dived before; hiring an old Nissan Patrol in Lae and driving from Lae to Mount Hagen and back along the old unsealed Highlands Highway, and 'the whole experience of another country and culture'. Ian Ogston said, 'No one from Goldie would not include the encounter with the Education Centre cleaner, George Tolata, as being one of the great experiences of the time in PNG.'

Other memories included: dodging the betel nut spit at Saturday markets; live turtles being sliced at the markets; the heartbreaking accidents and deaths of locals, due to alcohol abuse; learning to live with long life milk; the joy of fresh apples when the supply ship arrived; total lack of telephone communication with families back home; millions of geckos and huge frogs; travelling on a DC3 from Moresby to Lae and Madang; viewing the natural wonders of the country while flying over the mountainous terrain from Moresby to Lae; attempts to learn Pidgin, and listening to the 6.00 am news each morning on the ABC with the news read in English, followed by Pidgin and finally Police Motu; the remarkable experience of flights with incoming RAAF pilots in Caribou aircraft; sitting on the upper deck of our living quarters firing arrows at toads; seeing an indigenous soldier having his midday nap in a large cardboard box with his arms and legs over the sides.

Greg Farr said he had a Papuan baby named after him, but was at pains to point out this was due to an act of kindness on his part, not because of any biological contribution. Driving along a road in Port Moresby, Farr was flagged down by a distraught truck driver whose vehicle had broken down as he was on the way to Port Moresby hospital with his wife, who was in the early stages of labour. 'He and I transferred mother with baby still attached [i.e. unborn] to the front seat of my 1948 bull-nosed Morris and father sat in the back,' Farr said. 'Now this car had limited capabilities and would struggle up PM hills even without passengers. I could only think that God was on our side that night, for we made it up one of Port Moresby's steepest hills to the hospital, but only just.' When Farr visited the couple next day, he said they were very thankful and happily informed him that they had decided to give the baby his name.

Some Education Sergeants played sport with some success, such as Norm Hunter, who led the Army rugby team to the Port Moresby premiership in 1968, and was subsequently the only 'white man' selected in the national rugby team. A 1971 report from Murray Barracks Education Section noted that 'as usual the National Service contingent consisting of thirteen Sgts and one Officer is actively involved in numerous sporting fields'. It cited Dick Morgan as a 'flashy breakaway,' in the Army rugby team, and Rob Daniel, Gerry Keegan, Tony Rogers, Denis Jenkins, Graham Miller and Lieutenant Knight in the Murray Barracks Australian Rules team. Sergeant Norm Isenberg was coaching the second soccer team, Sergeant Miller was the squash representative, and Lt. Knight the badminton rep., Graham Edgerton had entered a table-tennis team in the local competition, and Brian Haines was playing for the Army hockey team. In Lae, West Australian Reg Radford played for the town's cricket team in the PNG Championships in 1972–73 with some success.

Peter Chard's experience shows how significant we came to regard rank in the Army and how we recognised our place in the hierarchy, and also why some Chalkies were glad to get away from it after two years. Before he was called up, Chard played first grade squash in the Sydney Pennant Competition and continued playing when he arrived in Moresby in 1968, helped by the fact that Taurama Barracks (like other barracks in PNG) had a squash court attached to the gym. Apparently hearing of Chard's prowess, 'the CO at Taurama, Colonel Pears, asked (ordered!) me to have a game with himself and the ranking officer in charge in PNG,' Chard said. 'How I did it I don't know! I must not have offended either of them because I didn't get any extra duties. It was an unenviable position as it didn't matter how easy I played, I could beat them, but I couldn't let them win otherwise they'd know that I threw it!'

When Phil Adam was at Murray Barracks in 1969–70, the Regimental Sergeant Major (RSM), the highest ranking NCO on the base, decided to hold a formal dinner in the Sergeants' Mess to 'teach the younger members of the Mess how the Army behaves'. 'This turned out to be a complete fiasco,' Adam said, 'with incredible drunkenness, fights, broken furniture, etc. ... The Chalkies were merely amused spectators to the whole thing. He never did it again.'

Given that the Chalkies were young men occasionally needing to let off steam, it's probably inevitable that alcohol would feature in some of their stories. At 1PIR Taurama, after a night of celebratory drinks for Ian Hodder's 22nd birthday, he and three other Education Sergeants decide to test their skills with newly acquired bows and arrows, purchased at the Goroka Show. 'We drove around the camp roads looking for cane toads to "shoot",' Hodder said. 'We'd obviously had more than our share to drink because we were unable to score a "kill" at point blank range.' At Taurama, Phil Parker and his fellow sergeants drove their old FC Holden around the base with a spotter on each front fender giving directions to the driver as to where there was a toad to squash.

Cars and motorbikes were prominent in the off-duty lives of many Chalkies because they allowed them to 'escape' from the Barracks, especially where those barracks were out of town. When Ian Ogston and John Morris were posted to Goldie River Training Depot, they bought a battered VW between them. Sometimes such vehicles were onsold to the incoming Chalkies, but in this case, just as the sale was proceeding, prior to Ogston's and Morris's departure, the VW's engine caught fire, and no money changed hands. A more serious event was the death in 1970 of Sergeant John Martin, based at Murray Barracks, and teaching at Iduabada Technical College, who was killed in a motorbike accident.

Living in single quarters in the Sergeants' Mess also brought its problems. For example, one of the regular Australian sergeants at Taurama was fond of a drop, and after the Saturday evening movie at the Mess, which he always attended, 'he would stagger off to his room with a skin full of grog, lock himself in his room and listen to the ABC on his radio VERY LOUDLY,' said John Ford, whose room was next door. He would fall asleep with the radio blaring, 'which was bad enough,' said Ford, 'but at 1.00 am the ABC would cease broadcasting and then for the rest of the night there was a piercing beep every 30 seconds.' The other sergeants would pound on his door, yell until they were hoarse and shine lights into his room, but their drunken colleague continued to snore, making sure no one else slept that night.

On a more serious note, Ian Curtis said he saw 'many instances of violent reaction – caused by close living in the Sergeants' Mess. Many would not talk to or even acknowledge certain people. Grudges were nursed. It was generally conceded that certain amongst us had "gone troppo"'. On the other side of the ledger, when Terry Edwinsmith was at Taurama in 1968, almost the whole Battalion marched in the funeral procession for RSM Warrant Officer Class 1 Frederick Wilson following his unexpected death at age 43.

In one instance, the 'division' between the regulars and Nashos was highlighted during a visit by the Defence Minister, Malcolm Fraser, to Taurama Barracks in late 1969. According to Chard, Fraser was 'taken around the Sergeants' Mess and introduced to every member *except the Nashos*. ... It was probably a diplomatic move on behalf of the RSM, J.D. McKay, knowing how much we all hated the army!' As has been noted already, however, that hate was not universal among the Chalkies.

Ivey had an opportunity to compare the culture of Army training with that in the Police Force when he was seconded for three months to the Bomana Police College in Port Moresby. 'The Police Senior Officers were British, some with experience in Africa,' Ivey said. 'Their attitude towards the PNG recruits was very strict, while the recruits were dressed and housed very simply compared to their Army contemporaries. The recruits were expected to display great respect to their Instructors. Although not an Officer, I was always saluted by the recruits, possibly only because I had white skin.'

Ron Inglis, who spent time at both Moem Barracks, Wewak, and Igam Barracks, Lae, said he became aware of 'the curse of racism' among some expatriates in PNG. 'Even within myself I could see racist elements that had automatically become part of me while growing up in Australia in the 50s and 60s,' Inglis said. 'I remember being shocked by the derogatory way in which some expatriates spoke about the locals. "Rock apes" was a term used in white conversation. White superiority and pessimism for the future of an independent PNG were strong characteristics of the colonial society and I found these to be very distasteful.' Another Chalkie said he saw racism in practice, when regular Army personnel living in provided married quarters abused their Pacific Islander house-maids or child-minders. 'One dreadful incident was all over an officer's wife's blouse being singed by the iron!' he said scathingly.

Within the Army, there was occasional unrest within the indigenous ranks, usually over pay. Steven Hill experienced an incident at Murray Barracks where a number of soldiers wanted to be discharged. 'Four apprentices who were finishing their time went around Murray Barracks one evening saying that the Brigadier wanted to see them [the troops] on the oval next morning,' Hill said, 'When they turned up, the four stood up and started calling strike.'

Civic action patrols, which for some Chalkies was an expectation at their barracks and for others meant volunteering, provided some long-standing memories, and Chard, who otherwise found Army life not to his liking, said a patrol to Bougainville was the highlight of his time in PNG. With C Company from Taurama Barracks, he flew to the town of Buin, on the island of Bougainville, and walked over the mountains to another town, Kieta. On the way they came across World War II wreckage and numerous artefacts. While they were camped on the beach at Kieta, awaiting a flight back to Moresby, it was announced that the live ammunition would not be flown back. 'And so a "whoopy shoot" ensued,' Chard said. Although he had received no training in its use, 'I carried a regulation issue pistol (9 mm) and blasted off many rounds out to sea. It's the only time I've ever fired a pistol.'

A civic action patrol to the Gulf was a highlight too for John Meyer, but its impact was problematic. It ended up being a "typical Army stuff up", Meyer said, 'because we didn't build the medical aid building; we left it in the grass and returned to Moresby. Army Engineers decided on a site that was under water at king tides so we were unable to complete the project. We took with us our own Cool Room, generator and alcohol supplies and we managed to consume the entire stock.'

Tom O'Meara's 'stuff-up' was of his section's own making. While out on a patrol, a section of the platoon was given approval to look for food (cuscus/possum), and he went with them. They eventually found a cuscus in a plantation, but after further exploration into nearby jungle, O'Meara noticed the two PI section leaders, both well-educated corporals, conversing seriously in pidgin. Next moment, they turned to tell the Education Sergeant unselfconsciously that they were lost, and handed him the map and compass.

'I basically failed map reading at "Pucka". Ditto compass reading!'

O'Meara said. 'Hoping that I had both map and compass up the right way, I "studied" them with intense levels of concentration, looked about me dramatically, paused dramatically, and announced, "This way, men!" Lo and behold, after only about 20 minutes or so, we hit a majorish road!'

I was most impressed,' O'Meara said, 'but "my" men (as they now were) expected nothing less, and did not break into wild cheering and raucous gratitude. I thought my work was done. But again, the two corporals waited patiently. Oh, I see. Left or right? Study map. Shake compass. Look about confidently. Pause. Pray. Some two hours later, we hooked up with the rest of the platoon.'

Russell Jenkin also had a memorable map-reading excursion when he was given a group of PI soldiers to take on a compass march, up and down heavily timbered slopes. 'I had a map and knew where I was going!' he said. 'All but one of the native soldiers, eventually defied my directions and went their own way. One stayed loyal! As it turned out, I understood a map, but the others understood the territory! They found their way down to a river and followed its course back to base. My colleague and I slipped and slid up and down steep slopes and got back to the same base – exhausted! I had been taught a lesson, but I chose not to share my experience of this exercise with the CO!'

It was estimated that the seven rifle companies of the PIR spent up to three months a year on patrol duties, with about a third of that time allocated to civic action projects.[131] Despite their prevalence and the good times Chalkies had during them, civic action patrols were often criticised in PNG, however, for showing the Army in a good light at the expense of the Administration. The argument went that in undertaking community assistance programs, the people saw the Army as the organisation that benefitted them more than the Administration did, and that this laid the groundwork for an Army takeover in the future. Some claimed that in cultivating good community relations, the Army was actually dividing people's loyalties. Brigadier Hunter countered: 'It is better to have the army out with people, learning to understand them, than to be sitting in their barracks getting big heads.'[132] Even within the Army, however, some officers disliked civic action because it didn't have a proper military purpose, while external critics believed such patrols strengthened the Army's claim to existence in an emerging nation that couldn't afford to support a significant body of troops.

In 1970, there was an occasion when the positive image the Army had built up for itself went close to being severely tested, and I and several other Education Sergeants found ourselves in the middle of it. It was the only time between 1966 and 1973 that Chalkies could have been involved in an action that might have resulted in not only violence, but bloodshed, and would undoubtedly have been disastrous for the PIR, the Territory and Australia's future relationship with an independent PNG.

By the middle of 1970, midway through our tour of duty, the Chalkies in PNG had pretty much sorted out what the Army expected of us. At Taurama Barracks our teaching revolved around the rhythms of the battalion, with our courses scheduled around their training program, parades and civic action patrols. Orderly Sergeant and other Army duties, sport and social activities were tacked on to that. So I was surprised when I returned with my family to our married quarter at the barracks one Saturday afternoon in July to find a note taped to the front door, 'See Major Howard urgently'.

Leaving my wife and three-month-old son on the doorstep, I ran up to the Admin building, where Major 'Hori' Howard, OC Admin Company, was just coming out the door. 'What's going on, sir?' I said.

Major Howard said, in effect: 'The Australian Government is considering sending troops to Rabaul to assist the police there. Because New Guinea is a United Nations Trust Territory, we need to document every action we take. You Chalkies have been given that task. Riot training for the battalion begins in the morning at 0800. Pack your gear and be ready to move out tomorrow.' Another Chalkie at Taurama, Ian Mackay, remembered that we were told, 'Don't tell anyone, including your wives, what's happening – just go to work, as usual.'

The situation in Rabaul, on the island of New Britain, had been deteriorating for some time. In 1969, the Administration had proposed establishing an elected 'Multi-racial Local Government Council' for the Gazelle Peninsula. The local Mataungan Association, a Tolai group, opposed it on the grounds that it would be dominated by European interests. A demonstration in May that year had attracted 5,000 marchers, some carrying anti-Administration and anti-European placards, and Mataungans began squatting on land they said was rightly theirs.

Opposition Leader Gough Whitlam stopped off in Rabaul on a PNG tour in December 1969, just as I and the new Chalkies were settling into our postings across the country. For us the dispute was something happening on a distant island, which we read about in the local *Post Courier* or heard about on the ABC, virtually our only access to quality news. Whitlam told the Mataungans he supported their cause, but not the violence, and promised early self-government and independence for the country.

The issue continued to fester, and around 1000 police were sent to the area to try to keep protests and altercations in check. Early in July 1970, the Australian Prime Minister, John Gorton, as part of a PNG tour made a visit to Rabaul in an unsuccessful attempt to placate the protesters. An unsympathetic crowd of 10,000 forced the PM to retreat. He allegedly had a pistol secreted in his clothing, just in case, and later claimed that he would have used it if his wife had been in danger.[133] The mind boggles at the likely fallout if the Prime Minister of Australia had brandished a weapon in the faces of thousands of hostile Tolais.

Soon after his return to Australia, Gorton responded positively to an Administration request to send troops of the Pacific Islands Regiment to Rabaul, 'in aid of the civil power', which is why I found the note on my door that quiet Saturday afternoon at Taurama Barracks.

Next morning the seriousness of the task was brought home to the Chalkies when we were issued with 9 millimetre pistols (*sans* ammunition) and given a five-minute lesson on how to use them. Then, with the pistols clipped in holsters strapped to our hips, we headed for the parade ground to learn riot control. On the other side of the country, the Chalkies at 2PIR were doing the same. Major Howard was 2IC of the proposed force. 'The Tolai soldiers were given the option of remaining behind,' he said later, 'but I think all volunteered to go.'[134]

With eyes wide, I watched as the troops formed a 'hollow square' around a jeep containing the platoon commander, a sergeant, a radio operator, and a medic – and me, as scribe. Apparently based on methods the British used in Malaya against communist guerrillas in the 1950s, the idea was that rioters would be warned in various ways about an unlawful assembly, and then the troops would move to a kneeling position and prepare to fire. Even in training, my hand was shaking as I jotted down the sequence of events in the small green cloth-covered notebook issued for the purpose. This was serious stuff. Someone could get hurt, or worse. It could even be me.

'The problem as I saw it,' said another Chalkie, Steve Beveridge, 'was that all the troops were lying [or kneeling] down with rifles at the ready, and we were to stand up alongside the officer! We did stick out a bit!' Ian Mackay had similar thoughts: 'Sometimes, the only non-PNG soldier was the scribe. Stood out slightly!!!!'

Following our brief training, we piled on to trucks, awaiting orders to head to the airport. C130 transport planes were waiting there to take us to Rabaul. The soldiers were surprisingly quiet, no doubt also aware of the possible consequences of what we were about to do. For my part, the sweat running down my back was not only from the humidity.

While we waited, we had no idea what was happening in Rabaul and Canberra. It was only later that I learned there were two other dramas being played out that day, as well as the one in which I was reluctantly playing a bit part.

On the Gazelle Peninsula, the situation on the ground was tense, but not as bad as had been painted. Thousands of Mataungans were confronting lines of armed police, but there had been no violence. According to Steve Beveridge's source, authorities were concerned, however, that the local populace might have access to left-over weapons from World War II, and might use them against the police.

What happened in Canberra emerged later: the Defence Minister, Malcolm Fraser, refused to accede to Gorton's demand that he sign the request to the Governor-General to call out the troops, the Defence Committee advised caution, and the frustrated Prime Minister eventually signed the request himself, but failed to persuade the Governor-General it was a good idea. Gorton was forced to take time out to discuss the proposal with senior colleagues, including Fraser.

In the meantime, according to Hori Howard, when the request had first come through to PNG Command, Brigadier Ralph Eldridge decided that with the situation stable in Rabaul, and since it was getting late in the day and there were no air navigation facilities there for the transports to land safely, he would wait until next day to commit troops.

That next day was sufficient for the Government to reassess its position and, while the idea was not knocked completely on the head, they decided there would be no immediate call-out of troops.

As I sat in the truck, I saw Hori Howard striding towards us. 'Thank God common sense has prevailed,' he said, looking relieved. 'The government has decided against sending troops. You can all stand down.' 1PIR troops returned to their barracks; in Wewak, 2PIR did the same.

Howard's words made me realise for the first time that the 2IC of the task force had a personal position on the proposed use of troops, and as an experienced officer would have seen even more clearly than we did the damage such a move would have caused the PIR. I let out my own sigh of relief, glad that none of the scenarios that had gone through my head had come to pass.

In Rabaul, the non-violent confrontation continued as before, however. Then police observed a van of some sort driving slowly into the crowd, their lines parting to let it though. The authorities were concerned the truck was being used to hand out weapons (possibly those that had been found and secreted from World War II). A moment later the vehicle was identified – a Mr Whippy van taking the opportunity to sell ice-creams! That broke the tension, and when rain started to fall shortly afterwards, the crowd began to disperse.

And so the three overlapping dramas were over, at least for the time being. As for the Chalkies, we were glad to hand back our pistols and go back to our classrooms.

In rejecting a request the previous September to put PIR troops on stand-by, the Defence Committee in Canberra had said, 'It should be pointed out to the Administration that none of the PIR are trained, or psychologically prepared, for the purpose of controlling civilian disturbances, and this in itself carried risks of the greatest importance to the future of the PIR and to the Territory as a whole.' [135] When the occasion arose again, we Chalkies were arguably even less trained or psychologically prepared, since apart from the occasional civic action patrol, we hadn't touched a weapon or done any infantry training for about a year. Our focus had been on the classroom. We were part of the battalion, and readily at hand as well as having the necessary skills, so it made sense to use us, but it was hardly the sort of role we could have foreseen when we were posted to Army Education.

In Canberra, following another meeting between Gorton and his senior ministers, an order-in-council to call out troops if necessary was signed as a precautionary measure, but not put into effect. The confrontation in Rabaul continued and, regrettably, the following year eventually resulted in the murder of a respected senior Administration official. Police action followed, but no troops were called out.

***

Sometimes the Chalkies were able to tag along on trips that were not civic action patrols but some benign military or aviation activity in another part of the Territory. For example, Werder picked up a number of Caribou and helicopter flights with the RAAF. 'On one of those occasions, my life flashed before me,' Werder said, 'as the pilot nearly crashed into trees as he approached the strip in very heavy rain. My scream of "trees" saved me and the aircraft.'

Chard also wangled a flight on a Caribou, to the Trobriand Islands and West New Britain, and sat in the jump seat between the two pilots as they made the heart-stopping return journey to Moresby through the lowest point in the Owen Stanley Range, the Kokoda Gap. 'I learned that day to beware of overhead Caribous,' Chard said. 'To have a leak, you peed into a funnel attached to a hose which went out through a hole in the fuselage!'

The Kokoda Gap is on the Kokoda Track, and John Morris had the chance to walk the famous track in 1970, thanks to an invitation from his Education boss at Goldie River, Captain Dick Robinson, who hoped to find some war relics. Robinson wanted to walk the track as far as Imita Ridge (a key point in the Australian troops' repulsion of the Japanese advance in World War II), after a new Army recruit had mentioned a 25-pound cannon in the area. 'The entire day was memorable,' Morris said, '– the rugged and slippery climb, the trenches dug by the diggers during WW2, and the hardship that they must have endured over many months, the tropical landscape, crossing the Goldie River with water up to our waist, and then the need to dispose of the leeches in our clothing, the 20-cent pineapple bought at Uberi Village on the return trip, and the relief climbing up that last hill to Owers Corner to see the vehicles ready to take us back to Goldie.'

What the Second World War diggers would have given for that same sight.

Doug Rathbone, a Victorian Technical School teacher, went climbing in the mountains for a different purpose. Along with two other Chalkie sergeants, Bill Semple and Bob Strachan, in June 1972 Rathbone climbed to 14,000 feet on PNG's highest peak, Mount Wilhelm, to place a memorial plaque for Education Sergeant Christopher Donnan, who had been based at Murray Barracks, and disappeared while making an ascent of the mountain on 28 December 1971. The final words on the plaque read: 'If heaven is in a high place, Chris is indeed privileged to rest so near to God.'

Another unexpected experience for the Australians were 'gurias' or earth tremors, which are a frequent occurrence in geologically volatile

PNG. Ian Hodder was crossing the parade ground at Moem Barracks in 1967 while on Orderly Sergeant duty at five o'clock in the morning when 'things began to shake and move beneath my feet and the surface of the ground literally rippled like a pond of water and passed below me,' he said. Jim Davidson said that the soldiers at Moem would run out of their rooms when a guria struck after hours. 'Didn't matter whether it was ground floor or first or second storey. A stunning sight to see men running in mid-air, hit the ground still running and un-damaged, then disappear into the foliage.' Davidson was impressed by the elasticity of the human body.

John Teggelove saw a similar incident at Goldie River, when the fire alarm and automatic sprinklers went off in the middle of the night in mid-1967 in a newly occupied accommodation block. 'Bodies and bedding bolted for the bush in all directions,' he said. 'Three hours later and troops were still being rounded up.' Teggelove also noticed that, 'Amazingly, despite the separation in accommodation of soldiers from different villages and tribes, most were in "Wantok" groups when they returned to Camp after the big scare.'

According to Jim Davidson, there was a similar response from the troops at Moem Barracks in 1968 when the Quartermaster (QM) decided to torch all the second-hand clothing that had been handed in by soldiers in exchange for new uniforms. A detail of soldiers helped transport a huge pile of clothing to a large clearing, where it was liberally doused with petrol. The QM laid a trail back a long way from the pyre, told the onlookers exactly what would happen, and called for a volunteer to strike the match and light the heap. There was 'an almighty kerwoomph, a huge flash of flame, boots and clothing hanging from the trees,' Davidson said, 'and not a member of the detail other than we two to be seen. The detail eventually emerged from various hideouts, with eyes still well popped!'

The responses of PI soldiers to unexpected incidents in the classroom was often a source of amusement and delight for the visiting sergeants. In the classroom at Murray Barracks, Ed Diery caused pandemonium among the soldier students when they were dissecting cane toads in a science class and the creatures started to come back to life because Diery hadn't fully anaesthetized them. At Goldie River Glenn Hall had to be creative with a similar activity. 'I had the RSM in my Science class,' Hall said. 'He was a PI and had been one of the WW2 Fuzzy Wuzzy angels. He needed to pass Year 10 Science and he had attempted it several times. Every time he got to the part in the set curriculum to dissect a frog he quit the class! I came to the arrangement that I would do the dissection and that he would watch. He accepted this and consequently was able to complete the course. I'm not sure this arrangement would stand with the NSW Dept. of Education rules, but it worked for us!'

Other Chalkies used the Army system to their advantage, with Steven Hill and his colleagues at Murray Barracks having an end-of-course picnic on Fisherman's Island under the guise of studying the ecology of the reef. The island lies just off-shore from Port Moresby and is renowned for its sandy white beaches and gentle blue-green waves. The Brigadier, who no doubt knew the true purpose of the exercise, signed it off, 'and using Q Store tents and seats and barbecue, transport buses and the Engineers' landing barge, we had a picnic on Fisherman's Island,' Hill said, 'taking the nuns and children from the Spastic Centre.' These days the place is known as Daugo Island, and civilians can arrange the same sort of picnic by boat from Moresby for around 850 kina (about AUD$400).

John Humphrey had a similar idea at Moem Barracks, where they were discussing the formation of coral reefs, which happen to surround the area. So what better thing to do than have an excursion to the beach, for swimming and studying the reef. 'Next thing,' he said, 'the men had caught a few crays, we lit a fire on beach and had fresh cray for afternoon tea!!!' All was not quite idyllic in this tropical scene, however. 'We got a bit of a scare when one man stood on some sort of stonefish, which injected barbs into the sole of his foot, and ended in a trip to the hospital.'

Ian Hodder's ocean-going effort at Wewak also had a downside. He and his mates borrowed an assault boat for a fishing expedition outside the fringe reef, and lost the outboard motor off the back. 'We were all docked pay after that one!!' he said.

Orderly Sergeant duties provided opportunities for unexpected actions, or, as Terry Clarke learned, potential actions. While sleeping overnight in the duty sergeant's office at Igam Barracks, Clarke discovered that the office was the storage point for WW2 unexploded ordinance until it could be disposed of. 'I spent one night sleeping next to three or four unexploded 'huge' bombs – did not like it!' he said. At Moem Barracks, Greg Smith was also sleeping overnight on duty in the Battalion HQ, having stripped off his uniform, when there was an emergency call about a fire. 'I struggled to get dressed back into uniform with just one hand,' he said, 'with the other hand constantly on the barracks alarm to alert everyone of the emergency.'

Snakes also figured in Orderly Sergeants' lives. At Goldie River, in 1971 Frank Nolan was called upon to remove a python from the ORs' mess (which had quickly been vacated). A year earlier, Alex Thomson was dozing in the office at Goldie while the duty officer checked out the camp. 'I heard the Land Rover pull up,' Thomson said. 'Next moment a taipan is flying through the air towards me. I think I broke the world high jump record even though it was dead.' His tormentor was another Nasho, Lieutenant Rick Hawley. An army doctor at Igam Barracks whose special interest was pythons kept several at his surgery in tea chests with wire netting covers. As a security measure, Peter Darmody kept a rubber snake in his locker at Murray Barracks because, he said, the local men who did the soldiers' washing and ironing were afraid of snakes.

There were also more serious occasions. 'The guard at Murray fixed bayonets and were going to deliver tribal justice to an Australian soldier who had tried to run them down then round them up on a large motor bike,' Ian Colwell said. 'I was able to defuse the situation with no bloodshed, nor recriminations against the guard. I had full sympathy with the guard and probably used this in persuading them to return to the guard post and let me sort things out. The Australian was returned home within a few days.' Also at Murray Barracks, Richard Morgan became involved in a brawl while on duty as Orderly Sergeant, with a drunk soldier at a football match. 'Potentially disastrous!' he said.

Cultural differences were always near. While Bob Coppa was on Battalion Orderly Sergeant duty at Murray Barracks in 1970, he was in an Army vehicle on his way to the airport to collect the mail when he was directed to pull over by the police. 'As I was in uniform the police were quite respectful and cooperative,' he said. 'They were investigating a death. I was taken into the nearby scrub and shown a body with a spear lodged in the body. The policeman told me that the victim had not paid the full marriage price for his meri [wife].'

On another occasion, Coppa was not on duty but became involved in a potentially dangerous situation when he happened to ring an Australian woman who was house-sitting in Port Moresby and she told him that local men were trying to break into the house at that very minute. She was desperately trying to barricade the doors. Coppa grabbed an Army mate and they drove to the house at high speed. 'Our weapons were our army belts with the brass buckles,' he said. 'We pulled up and charged up the driveway yelling and whooping and whirling our belts in the air. There were at least eight locals trying to break in. They took off into "bush" with us in hot pursuit, but they ran much faster than us.'

Bill Larsen recalled that while stationed at Vanimo, away from his wife, he experienced a cargo cult. 'I was very concerned for her safety travelling from Moem into Wewak each day [for work],' he said. Cargo cults developed as a sort of religious belief in Melanesia from the late 19th century, when certain groups of uneducated villagers attributed the arrival of Europeans' material goods ('cargo') to some sort of 'white man' magic or spiritualism, and attempted to create situations where such largesse might be redirected to them. In Papua and New Guinea, the sudden influx of wartime provisions in the 1940s saw an upsurge of interest in acquiring such goods, and sometimes a belief that white people were interfering with indigenous people's rights to access them.

One of the enduring memories of many Chalkies was of charter flights across Papua and New Guinea, many arranged by regular Army Education WO2 Dan Winkel, who was based at Murray Barracks 1966–69, and also later by two Chalkies, Doug Rathbone and Tony Johnstone (Murray Barracks 1971–72). Rathbone and Johnstone in 1972 offered a one-day charter flight from Moresby to the Goroka Show for $30, and a two-day excursion from Moresby to the highland towns of Mt Hagen, Minj and Goroka (including a bus tour and overnight accommodation) for $57 a head.

According to Winkel, the initiative for the tours he organised came from the very top. 'A couple of months after the first group of National Service Education Sergeant Instructors arrived in Port Moresby,' Winkel said, 'I received a directive to organize opportunities for those who so desired to extend their PNG experience by viewing certain areas away from the Murray Barracks area. The directive came to me from the DADAE (Lt. Col. Alan Payne) where it had originally come to the Commandant, Brig Ian Murray Hunter from the then Minister for the Army (Rt. Hon. Malcom Fraser).'[136]

Fraser was Army Minister for two years from early 1966, and Winkel believed the initiative stemmed from a Nasho's complaint about lack of travel opportunities in PNG, which he sent to his father, who was a friend of Fraser's. Winkel's first effort was a fishing trip out over the reef in the Army work boat, and Lt. Col. Payne went along too. After that however, Winkel expanded his travel vision during his three-year tour of duty to develop a series of charter flights across the Territory. Winkel's account of the first of these flights gives some idea of what was involved:

One of my WO friends who happened to be posted to the PNGVR as a Depot Instructor, advised me that the Mt Hagen Show was coming up and that it would be a great opportunity for the NS Sergeants to see something of the Highland culture, if I could organize a means of getting them to Mt Hagen. At that time in 1966, there was a RAAF Detachment stationed in Port Moresby with its staff located at Murray Barracks. I frequently passed the time of day with the Squadron Leader in charge, and so one day I stopped to ask him if there was any possibility of one of the RAAF Caribous being available for a flight to Mt Hagen. The reply was negative but if I could hire a DC3, he or one of his staff would probably be willing to fly it for us, thereby allowing the pilot to spend the day at the Show.

After quite a bit of phoning and inquiring, I was able to hire a DC3 from TAA ($90 per hour + fuel). Bookings filled all the 40 seats within a few days. (Most were NOT NS Sergeants but ARA people and wives.) When the Saturday of the scheduled flight came around, I was very surprised to see the Sqn Leader and a Pilot Officer at the Airport when I arrived. Ferris Leischer from TAA was there and once the formalities of my signing for the aircraft and handing over the $1200 for aircraft hire, Ferris allowed the Sqn Leader to take possession. The Pilot Officer and I organized the loading of the 'hot box' breakfast that we had collected from the Sgts Mess kitchen and then it was 'All Aboard'.

By the time the P.O. and I had everybody seated side saddle, the Sqn Leader had both engines up to running speed and it was 'down the runway into the sea breeze'. Once in the air, we did a lazy circle and gradually climbed to clear the Owen Stanley Range. After approximately 1½ hours we had seen Lae in the distance on our starboard, and had turned another right angle to head almost due west up the Markham Valley to our final destination, flying at around 10,000 feet most of the way. We touched down and parked amongst numerous other aircraft (some bigger, some smaller) at around 9.30 am.

For the next 3 hours we were delighted to take in and photograph the exotic sights and smells. At around midday, I took as many travellers as I could round up off to the Mt Hagen Club for lunch. By 1 pm we had to be in the air again. Because we dallied at the Club and then had to wait in a queue for permission to 'take off', the Sqn Leader made the decision not to follow the same route he had taken in the morning because of the possibility the gap in the Owen Stanley Ranges would be clouded over. He flew directly west until he reached the head of the Fly River and then followed the Fly to the Gulf of Papua. Once in sight of the sea, the pilot made a 90 degree turn to port and then back to Moresby.

It was a long tiring day and I had to wait until Tuesday to get the final account for fuel used. The fuel used was less than anticipated which allowed us to have a slide night party at my married quarter a few weeks later with the funds left over.[137]

Given that many Chalkies had made their first flight when they had flown from Australia to Moresby, the excitement of flying at relatively low levels in a twin-engined propeller-driven aircraft, the Douglas DC3, to see other parts of the country and significant cultural events brought them face to face with other facets of the 'land of the unexpected'. It was also a welcome chance for them – and, for the married ones, their wives – to escape from the confines of the Army.

***

The range of experiences recalled in this chapter says a lot about the nature of the Chalkies' interactions with PNG. There are events and incidents that had sunk into their memories after almost 50 years. Some of them were cultural, significant because of the extent of their difference from Australian expectations. Others were responses to the natural environment or to humorous or serendipitous happenings. The near call-out of troops was probably the most nationally significant event for any Chalkie, but at the local level there were anxious moments too. Alcohol also played its part, not always without consequence. Once again the recollections show the Chalkie as both teacher and soldier, as well as attempting to have a life outside the Army. For married Chalkies, there was an additional role – as a husband, and in a few cases, as a father.

11

'Called forward': Chalkies' wives in PNG

Although wives could join their Chalkie husbands in PNG, the Army in most cases wouldn't let them do so immediately, apparently because it wanted the new sergeants to focus on their initial orientation. This usually also meant living in the single men's quarters, be they tents as they were originally at Murray Barracks, or rooms in the Sergeants' Mess as they were at Taurama – an enculturation process. Also, we were told in advance that Army married quarters would not be provided, and that we had to find our own private rental accommodation, but warned that it must be 'inspected by Command Catering Staff to ensure it is suitable and satisfactory before families can be called forward'.[138]

In the event, some Chalkies *were* given married quarters, depending on what was available at the barracks they were posted to. Most Nasho Chalkies were single, however, and lived in the Sergeants' Mess on base.

As might be expected, Chalkies' wives were also in their 20s, and as individuals and couples they experienced their temporary home in various ways. One duo, Kevin and Lindy Horton, were married in 1970, towards the end of his first year of Nasho, and just before he went to PNG with Army Education. 'As a 21-year-old bride, I waited with much anticipation for the start of married life as the wife of a National Serviceman in Taurama Barracks in Papua New Guinea,' Lindy said. 'It took five weeks for the 'call forward' to come through after suitable accommodation had been found in Boroko.' It was a two-bedroomed privately rented unit, with so-called 'boi-wire' on the windows to deter burglars (unsuccessfully as it turned out). In February 1971, just a few weeks after her arrival in Port Moresby and four months into their marriage, Kev was sent on a patrol to New Ireland with C Company,

1PIR. 'While this proved to be one of the best times for him, it was by far the worst for me,' Lindy said.[139]

While her husband was away on patrol, one night Lindy's neighbours in the block of flats invited her to go to the outdoor movies with them. 'Because of the rain, you sat in the car during downpours with cut potato wiped across the windscreen to keep it clear. You kept cool on deck chairs beside the car for the rest of the evening,' Lindy said. 'We arrived home to find our flats had been flooded. On opening the door, the first things to float out were our Wedding Album and the last photos of my mother. Luckily another tenant was a photographer and rushed these to his studio for drying.' Understandably, Lindy was pretty upset.

'The next morning I decided to drive out to the barracks to see if I could get in contact with Kev in New Ireland,' she said. 'I arrived at [CO] Colonel Lange's office calm and collected, but then burst into hysterical weeping and scared the poor man half to death. Like all good men in a crisis – he called his wife! A group of soldiers was sent to clean up the flat and, much to my amusement and dismay, I found everything washed in the washing machine – including my leather shoes and bags!! Every cloud has a silver lining, and on Kev's return we were given an Army House in the barracks.'[140]

West Australians June and Robert Daniel had been going out for two years before he went into National Service in 1970. 'I knew that Rob had been called up when I met him, so that was always part of the deal as our relationship progressed,' June said. It was not until Rob received his RAAEC posting to PNG, however, that they decided to get married. 'That decision was firmly based in the knowledge that I could join him there.' While Rob was training, June continued to teach in rural Western Australia.

In October 1970, after receiving the 'call forward', the newly-wed Mrs Daniel headed to PNG to join her husband, with a mixture of excitement and trepidation. 'However, a firm belief in ourselves and our ability to cope with whatever came our way was foremost in our decision to face this part of our lives together,' she said.

Rob was posted to Murray Barracks, where no married quarters were available, so the couple lived off base in a block of eight flats in Boroko, a Port Moresby suburb, along with three other Chalkie couples. June picked up a job for the Department of Civil Aviation in Port Moresby as a Clerk class I. 'The cruisiest job I have ever had,' she said. 'As a Commonwealth Public servant I was paid at the highest level possible for that class as I was a tertiary graduate, had a post graduate qualification, and was 23 (the top of the age pay scale).' She worked in the newly established Aviation Training College, set up to train indigenous air traffic controllers and flight service officers.

Shopping at the local supermarket was supplemented by local produce from Koki Market. Imported food was expensive – fresh milk from the Atherton Tableland in North Queensland, frozen lamb from New Zealand, lettuce from Australia, but wine was cheap.

The Daniels' time in PNG gave their married life a financial kick-start, enabling them to buy a new car and a block of land on their return to Perth, and a modest home loan meant they had money left over for furniture and furnishings. 'We remember our time in PNG fondly,' June Daniel said, 'and are glad to have passed so much of Rob's time in NS in such an interesting and safe place.'

Another West Australian school teacher, Jill Larsen, also said that the time she and her husband Bill spent in PNG set them up financially. She said they were both strongly opposed to the Vietnam War, and were devastated when he was called up, however. They brought the wedding forward, and had been married five weeks when Bill left in January 1970 for recruit training at Puckapunyal.

After some initial confusion about his final location with the RAAEC, Bill ended up at Moem Barracks, Wewak. When the Army sent Jill to join him, they told her he would be at Moresby to meet her when her plane touched down. 'Of course, he wasn't!' she said, as only someone who has dealt with Army organisation can. 'My plane had an emergency landing just after take-off from Perth so I was delayed by two days before I finally arrived at Wewak airport. Poor Bill had no idea where I was, and he had been waiting for the plane for three days, as all my messages had been sent to Moresby.'

The Larsens lived in married quarters at Moem Barracks, and Jill said she was very proud of the work Bill did there. 'He got to know many of the PIR soldiers he was teaching. He was the coach of the Aussie Rules footy team and had a wonderful time getting to know his players. We found army life pretty restrictive. We found some of the rules restrictive. We also found racism was rife – which was probably quite normal for that time.' One difficult aspect of Army life was coping with negative comments from long-term sergeants. 'Some of them hated the young Chalkie sergeants,' Jill said.

There were not enough local teaching jobs in Wewak for all the Chalkies' wives, but Jill found work at a Chinese trade store, which she loved. She and Bill made good friends with the family, and Jill developed a new range of business skills. 'We were both married so young,' Jill said, 'that married life in Wewak was a new adventure every day.'

Among her memories of that life are: coping with zillions of ants, cockroaches and giant frogs; watching Bill surfing at a local beach and seeing a shark pass under him as it chased a school of fish; going inland in their Mini Moke and nearly getting stranded trying to get back over the flooded Sepik River – several big blokes had to stand on the sides of the Moke whilst she drove slowly over the flooded causeway; driving over a huge snake on her way to work; terrifying alcoholism abuse by locals; sheet lightning every night, and torrential rain. The Larsens also discovered that the houseboy hired to do their washing and ironing ate their cat.

International communications in most parts of the Territory were poor, which meant virtually no phone contact with families in Australia. 'We managed to set up one call from Wewak, as my dad had just recovered from a terrible crushing accident,' Jill Larsen said. 'I just managed to hear dad's voice when the line went dead. I was devastated!' Jill returned to Australia with an unwanted northern legacy – a stomach parasite that her father subsequently caught. 'He was ill for months before his doctor asked about any tropical connection,' she said.

Despite the variety of sometimes challenging experiences in the Territory, Jill said that 'as much as we hated the idea of conscription, we have always thought that going to PNG was our Lotto win. Still do! Our life would probably have been very different if Bill had gone to Vietnam.'

Another West Australian teacher, Graham Leader, was in the same intake as Bill Larsen in January 1970, but Graham's wife Merlyn didn't have as positive a view of her subsequent experience in PNG as Jill Larsen did, although the two shared the same anti-conscription views, as well as accommodation for a while.

Merlyn and Graham Leader had been married for a month before his call-up. Whilst her husband was at Puckapunyal, Merlyn worked as a teacher in Perth, and when he was transferred to Singleton for Infantry Corps training, she moved across the continent to Newcastle, sharing accommodation with Jill Larsen. The two women saw their husbands most weekends.

Subsequently, Graham Leader was posted to 1PIR Taurama, and at age 22, Merlyn joined him there in November 1970. Sergeant John Ford, another West Australian, picked her up at Jacksons Airport in his pride and joy, a Jaguar X6. The Leaders were allocated a married quarter at Taurama Barracks, which provided both comfort and security when Graham was on overnight duty or teaching a course in Lae. However, Merlyn found it 'daunting' to be living in a camp of regular soldiers. 'The Army was very regimented and unfriendly,' she said. 'Felt isolated because we had not earned the rank – or that is what they thought. Regulars and their wives were not very friendly. Chalkies consequently kept together as a group.'

Initially Merlyn was a 'check-out chick' at the Army canteen on the base, but then accepted a job as a teacher at Taurama Primary School, which was for the children of 1PIR soldiers. The previous year, two Nasho sergeants, Darryl Stewart and Mick Mulligan, from Victoria, had taught there (and coached the Battalion AFL team). Merlyn said the school had an Australian principal and was not very big – about five classes in total. 'My class (Standard 1) had 26 and was a mixture of locals and Australians,' she said. 'The school had few resources and that made it difficult to motivate the students.'

When Graham was temporarily in Lae, Merlyn went with some friends from Murray Barracks to a beach and became involved in a riot of locals and so had to hurriedly reverse the car to escape the melee. 'Very frightening,' she said.

As another reminder of where she was, Merlyn developed a tropical ulcer as a result of being scratched by a shoe buckle. 'The Army nurses had little or no supplies,' she said, 'and so after week or so I had to go to a civilian doctor who cured it very rapidly.'

Merlyn Leader had trained as a secondary teacher, but her experience at Taurama school led to her becoming a primary teacher when she and Graham returned to Perth at the end of 1971. 'In that respect the time in PNG was of tremendous effect,' she said, but her final verdict was: 'Couldn't wait to come home. It was just a negative pause in our life.'

On the other hand, Bev Morgan's husband extended his time in Nasho so that he could go to PNG, and the two of them spent two years in the Territory in 1971–72. After completing primary teacher training in New South Wales, Richard Morgan went into recruit and Artillery

Corps training in the first half of 1969, and was subsequently posted to an Artillery unit at Townsville. He applied for a corps transfer to Education and was initially posted to the Education unit at Lavarack Barracks, Townsville, and then to 1 Australian Logistic Support Group, based at Vung Tau in South Vietnam. The second posting came as a surprise. 'We had anticipated a posting to Darwin, and would not have married at that time had we known about a change of posting,' Bev said. She continued to live with her parents and to work during this time.

At the end of his time teaching in Vietnam in 1970 (which is another story), Richard extended his period of National Service and applied for a posting to PNG, and was sent to Murray Barracks, with his rank of sergeant now permanent. This time Bev went with him, after completing the required series of immunisations and following the strict procedures for uplifting their personal effects, 'right down to counting every piece of cutlery prior to departure'.

Like the Chalkies who had gone before her, when Bev stepped off the plane in Port Moresby in April 1971, she was greeted by a wall of dense air. 'I also realised very quickly that I had arrived in someone else's country,' she said.

Finding herself unexpectedly pregnant, Bev wasn't able to apply for a job, and her working life 'came to a grinding halt'. At age 21, she had their first child in Port Moresby General Hospital, and her days in Moresby until the family's departure in December 1972 were generally spent looking after the baby, which included pushing a pram to the shops, as she didn't drive at the time. 'Having a child in TPNG was a positive experience for me,' Bev said, 'as I observed that motherhood was a much more natural part of life for the Papua New Guinea women.'

On one occasion, after a nerve-wracking flight in a small plane to a Mission station in the highlands, and sleeping in a hut with snakes lurking below, Bev had to rescue her son from local villagers who tried to carry him off into the bush, after giving her a shell in exchange. 'The people were so taken by his white skin he was kissed all over,' she said. 'I had to chase them and grab him out of their arms.' Nevertheless, Bev Morgan said that experiencing a vastly different culture to the western suburbs of Sydney was a bonus of living in the Territory.

Bev said there appeared to be a recognition that life could be lonely in PNG and she recalled with appreciation that the church she attended 'ensured that everyone had someone to share Christmas Day with. I think this kind of attitude prevailed amongst other groups too.'

'These days, the two years spent in TPNG seem to belong to another life,' she said. 'In many ways they were challenging days away from family and the security of one's usual environment. Not sure I would like to do it again at my current age but am very pleased to have done so when I was younger.'

South Australians Anne and Peter Shackleford had been married 12 months when he went into National Service early in 1972, and it was another five months before she was able to join him in PNG. The time in between was hard she said. 'We had no idea how long we would be apart or whether, where and under what circumstances we might resume married life.' By this time the period of National Service had been reduced to 18 months, and Vietnam was no longer an Australian Army posting. Anne had been working as a nurse and was part-way through midwifery training when she left Adelaide.

Anne remembered the heat when she arrived in Port Moresby in May 1972, aged 22, but also the joy of being back with her husband of 15 months, the excitement of spending time overseas, and 'some sadness at the prospect of not seeing my extended family for over a year'. The couple moved into a rented flat off-base in Boroko, and took up a reasonably regular life, since Peter was teaching at Iduabada Technical College, five days a week. Murray Barracks was merely his pay station, and occasionally he had Orderly Sergeant duties in the College vacation periods. Without midwifery qualifications, Anne couldn't be employed as a nurse, so she took a secretarial job at the Joint Intelligence Office in Port Moresby. 'Our life was more or less normal i.e. much as might have been expected had we been in Australia.' she said. 'Apart from betel nut.' Their social life was mainly centred on the church they attended.

Other reminders that they were not in Australia were: a car full of mosquitoes when they left the windows down while snorkelling at a nearby beach; one of the car's headlights falling out of it's casing on their way back from the start of the Kokoda Track in the dark; going to the main town oval on one occasion where the locals were dancing and singing, and hearing the amazing harmonies. On another occasion they were sitting in the car on the edge of a soccer pitch watching a game, when the crowd suddenly surged onto the pitch and began charging up and down. 'Uncontrollable and very menacing,' Anne said.

Nevertheless, when Peter had the option in December 1972 of

completing his National Service at that point, following the election of the Whitlam Government, they decided to stay on for the final six months of his original term. 'It was one of the best times of our lives,' Anne said. 'We count ourselves blessed for having been given the opportunity. Having said that, if I'd stayed in Adelaide I would have completed my midwifery training which may have impacted on my return to the workplace following the births of our [three] children.'

Victorian Marg Humphrey was another Chalkie wife whose career was interrupted by her husband's posting to PNG. John Humphrey had already been called up when Marg met him, but it was about three years before he completed his secondary teacher course and headed to Puckapunyal for recruit training in January 1970. The couple married later that year, six weeks before John left for PNG. After the honeymoon, Marg went back home to her parents in Melbourne, and John came down at weekends from his temporary Education posting at Bandiana.

John was posted to Moem Barracks, Wewak, and one night in December 1970, 23-year-old Marg flew out of Melbourne to join him, the first time she'd ever been on a plane. At Sydney she waited until after midnight for a plane that went direct to Lae. 'There were three passengers and one crew and NO food on the plane,' she said. 'We arrived in Lae very early in the morning and I was advised by one of the passengers NOT to leave the airport, even though my flight to Wewak was not until late afternoon. The airport was full of natives breast feeding the baby on one side and the pig on the other. When I boarded the plane to Wewak I was the only European on the full plane, even the crew were all natives. I was VERY glad to see John waiting at Wewak airport.'

Like the other four Nasho couples at Moem Barracks, the Humphreys were allocated a married quarter. 'Our daily life was much the same as at home, except there was no TV, no phone and you wrote letters to family and friends,' Marg said. 'You couldn't get in the car and visit friends or go for a drive or weekend away.'

Marg's father had been in the CMF when she was a child, so she had a pretty good idea of what Army life would be like. 'At the time you just accepted what they had to do for the Army,' she said. 'Every day including Saturday and Sunday the men had to go on parade and get their malaria tablets. You never questioned why, it was just part of their Army life. John left for 3 months in Vanimo about one month after I arrived in Wewak.'

In Melbourne, Marg had been a craft teacher; in Wewak she took a job as with Post and Telegraphs, typing telegrams received over the radio from the outstations. 'I enjoyed the job, and it could be picked up on a normal radio,' she said. 'John would listen to me chatting to the outstations at home on Saturdays when I worked.'

Unfortunately, relations with non-Nasho Australian wives at Moem Barracks were not a highpoint, as Jill Larsen also mentioned. 'We had NO interaction with regular Army wives,' Marg Humphrey said, 'as they could NOT accept that our husbands were Sergeants after three months in the Army, and it took their husbands years and a tour of Vietnam to become a Sergeant.'

The enmity showed itself in unusual ways. 'One day, one of the married Nashos' wives decided to have a party, and when she went to the Army canteen at Moem to buy the food, the lady wouldn't serve her, as she was NOT invited to the party. The Chalkie's wife had to drive into Wewak [about 8 km] to buy the supplies.'

Despite the limitations of life at Moem Barracks, 'it probably was a great way to start married life,' Marg said, 'as we had to fend for ourselves, had no family to rely on and no take-away food. We had to do everything for ourselves and spend every night as a couple, as there was nowhere else to go except home.' As Anne Shackleford also found, there were career consequences for Marg after her 12-month sojourn in PNG, however: she never did return to teaching, because she would have had to update her qualifications.

The two characteristics that link all the married couples in PNG is that they were all relatively young at the time, and newly married, some for only a few weeks before they were temporarily separated, and whether through self-belief or naivety, they faced up to the challenges, even if they didn't always find, as Jill Larsen did, that married life was 'a new adventure every day'. For some couples, PNG was an unexpected bonus in their new lives together, for others, an unwanted intrusion.

Pam Wedgwood's story of her time in Papua New Guinea is different to those of the other Chalkie wives because she had lived there since she was a small child. The Army sent Queenslander Peter Wedgwood to Port Moresby with the first cohort of Education Sergeants in August 1966. He was posted to Murray Barracks, and first met Pam at her local church, St John's. They were married in Moresby in May 1967, both aged 22.

Pam had joined the Department of Agriculture, Stock and Fisheries the previous year and was working in the laboratories with a team trying to establish ideal elemental levels for the cash crops (coffee, cocoa, coconuts, tea) of the territory, with the intention of producing manuals that could be used by the locals when independence came. After the wedding the couple lived in a 'leave house' for three months, then with Pam's parents for two months, and their final two months in Moresby was spent in another 'leave house'. None of the other Chalkie sergeants at Murray Barracks was married at this time – it was only later in the National Service period, perhaps when teachers tended to be slightly older because of deferments, that more wives came to join their husbands.

In Pam Wedgwood's case, her husband-to-be came to join *her*. 'As far as the Army was concerned, they sent Peter to the territory as a single man with just his kit,' she said. 'When it came time to discharge him, they had to pay the air fares for a wife, all her kit and quite an amount of household goods including my car, which was shipped to Brisbane.'

Brisbane was Peter Wedgwood's home town, and once again Pam's arrival in late 1967 tipped the usual Chalkie situation upside down. 'I had to leave my family at the end of his tour and relocate to Brisbane – a whole new life for me,' she said. 'In the first instance I had to meet his parents (they were unable to attend the wedding), and then be accepted into his circle of friends.' (Her father-in-law had told Peter's friends that he had married a Papuan, and Pam said they expected her to be black when she stepped off the plane.)

'This is a complete reverse to the experiences of other Nasho wives for whom Australia was home,' Pam said. '*PNG was my home* and had been since 1949 (although I had spent 1955–64 in North Queensland between boarding school and Uni).' Pam Wedgwood said that living in the Territory for so long gave her a very different perspective to that of the Chalkies and their wives who were there for a relatively short time. 'Among our friends to this day are people who taught at the Sogeri school, which produced many of the territory politicians,' she said, 'and I feel they made a much bigger impact.'

One woman who was in PNG for a particularly short period was not a Chalkie's wife at the time, but a fiancée. Queenslander Ross Beer was posted to Murray Barracks in Port Moresby in August 1968 and lived in the Sergeants' Mess. His fiancée, Geraldine, arrived in the Territory in January 1969 and took up residence in a hostel in the Port Moresby suburb of Hanuabada. Geraldine and Ross were married after she returned to Australia in October 1969, presumably without the Army having to pay the return cost of her air fare, her kit or her household goods, which at least would have saved her having to count the cutlery.

12

Back to the future: Post-Nasho career directions

When Australian Opposition Leader Gough Whitlam in 1969 espoused self-government for PNG as soon as Labor gained government, with independence to follow within the first term of office, Woolford noted that he 'spoke as if a Labor victory in 1972 was certain'.[141] Whitlam's notorious self-confidence was vindicated when in December 1972 his party, proclaiming the slogan, 'It's time', defeated McMahon's Liberal-Country Party coalition by 67 seats to 58, after 23 years of conservative rule. With an initial two-person 'ministry', Whitlam immediately moved to fulfil one of his election promises: to abolish conscription.

On 6 December, four days after the election, Deputy Leader Lance Barnard announced: 'There will be no further call-ups. Those who have already received a notice of call-up will not be obliged to act on it. So, as from today, notices will be going out to those who have received a call-up notice that they have no further obligation under the National Service Act. I expect that before the end of this week the necessary regulation will, have been provided; that will enable the discharge of those national servicemen who are now in the armed forces to take their discharge.'[142] Barnard said there would also be benefits in staying on, if conscripts chose to do so.

The consequences of the new policy were almost immediate for serving Chalkies and the Educational Corps. Martin Forbes, the didiman at Moem Barracks in 1972, recounted the way events unfolded at Wewak: 'The night of the election is still something I remember vividly. Being the only married Sergeant of our group, we hosted a late afternoon BBQ which deteriorated into a very noisy celebration as we listened on short-wave radio to the election results. Most of our lot were pretty quiet, but they made up for it that night! I distinctly remember one (though it was probably several) of us announcing to the whole MQ area "WE'RE GOING HOME". We had even imported the famous "It's Time" blue T-shirts and some had been wearing them for a few weeks prior to the election.'

'The aftermath of the election was amazing,' Forbes said. 'On the Sunday, everyone had to elect whether they were staying or going. Those going were told to pack their bags and on Monday a C130 arrived to take them all home. It picked up the others in Lae and Moresby and so most were back in Australia within 48 hrs of the election. The one Chalkie doing penance in Vanimo couldn't get a flight back to Wewak and went home on the Tuesday by civil air.'

For those on the other side of the country, decisions also had to be made. 'We all gathered at a night club to celebrate the fact that we could now go home and not wear those daggy PNG uniforms any more,' said Queensland primary teacher Warren Ison, who spent his PNG term in 1972 first at Taurama and then at Goldie. 'THEN almost all of us volunteered to stay on another 6 months to finish our mission.'

The following year the Corps reported the fallout for the RAAEC in PNG: 'The cessation of National Service has probably affected us more than most. Had all the National Servicemen in the Force left immediately they were able, we would certainly have been in dire straits; happily, many chose to serve out their terms, and some chose to soldier on for longer periods. Could it be that they have come to like us? Perhaps they found that the pay wasn't so bad. Whatever the reason, those who did stay on provided us with valuable breathing space.'[143]

Forbes's decision to remain at his post was not entirely because he wanted to complete his term of Nasho: 'Truth was, I had just taken a bride, and the jobs outlook in Australia at that time was rather bleak. In fact, I stayed in the Army for 21 years – 15 in RAAEC and six in RASigs.'[144]

In 1973 the Corps noted that Education work had ceased at Wewak and at Lae Area, except that at Moem Barracks, 'Sgt "Farmer" Forbes continues to run the agricultural project and show a nice profit for Regimental funds from the sale of produce – mainly eggs and pigs.'[145]

The new Government also fulfilled another policy promise. On 1 December 1973, Papua New Guinea became a self-governing country, with Australia's powers now limited to courts of law, the House of Assembly, electoral affairs and foreign affairs and defence. The Pacific

Islands Regiment and associated units had already transformed into the Papua New Guinea Defence Force (PNGDF) the preceding January. In acknowledging the Army's handover from the Australian Government, the Chief Minister, Michael Somare, said the people of Papua New Guinea 'did not forget what had been done in the past by the elements which now made up the new force, but they looked back to the past and its traditions only to gain strength for the even greater challenge which lay ahead'.[146]

In Australia, the Army itself underwent a major restructuring under the new Government, which also inevitably affected the RAAEC. The Editor of the Corps newsletter referred to the '1973 holocaust' but assured staff that while Army Education now sat differently within the Army organisation, it still had a significant role to play.[147] In December that year, Army Education staff in PNG were transferred from the PNG Defence Force to the Australian Defence Force Assistance Group (PNG), and the Editor noted a proposed establishment of 28 RAAEC officers in PNG in 1974 compared to 19 the previous year. This may have been so on paper, but it turned out to be wishful thinking.

The Editor predicted that Army Education was likely to become 'more adult-human-being oriented than it has been in the past, and at the same time will become more relevant to the needs of the Service as they relate to the wide array of underdeveloped talents that are part of each individual soldier.' He also promised that, 'In New Guinea we shall continue to play our part developing the minds of Pacific Islanders along the patterns of Western concepts up to university entrance level.'

By 1974, with no new National Servicemen as supernumeraries, and the Corps unable to make new appointments because of the Army reorganisation, however, the work in PNG contracted severely, with staff posted only to the Joint Services College (formerly Military Cadet School) at Lae and the Training Depot at Goldie River, in addition to Martin Forbes in his final year as a didiman at Wewak. In February 1974, the ADAE, Lt. Col. Henry Dachs, who had returned to PNG the previous year on his third tour of duty there, presented books to Kila Kila High School and Gordons High School in Moresby which had been purchased from the Memorial Trust Fund for Chris Donnan, the Chalkie who had disappeared while climbing Mt Wilhelm in 1971.

By this time the Corps had begun recruiting locally, with Lieutenant Geoff Malaisa instructing at JSC, and Sgt Bawasu, a graduate of Goroka Secondary Teachers College, an instructor at PNGDF Training Depot.

In addition, the PNG Defence Force was sponsoring four students at UPNG who were undertaking a degree plus a diploma of education; two soldiers studying at Goroka Teachers College were expected to graduate at the end of 1975.

The change from the heady days of annual waves of conscripted Chalkies posted to every barracks was stark: 'At PNGF training Depot, the emphasis has shifted from basic education to post Form 4 education for recruits selected as potential officers and apprentices. DFCE [Defence Force Certificate of Education] 1, 2 and 3 courses are still run for solders requiring them, but there are now only a few courses programmed, and a small mobile team runs other courses on an "as and when required" basis, i.e. units now bid for courses.'[148]

In June 1975, Chief Minister Michael Somare, who as Leader of the Pangu Pati had met the 1971 Chalkies during their orientation program, announced that PNG would become an independent nation on 16 September, 1975.

'It had, by Third World standards, been a long time coming,' Woolford wrote. 'Freedom came slowly because the demand for it came slowly. ... In many respects it was the Australian government, rather than Papua New Guineans, which finally set the pace. Demand was slow partly because of the uneven pattern of administrative contact, which meant that by the 1960s the Highlands were in a state of development roughly comparable to that of the coast before the war; partly because of Australia's refusal until the mid-1960s to permit the emergence of an educated leadership; partly because of the paternalistic nature of Australian rule, which induced an unhealthy dependence.'[149]

***

The early teacher conscripts, plucked from other Corps, arrived in PNG Command in August 1966 and spent up to 17 months there; for those arriving later, the average term was around 13 months, while the changes to Australian Government policy on National Service in 1971 and 1972 shortened the terms of some of the later conscripts in PNG Command.

Once their allotted time in PNG was over, the Chalkies headed south to begin the demobilisation process and in most cases to pick up their civilian lives again. Education officers at Taurama Barracks commented in August 1970: 'At this point in their tour of duty, our NS SGTs are familiar with the PI soldier's problems, but unfortunately it is also the time when they start thinking about their return to Australia. This is unavoidable, but we are sorry to see them go. At a later date, they will perhaps remember their days of teaching in 1PIR with some feelings of nostalgia: we rather hope that their experience here has enriched their own expertise as teachers, and that they have received as much as they have given.'[150]

The 73 Chalkies surveyed for this book were asked not only what they remembered about their teaching days in PNG, but also about what impact they thought their teaching experience in the Territory, as well as their time in the Army generally, had on their subsequent professional life and career. As might be expected, there are divergent views on the topic, with negative, positive and qualified viewpoints.

Not all of them went back into teaching after Nasho. In the survey, almost 20% said they moved straight into new careers – four signed up for regular Army commissions, and other new pursuits included engineering, pastoral ministry, national and State public services, and establishing their own computer business. Frank Cordingley used the option of paid full-time study to prepare himself for a career in computing science, and Les Rowe had already lined himself up a job in the diplomatic service before he left the Educational Corps. Rowe said his Army service gave him an understanding of military processes and modus operandi which was helpful in certain diplomatic postings. Terry Edwinsmith reversed the process – he went into accountancy immediately after Nasho, but after two years returned to primary school teaching.

60% said they returned to teaching, sometimes after undertaking a year of full-time study at government expense, while some did part-time study under the same scheme. There was a variety of tracks across the subsequent years, including moving into educational administration, teaching in TAFE colleges, taking secondments into 'head office' and even with private companies, and heading off into consultancies. Several went on to teach in universities, full- or part-time. Just over 20% returned to teaching immediately after National Service, but gave it away in favour of other careers, as diverse as intelligence analyst, real estate agent, dairy farmer, human resource manager, sugar cane inspector, university teacher, and tourist officer. One went into the taxi business and ended up as a senior police officer; another eventually re-enlisted in the Army and became a computer systems expert, several ran their own companies, and at least one joined the Australian Public Service.

West Australian John Fragomeni said that while the time in Army Education gave him an opportunity to review and assess his teaching career, a 'real black spot' was that the two years' interruption set him back 'many years' in seniority, status and promotion. His studies were also interrupted, and when he returned to Australia he discovered the university had changed the structure of his degree, forcing him to undertake considerably more units before he could graduate. 'How do you measure a handicap like that,' he said, 'as far as how your career has been held back by the National Service obligation you were singled out for goes?'

Keith Werder (1969–70), who said that the impact of his Army Education and PNG experience on his professional life was 'absolutely nil', also complained that he missed out on early promotion in his civilian teaching career. 'Maybe because I was willing to take any country posting, my thirst for promotion was sated,' he said, 'but without National Service, it is possible I could have gained these promotions without having to endure some rough country living conditions to effect this.' Another Queenslander, Phil Adam, and Victorian Phil Parker believed it gave them a broader experience and perspective on life, but not much else. West Australian Bill Larsen said its only legacy was greater knowledge of a developing country, and another WA teacher, Keith Bryant, reckoned its outcome was to make him sure he didn't want to stay in the Army, despite the offer of a commission. There was a standing offer to Education Sergeants in every cohort to sign on for a short-term commission in the RAAEC.

New South Welshman, Robbie Scott (1971–72) said: 'My time with the RAAEC definitely held me back as far as promotion within the education system, but I would not have traded my time in National Service for anything. My experiences and friendships made are worth much more that any increased pay packet.'

Adam thought that conscription itself may have had a negative effect on his professional life 'because as a consequence of the interaction of that experience and my own particular personality and beliefs I was never prepared to be dictated to by people whose capacities I did not appreciate. I found too many senior officers in Education to be lacking in competence and professional integrity and I found it difficult to accept their authority at times.'

Warren Dunn said it was impossible to compare the discipline of an Army system to the challenge of teaching teenagers in a civilian high school, many of whom were 'hostile learners'. On the other hand, Frank Cordingley, who had once been anxious about his ability to control a squad of troops, said that even though he was only 8 stone in weight when he returned to a civilian classroom, 'the students knew I was a sergeant in the army and so discipline was not a problem'. Nevertheless, Cordingley's ability to control a class meant that most of his allocated classes were of students 'with poor attitude and little prospect of a good education', and eventually led to him changing careers.

Peter Shackleford said conscription had only a 'serendipitous' career outcome for him because National Service delayed the start of his Australian secondary school teaching career by 18 months, and this positioned him for a postgraduate research and tutoring position in physics while he was teaching at the South Australian Institute of Technology, which led to a public service career.

Nevertheless, the paradox of working in their chosen profession and in a culturally challenging environment while a reluctant conscript in the Army reaped diverse personal harvests, as John Dark found. The Queensland primary school teacher was 24 when he entered National Service, and said he thoroughly enjoyed his time in Army Education. 'On reflection, I should have continued on and maybe the road would have been a little smoother.' He did in fact reapply to get back into the RAAEC some years later but was unsuccessful. Despite the satisfaction of teaching in the Army, however, 'I really felt that two years was a big chunk out of my life,' he said. 'I felt rather disoriented when I came back. I have had two failed marriages and am in my third relationship.'

Andrew Remenyi had mixed feelings about his time in Army Education in 1971–72. He felt disadvantaged by his time in the Amy, with no compensating benefits from being in the Education Corps. 'I had to change my career plans drastically,' he said, 'as I knew I could not get back into either a Philosophy career (which was my first goal) or a Literature career (my second goal).' Remenyi chose Psychology (his third major in his undergraduate degree) because while he was in PNG he was offered a position as an Educational Psychologist in the Special Services Division of the Victorian Education Department. On the other hand, 'National Service, the Army experience, did sensitise me to practical psychology (why do we do what we do?),' he said.

More than 70% of the Chalkies surveyed thought their time in Army Education in PNG had a positive impact on their subsequent professional career, although some took a while to come to that judgement. A further 14% believed it had no impact, a small group saw it as having a negative impact, and a couple had mixed feelings about it. Some separated the Army experience from the Territory experience. A number used the term, 'significant' or 'pivotal', including Norm Hunter, who said that the leadership responsibilities and high expectations placed on him 'probably influenced my future confidence re starting a new school and becoming a principal'. Ian Colwell also thought it made him a better teacher and principal. 'It taught me to treat the bureaucracy with quiet disdain and to cover myself as best I could,' he said. 'I found the army was a far more humane system than Education Queensland.' Peter Wedgwood took some of that humane system with him – when he resumed teaching in Queensland the former Education Sergeant spent 17 enjoyable and rewarding years as an officer of cadets.

Since most Chalkies had experienced, at most, one year of civilian teaching in Australia before their call-up, their time with Army Education in PNG was often crucial to their professional development. Tom Derham, who was posted to the Territory as second lieutenant in 1972, and had twelve months teaching a Grade 4 primary class before he entered National Service, found that teaching secondary-level maths in the Army helped to secure a mathematics teaching position in Victoria, and began a long term interest in teaching mathematics (and he subsequently gained more qualifications in this area). 'The whole experience in PNG broadened my teaching and life experience,' he said, 'and made me more open to taking on new challenges in different places and areas of education throughout my career.'

New South Wales science teacher Steve Beveridge initially thought National Service was a waste of time, and was upset that former colleagues not called up kept pursing their careers, and that he was going to be two years behind. 'With the benefit of time however, it proved to be a valuable experience for me personally,' he said. 'I'd been to a selective high school, then university, then taught (one year). There was a whole cross-section of the community I'd never really interacted with – and I was in the Army with them. Living and working with them day-today in a team environment. It was a socialising experience which I probably needed, given my 'sheltered' background.'

Others, such as Ian Ogston and John Hain, talked about having their eyes opened to the world, and collecting resources that benefited their subsequent teaching. For Glenn Hall the benefit was in working in another education system and having the opportunity to talk to teachers from across Australia; for Ron Inglis it meant experience in teaching across cultures, to students who had limited grasp of English, learning to teach with few resources and creatively using whatever resources were available. Mixing with other teachers also helped Bruce Nulty realise he needed better qualifications to advance in his career, and after subsequently completing a Science degree, he chose to teach in the Northern Territory 'because I knew I could, after the TPNG experience. I was more sympathetic of other cultures.' John Morris said that not only did he learn to stand on his own two feet in a supportive environment in PNG, but that 'after having the 'red brigade' – half colonels and above – swanning through my classroom at Goldie River, school inspectors were relatively easy to cope with.'

Sometimes it was a mixture of personal and professional development as John Humphrey explained: 'I think that my time in the Army made me a more mature person, ready to confront the complexities of teaching and life in general.' Warren Ison also thought there were multiple benefits, 'firming up' his character as an individual, an educator and a Christian, and preparing him for the intercultural education that became his work focus in Australia. 'In short, what could have been seen as a career interruption, proved to be a part of a career preparation,' he said. Roger Grigg had a similar story. He said that when he left the Army he was still very naïve and immature and may have stayed that way if he'd not had the chance for further study. 'In the army all I learnt was that you can beat the system,' he said, 'but at University I learnt to question whatever was presented, and it provided me career opportunities that would not have happened had I not be conscripted. … If I had not gone into the army I believe I would have finished up as an uneducated primary teacher in the bush.'

A number of Chalkies mentioned how they thought the experience 'matured' them, or better prepared them for a lifelong teaching career. 'I was always looking for adventure in my life and to 'get away from home' but was too immature to achieve it by myself,' said Graham Lindsay, who was 20 years old when he was called up in 1966. 'Being sent to PNG opened up new vistas and new understandings of the needs of others. I became more able to deal with people, especially those in authority. As a child I had grown up fearing those in authority.'

Maths teacher Alex Thomson said the Army taught him not to be afraid of something you thought you couldn't do. While still in

Australia, he remembered saying at Holsworthy Army Camp, NSW that he couldn't teach Australian history. 'I did. And I loved it,' he said. This new-found confidence permeated his teaching: 'The PNG recruits had a huge eagerness to learn, and I think my [later] expectation of Aussie kids led them to have no choice but to want to learn.' For some, the realisation of a legacy came slowly, as in Bob Coppa's case: 'I was very annoyed with the whole experience for quite a while, but as I gained more teaching experience I realised that meeting and teaching such a wide variety of people stood me in good stead in understanding the pressures and expectations on people who came from totally different backgrounds to me.'

Other saw the impact of their time in PNG in inter-cultural terms, making them more appreciative of other ways of thinking and doing, and of the challenges facing the country when it became independent. 'My time there was experiencing life in a third world country, in a society in rapid transformation and in an environment fuelled by optimism for the future,' John Ford said. 'I could see the world from a whole different perspective to that of the Perth Education Department viewpoint.' Richard Morgan had similar thoughts: 'I gained an appreciation of a very different culture and thought a lot about an emerging country. It was clear to me that independence would be a challenge for PNG, and this has proved to be the case.'

Some Chalkies were so taken by the country they went back to work there after discharge from the Army, sometimes before and sometimes after independence. In John Herlihy's case, it happened while he was still in the Army. After his initial PNG posting as a second lieutenant, Herlihy signed on for a short-service commission and in 1971 received the posting to Vietnam he had sought, but after that tour of duty asked to be reposted to PNG, where he served for three more years (1972–75), as Adjutant at Goldie River and then for two years as OC Recruiting for the PNG Defence Force. John Meyer stayed on: a year at the University of Papua New Guinea to complete a Diploma of Education (at Australian Government expense), then two years teaching at Malabunga High School outside of Rabaul. Richard Boddington didn't stay away long: He and his wife returned to Australia in October 1972, and he was discharged on Boxing Day that year. 'A few weeks later I returned to PNG as Learning and Development Manager for Steamships [Company],' he said, 'followed by appointment as HR Manager at the Housing Commission of PNG.'[151] At the Housing

Commission, Boddington was responsible, among other things, for the Commission's localisation program, ensuring that positions held by Europeans were gradually taken over by indigenous officers. He also became an evening and correspondence tutor for commercial subjects conducted by the College of External Studies, Port Moresby, and a part-time Accounting tutor at the University of Papua New Guinea, which had been established in 1965, following pressure from an earlier UN Visiting Commission.

Others also came back from Australia to teach and train: Michael Lee to the Administrative College and Ian Mackay and Ian Lovell to the Police Training College, and Peter Chard, who saw his time in National Service as 'a complete waste of time', to Corrective Services. Grahame Hurrell went back as Education Officer at Bougainville Copper. Two decades after Nasho, where he regarded himself as a 'not whole-hearted soldier', Phil Doecke undertook PhD research in PNG and became Head of Physical Education at the National Sports Institute, Goroka.

My wife and I also went back to PNG, after our experience of living there in 1969–70. On demobilisation I did a year full time at university in Brisbane to complete my Arts degree (at Government expense), and then taught for a year in a Queensland regional high school, before taking a three-year secondment in 1973 to teach at the Administrative College (Adcol), Port Moresby. By this time, we had two children, and a third was born in Port Moresby General Hospital in the final year of our term. At Adcol, I helped develop the skills of a range of indigenous civil servants-in-training – local court magistrates, patrol officers, police cadets, and administrative personnel, assembled from all over the country. In career terms, my time in Army Education transformed me from a high school teacher into an adult educator, and after PNG I spent most of the rest of my professional life in universities, with a short detour into government.

After some years with the Queensland Education Department, Greg Farr headed in a new direction in his teaching career, not back to PNG, but to a personally and professionally rewarding experience not too far from the country's southern border. 'A year in PNG gave me a taste for Melanesian culture,' Farr said, 'and it emboldened me to actively seek the position in 1981 of Principal of the most northern school in Australia at Boigu, a top western island in Torres Strait.' He doesn't think he would have applied for the position without the

PNG experience ten years earlier. 'Warmly welcomed as the first white family to call the island home, we were adopted into a family and participated actively in village life. Living the cross-cultural experience and working with Islander staff and students was more than interesting for it challenged any unfounded pre-conceived ideas, helped us form new friendships and expanded our knowledge and understanding of cultural practices, racial prejudice and discriminatory government treatment of indigenous Australians.'

The return to civilian life after two years in the Army, and anything from seven to seventeen months in PNG, brought a mixed legacy to Chalkies' subsequent careers. Almost a given was the greater knowledge of a developing country – 'an environment fuelled by optimism for the future', John Ford said, and some saw it as no more than that. Others believed their time with Army Education in PNG had a direct impact on their subsequent teaching, sometimes in terms of the confidence it gave them in a classroom, sometimes in terms of the understandings and resources they brought back with them. Perhaps this was also an inevitable outcome for many Chalkies, given that virtually all of us had done no more than one year's teaching in Australia before our call-up. So that all our teaching in PNG was grist to the professional mill, broadening our teaching and life experience, as Tom Derham said.

For some, this broadening came through contact with people from other education systems, including recognition of the need to upgrade teaching qualifications to remain competitive and up-to-date, as well as through interaction with a cross-section of Army types from outside Education. There were also some who learned not just teaching technique, but also took away with them a broader understanding of leadership and were able to apply that in positions they later sought out in Australia and elsewhere.

For others, the possible benefits of living and teaching in another culture could not outweigh the blow to career prospects in Australia caused by being two years behind their peers – 'a big chunk out of my life', as John Dark said. Those who felt most disadvantaged by their extended absence were understandably the most passionate about their detestation of the Army or conscription, or both.

The two years in the Army also brought about career changes for some conscripted teachers immediately after demobilisation, sometimes negotiated while they were in the Army, suggesting that those Chalkies had already decided that teaching was not for them.

In some cases, the change of direction was forced upon them when opportunities dried up or conditions changed while they had been away. Chalkies so affected were understandably aggrieved that their plans had been thwarted by their National Service obligation.

Others stuck with teaching for a while after demobilisation before changing direction – a divergence that is probably a characteristic of the teaching profession generally. There were also a number who returned to work in PNG – in one instance just a few weeks after demobilisation, in another 20 years later, suggesting that their earlier PNG experience, even within the strictures of the Army, had generated sufficient enthusiasm for the country and its people to convince them that they still had a contribution to make.

For some, the return to civilian life had a bump or two along the way. 'When I was being "demobbed", Melburnian Bob Coppa said, 'a sergeant whom I had never met before came up to me and told me that I could not join the RSL because I had not fought overseas and that I was only a temporary sergeant. I was thoroughly taken aback at such resentment. My reply was in good army vernacular which roughly translated as, I would not like to join any organization that he was eligible to join …'

West Australian John Fragomeni was also surprised by the vehemence of a comment made to him at the time of discharge in Perth in early 1973, after a few weeks in a 'very relaxed work environment' at Western Command, Karrakatta. 'Remembering that I was a sergeant (albeit temporary)', he said, 'I thought that being told, in a fairly blunt tone, "Here is your discharge certificate; you now have two hours to get home and take that bloody uniform off, and if you are seen in it after that, you can expect to be arrested," was somewhat unwarranted!!!'

13

'Not a time wasted entirely':
Reflections on National Service

There's now an Australian Army Infantry Museum at the Singleton barracks where some Chalkies experienced recruit training in the late 60s and early 70s, and where many of us went through the motions of Infantry Corps training before we were sent to PNG. When Steven Hill visited Singleton in 2015 and saw the PIR museum display 'the young faces and the innocence of most of us about the future of PNG was striking,' he said. How much we knew and how little we knew at that time.

Almost 50 years later, many of those same men, their faces now neither young nor innocent, reflected on their time in National Service and in PNG. In the intervening period, some had softened their earlier, harsher views; others remembered with regret, and sometimes bitterness, the time that had been taken from them; other ex-Chalkies saw their two-year term, or at least their time in PNG, as the highlight of their lives; for others there were mixed emotions about the experiences they'd had.

For Victorian Special Education teacher Bill Bailey, Nasho had a lot going for it. 'My time as a National Serviceman was very positive: I learned a lot of skills, I did things I had never done before, I visited interesting places and I made some good friends' he said. 'I was, of course, also very thankful that I did not have to go to Vietnam, or that I would serve my time as a steward in an officers' mess somewhere in Australia.'

This was the paradox of Nasho – up until 1970, you could be one of the 15,000 conscripts sent to Vietnam and take your chances of being killed or wounded, or you could be posted to an Army base in Australia, whiling away the rest of your term in some mostly mind-numbing menial task, as many of the 49,000 other conscripts were up until conscription was abolished at the end of 1972. Or, if you were a teacher, you might be among the 300 or so posted to Papua New Guinea and given a job that actually utilised your pre-Nasho training.

'I had an interesting experience that made my national service worthwhile,' said Andrew Dalziel, who started Nasho in 1971 and did the shorter version, 'whereas other conscripts I saw on discharge, who I had done basic training with and who were posted elsewhere, viewed their 18 months as pretty much a waste of time. There is no doubt that people who had the chalkie experience were able to utilise their training and skills in a meaningful way in a totally different culture that was very close to Australia.' As with some other Chalkies surveyed, Dalziel's views changed over the years. 'Over time … I have come to realise the experience did broaden my sense of self and gave me a greater understanding of the world,' he said.

West Australian John Ford, posted to Taurama Barracks in 1969 for 17 months, felt the same. 'It was a defining time in my life,' he said. 'It opened my eyes to the world at large. There were not so good parts, but PNG was overwhelmingly a positive experience for me. I felt I was doing something worthwhile in the Army, something I didn't think possible when I was first conscripted.'

Queenslander, Ian Ogston, who couldn't wait to get out of the Army when he returned to Australia at the end of 1971, said that although much of his National Service was a waste of time, 'the teaching at Goldie was one of the great experiences of my life; the Army context was irritating and difficult. Certainly the whole thing was probably the best sort of National Service anyone could have (cf. Vietnam or wasting two years in an Australian Army posting). There is no doubt in my mind that the teaching of the soldiers was incredibly worthwhile both for them and for their country.'

New South Wales science teacher Steve Beveridge was similarly sure of the benefits: 'PNG was a great alternative to Vietnam and much more interesting than staying in Australia,' he said. 'I'm pretty confident that I made a more significant contribution by being present in PNG than I would have in Vietnam. It was certainly a more useful role for the PNG troops, a large number who in due course would have gone back to their villages with a different understanding of disease, health and hopefully of science!' Vietnam was no longer an option by the time Ian Colwell did Nasho, but he otherwise echoed the thoughts of Beveridge: 'I take a small amount of pride that I was part of the transition to independence in a country that did not end in a military coup and bloodshed. It was a very good use of my time in the army.'

To be 'well-educated', soldiers had to be 'educated well'. Not everyone was sure the soldiers had been. Peter Darmody, who taught at both Murray and Igam Barracks over an 18-month period in 1967–68, said, 'I did not consider at the time that our teaching of recruits had much of an impact on our pupils. The courses were quite short and handed out like ration packs. Perhaps it was a different matter for our pupils. Even today I don't get too excited about the role of teacher National Servicemen in PNG, apart from the fact that it is an aspect of National Service which is not known by the general public.' Jim Davidson had reservations, too, commenting on the frustration of teaching at Moem Barracks in 1967–68 when the other demands on the PI soldiers were so great that he could rarely complete a series of lessons, if at all, without interruption or missing men. At Goldie River in 1971, Frank Nolan thought it was great experience teaching the recruits but noted that it was difficult for them to stay awake because of their long days of intensive training.

Much was expected of us, quite different from what we would have had as young teachers in Australia. 'I was fortunate to be selected for RAAEC and PNG as I was required to "grow up quickly" as there was no one to 'hold my hand,' said John Morris, who was 20 at the time he went into Nasho. 'I was able to teach without too much direct supervision, so I was trusted to "do the job".' Norm Hunter also noted the level of professional trust we were given, especially as novice teachers. 'We drew up courses ourselves,' he said, 'which, looking back, was an enormous amount of responsibility.'[152] For Hunter, teaching in PNG was a life-changing experience that was important in shaping who he is today. 'I learnt a lot about leadership,' he said: 'the motivating power of having high expectations of people, and the difference between positional leadership and authentic leadership that goes beyond rank.'

The lack of direct supervision by RAAEC officers and apparent assumption of the Education Sergeants' capabilities seems to have permeated all of the barracks, and came as a surprise to some Chalkies, after the close scrutiny most had been under as trainees or novice teachers. Perhaps the regular officers recognised their own relative shortcomings, as John Fragomeni implied: 'I thought it was a little amusing that we who went into RAAEC as conscripts, many of whom were three- or four-year trained or even more, and who did a solid six months of serious military training, were led by RAAEC officers, many of whom were only two-year trained and only had a token three-months course of military training.'

Phil Doecke, who was posted to Taurama and then the Training Depot, and had taught for 12 months in the Northern Territory before his call-up, said, 'Some [regular RAAEC officers] … tried very hard to be 'tough' professional soldiers, as their teaching wasn't necessarily very skilful. This approach didn't really succeed at all. Those who recognized fresh young energetic teachers with fresh new teaching ideas and practices and accommodated these, did well. A lot of the great teaching came from such young bloods, and where this was allowed to happen some great teaching and learning took place. I saw this at Goldie River.'

Nevertheless, in the main the relationships between the temporary sergeants and their regular Army officers in the RAAEC were professional and amicable. As the 1970–71 Education Sergeants left Murray Barracks at the end of their 12-month term in PNG, the regulars seemed sorry to see them go: 'We offer a sincere thank you for their loyalty and devotion to duty during their tour,' the regulars said.[153]

In general, the PNG Chalkies had the same sort of view of their posting that Terry Clarke did when posted to Igam Barracks 1970–71: 'I WAS LUCKY!!!,' he said. 'I am sure I would not have been positive if I had been posted a few thousand miles to the north.' Denis Jenkins, who taught as a 'civilian' at Iduabada Technical College 1970–71 said, 'I think I was in a rare and privileged position, compared to the vast majority of young school teachers conscripted at that time. … I don't dwell on it now, but I believe I was lucky that I was able to make as much as I did from what could have been two wasteful, dangerous or damaging years.' Jim Davidson's response about what the Army/PNG experience meant to him is more guarded: 'Not genuinely sure. Perhaps it made me more tolerant. I think it allowed me to develop the capacity to look at a situation from a variety of angles, note the idiocy of the occasional dilemma, perhaps pass a comment some would see as cynical, and move on. … Not a time wasted entirely; and something of a time which has been of use for instructive anecdotes over the years since.' 'At the time I was not so keen on the situation,' Graham Leader said, 'but with the passage of time I think it was a worthwhile experience.'

A number of former Chalkies commented on the mutual benefits of serving their time in PNG, including Victorian Les Rowe, who joined the Australian diplomatic service immediately he finished Nasho: 'If I had to be conscripted I felt that I hit the jackpot by being posted to PNG and to Lae. I travelled extensively throughout the country, and the experience of living in a totally different culture and environment possibly helped me in my subsequent career.' John Meyer, who later returned to work in PNG, reckoned his Army experience there was a 'massive eye-opener' and one of the biggest highlights of his life. 'The PNG experience was unexpected,' Steven Hill said, 'and only good things followed.'

John Hain said that in his seven months at Taurama Barracks in 1971–72, 'I learned a lot about PNG and its people and about myself. I felt proud of our small contribution to PNG's development.' Ron Inglis commented that his National Service could have turned out very differently, but that because of the PNG experience, it contributed 'far more positives to my life than negatives'

Others, like Greg Ivey, have developed a strong attachment to the country. 'I view the time spent in TPNG as enjoyable, awareness-raising, skill-developing and a constructive contribution to the careers of the PI servicemen,' Ivey said. 'It has left me with a continuing interest in PNG and the role of its Army.' Ivey has since twice returned on visits to PNG, and several other Chalkies have also visited or otherwise maintained links with the country.

One of these is Greg Smith, didiman at Moem Barracks 1969–70, who returned in 2007 to walk the Kokoda Track with his two sons and to briefly revisit Wewak and the barracks where he'd spent 14 months of his National Service. One of the disquieting sights was the ruins of the former Education Centre at Moem, burnt down by a group of rebellious soldiers in March 2002. It seems that the Education Centre was not targeted because of its purpose but simply because it was conveniently located for the protesters, along with an administration block. The latter-day soldiers made a number of demands, including speeding up payouts to retrenched soldiers, the immediate end of political involvement in the PNG Defence Force, and increasing the Defence Force budget. After two weeks of mayhem around the barracks and disruption to Wewak life, soldiers loyal to the PNG Government raided the rebels' quarters and disarmed them, with two shots fired and no lives lost.

The burnt-out building is a reminder that although the path since independence has not seen a military coup, the volatility in some parts of the country that was evident during the Chalkies' time there was still a concern almost 50 years later. John Morris said that in his 12 months at Goldie River in 1970–71, he gained a great understanding of PNG, particularly the people, the languages, their customs and traditions as well as their culture. 'It was a great opportunity,' he said, 'and we saw, at first hand, the difficulties that would confront the people after Independence.'

Sometimes awareness of the wider issues in the country ran alongside increased self-awareness as the Chalkies sought to adapt to the environment in which they found themselves. For example, a member of the last cohort of Nashos to be sent to PNG, Reg Radford, who was stationed at Igam Barracks, Lae, for 14 months in 1972–73, said: 'The Nasho sergeants at Lae Area were all very positive and joined in everything that was on,' he said. 'We were well treated. All three stayed on after the [Whitlam] election and finished our 18 months in Lae, while most went home immediately after the election. … It was a great 18 months and, on reflection, contributed greatly to the person I became and remain today.' Wolf Iwanowitsch said, 'It made me grow up.'

John Teggelove, who was posted to Goldie River Training Depot 1966–67, said that the experience improved with age: 'Retrospectively, I consider that my Army and TPNG time was a period of enhanced personal growth in experience, maturity and independence. Also, it enhanced future teacher career opportunities, pathways and seniority.' Ed Diery, who returned to Queensland to teach and later became Head of Science at a high school, also thought his time in the Army enhanced his career: 'I think my time in PNG was the icing on the cake,' Diery said. '… National Service provided me with experiences I probably would never have otherwise had. Also it provided a more interesting chapter in what would otherwise have been a fairly humdrum life (career-wise I mean).'

'Whatever I missed out on at home, I gained other skills, insights, good and bad habits and knowledge from the whole experience that I would not otherwise have had,' Graham Lindsay said. 'It is a part of my life I remember reasonably vividly and do not regret in any way.' Terry Edwinsmith thought his time was well-spent, meeting people from all walks of life. 'I was impressed with those whom I met in the Sergeants'

Mess [at 1PIR], he said. 'They were all good people.'

Greg Farr described his time in PNG as 'a most interesting cultural experience, even though it was spent almost entirely in Port Moresby. The Unit was well run, the teaching load was light but well organised and the teaching experience gained was a rare opportunity. I never felt I was wasting my time, although on reflection I might have used my spare time more productively and made better use of opportunities available. However, I did take up a fairly serious reading habit during that year.'

As a junior Nasho officer, John Herlihy was initially unhappy with his posting to PNG, but 'really enjoyed' life there because it opened up a whole new outlook on life and the wider world that he said he may not have developed had he just spent his National Service in Australia. From this first experience of living and working overseas, Herlihy developed a lifetime interest in Third World countries. 'It was a waste of time, it was frustrating, it most certainly was a good alternative to Vietnam, but it was also worthwhile as a life experience,' Victorian Bob Coppa said of his two years in National Service. 'As time goes on and you get a chance to reflect on the experience, the more you realize how it prepared you for the many challenges you successfully met in your career and personal life. The many immediate negatives fade over time and you concentrate on the positives that stay with you as part of your character.'

Victorian Phil Parker thought that his time in Army Education had little impact on his later professional life, but his time in PNG he often described to friends as 'close to being a tropical holiday', which is similar to Frank Cordingley's recollection of it. Another benefit, Cordingley said, was that his parents were delighted he didn't have to carry a weapon (unless, of course, he had happened to be one of those called upon to act as a scribe for a 'peace-keeping' force on a distant island!).

Greg Smith, who went to PNG as a 'didiman', an agricultural specialist, said it was a privilege to have the role, a position he knew nothing about when he went into the Army, 'let alone the opportunity for me to teach tropical agriculture to soldiers in the developing PNG Army!'. Another agricultural scientist, Martin Forbes said that, ironically, PNG might have been the only place he would have got a job when he graduated, the year before Nasho, because of the dearth of agricultural positions in Australia. Robbie Scott, also a 'didiman', said he had a number of very good mates who were 'jealous of his time in National Service and especially PNG'. Scott said his time in the Army had become a major part of his life with great memories and influences on what he had achieved and become.

A counter to these positive responses came from a study by psychologist Dennis Armstrong of attitudes towards Papua New Guineans held by some members of the 1968, 1969 and 1970 Chalkie cohorts.[154] From a statistical analysis of results of a 'before and after' questionnaire of 113 Chalkies from those years, Armstrong concluded that after six months in PNG, these conscripted teachers had moved from a simple, pre-posting positive view of Papua New Guineans to a more complex and less positive view, i.e. that they had become more judgemental with the reality of contact. Other findings were that the older, more experienced Chalkies tended to be more tolerant than the younger ones, and that Chalkies in PNG were significantly less satisfied with their lot at the end of their time of National Service when compared with National Servicemen who were based in Australia.

Overwhelmingly, the negative attitudes that Armstrong found though his questionnaire survey were not evident in the sorts of responses from the 73 ex-Chalkies who participated in the 2015 qualitative survey I conducted. The differences may be because mainly those with a more positive disposition towards the country and people of Papua New Guinea responded to the survey (see Appendix 2) and/ or because their attitudes had mellowed over the years in between.

***

For many Chalkies, the posting firstly to the RAAEC and then to PNG was a relief from what they had expected when they were conscripted. In June 1969, Major Henry Dachs told a group of us when we arrived at the Education unit at Enoggera Barracks, Brisbane, our first posting in Australia after our infantry training, that when we joined Education we left the Army. While it was true that we were generally no longer required to be part of the arms-bearing and constantly training body of the Army, we couldn't escape military tasks beyond the classroom and the fact that we were mostly NCOs in a hierarchical system where officers reigned supreme.

'The worst part was the Army attitude of, "Do what you are told and don't even ask questions afterwards", South Australian secondary teacher Bruce Nulty said. 'This was not so pronounced in the Education Corps.' Nulty said his National Service experience was so influential to his life that 'I resolved to do something more interesting, so that I would have other more entertaining stories to tell my grandchildren.' Nevertheless, he summed up his two years in this way: 'On balance, my time in National Service was worthwhile, but my experience of the Australian Army was mostly negative.' Russell Jenkin had a similar qualification: 'Apart from adapting to the demands of the Australian Army for two years, it was a major challenge to live in a vastly different culture and land and for so long. In hind-sight, it was life-changing, but most worthwhile.'

On the other hand, a couple of Chalkies thought the Nasho experience was so significant in their lives that a version of it would be good for the current generation. 'My experience in TPNG was so formative for my life that it makes a case for offering young Australians the option for Civic duty,' 1967–68 Chalkie Bruce Nulty said. 'Such Civic Duty should not be run by the Army and would not need to be overseas because there is much that needs to be done for Australia's Indigenous peoples in Australia.' A colleague in the same cohort, Phil Parker, agreed: 'I believe there could be an equivalent opportunity "offered" or "imposed" on today's young folk. Certainly wouldn't do them any harm, and the benefits could be very worthwhile.'

A number of Chalkies grappled with the paradox of the 'Army experience' versus the 'PNG/RAAEC experience', qualifying their belief in the personal and professional benefits with references to 'minor irritations', 'not so good parts', 'a few memories I'd rather forget', and 'the shackles of military life'. Greg Ivey said, 'I now view my time in the RAAEC as positive and developmental; and it overshadows the six-month infantry training period in Singleton.' Phil Doecke enjoyed his time in Education Corps, but objected to the attitude of some officers. 'Their attempt to impose the militaristic approach upon us was very uncomfortable,' he said, 'almost ludicrous in hindsight.' Nevertheless, Doecke, who returned some time later to again work in PNG education, said his time there during Nasho instilled a great connection with the country along with an appreciation of the 'value of cultural education, inclusion; a global view of education; learning through cultural 'lenses'; other ways of knowing which are equally valid, authentic; hegemonic issues of colonial power in education; importance of living, working alongside nationals in 'their space', to understand, respect, and value them.'

John Humphrey agreed: 'I loved my time teaching in PNG. I hope I was able to improve their educational outcomes, and was rather sad to leave. However, I was glad to be out of the Army, with all its rules and regulations and "kow-towing" to some people who I didn't think deserved to be treated that way.' Ian Lovell saw it slightly differently: 'I think the personal discipline I learned from military service and working in a large organisation taught me to believe that there is more value in corporate/group behaviour that the mere following of directions.'

Of course, overshadowing all the Chalkies' experience of the RAAEC and PNG was that they were National Servicemen, conscripted to Australia's military cause. They had much to say about that when they reflected on their two-year terms decades later. 'The experience helped develop a strong distaste for the notion of universal national service,' Rob Daniel said, 'not from a personal perspective, as I benefitted from the experience, but what I saw it do to so many individuals.' John Fragomeni remained opposed to the selectivity of conscription and 'the effect the lottery had on all those who were caught up in it', but acknowledged that 'those who went to PNG as part of RAAEC had a better time of it than many did,' a view shared by Richard Morgan, who has just completed primary teacher training before he went into Nasho, who served in Vietnam first before extending his National Service to go to PNG: 'I don't agree with random selection for National Service, but have to acknowledge that the time in the Army was beneficial for me.'

Jim Davidson, a 21-year-old Victorian primary teacher when he was called up, has continued to look upon National Service as something to endure over which he had no control, and was dubious there were many benefits, although he was grateful as an NCO for an insight into man management on a multitude of levels. 'The indigenous soldier/ local indigenous person looks at life in a greatly differing way,' he said. 'So I had the chance to look behind what was "obvious" to perhaps most European people and see that other races observe the same thing differently.'

Andrew Remenyi, who became an educational psychologist after Nasho when other career aspirations were no longer available to him, also believed his experience had few positives. 'I felt the rejection [by others] of Vietnam Vets very keenly personally, and experienced several incidents where I was criticised for being so morally weak as to enter conscription. I know this to be a reaction of many of my NS friends, for we were not conscripted for NS, we were conscripted for the Vietnam War.' Remenyi said that National Service definitely interrupted his professional life. 'I think I also came out of National Service with adjustment problems, mainly overdrinking,' he said, 'and feeling I was a lower-status citizen than my peers who had not been called up and who were now so far ahead professionally and personally.'

Keith Werder was also angry about being 'left behind' over the two years, and not only in his teaching career. 'I was at my peak as a cricketer and this was my chosen game,' he said. 'Those missing two years meant the loss of opportunities which could have resulted in even higher levels of representation. One of my mates used these years to further his cricket and ultimately, he went on to represent Australia. He was no better cricketer than I was. In short, my potential always remained unrealised.'

One ex-Chalkie, a 21-year-old teacher at the time of his call-up, also regarded National Service as detrimental to his career, as well as 'a huge waste of time for an illegitimate war in Vietnam. If the same situation occurred again today, he said he would advise his chidren to be conscientious objectors. 'At least, I would advise them to seek NATIONAL service as opposed to MILITARY service,' he said. Given the opportunity to reflect on his experience, the former Chalkie said: 'When I was in my early 20s, I was naive and "did as I was told". I was compliant. In hindsight, I look back and realise that the way in which National/Military Service was forced on some through a birthday ballot was immoral. Immoral because it was all about an immoral war which could never be won. Immoral because 'nashos' were liable to go overseas to a war zone when they should have been allowed to stay in Australia or volunteer for overseas fighting. But no, they didn't have a choice. Something like 200 lost their lives as a result, and when conscripted, they were below the voting age of 21 at that time. Hardly democracy at work!'

This former conscript's anger was shared by Peter Chard. 'I would regard my time in National Service as a complete waste of time,' he said. 'I hated the army with a vengeance because of the way we were treated and kept in the dark.' Chard said his time in PNG was the highlight, but only outside the army, and he liked the place so much that a year after his discharge he went back with his wife, for another six years, this time working in the PNG Public Service. He acknowledged one other plus from his Army Education experience: 'Teaching indigenous soldiers gave me adult teaching experience which was helpful when I taught in the Corrective Services environment,' he said.

These views are a reminder that not all Chalkies responded positively to their PNG posting, mainly because, like Nulty, they thought conscription was iniquitous in the first place: 'I was a Conscript, I did not want the Army to push me around for two important years of my life,' Nulty said. 'Am I supposed to be grateful that they sent me to TPNG, to a worthwhile and formative experience rather than a life threatening experience in Vietnam?'

Hugh Wilkinson, who went on to become Director of Army Education, said that many National Servicemen actually wanted to go to Vietnam. 'It was not that anyone was sympathetic to the cause,' he said. 'Rather, few actually wanted to do NS but, once in, you had to make the most of it. In those days the only way one could qualify for a war service homes loan was to go to SVN.' He cited a vox pop survey of some 60 recruits by platoon staff one day during initial training at Puckapunyal of willingness to go to Vietnam. 'Overwhelmingly, and spontaneously, the majority wanted to go,' Wilkinson said. 'Understandably, as it turned out, the only ones who did not want to go were married.'

On the basis of the responses from the 73 Chalkies surveyed for this book, the proportion willing to go to Vietnam was not as high among the Chalkies, although a number indicated they would have gone if required to. Others were quite certain that PNG was definitely preferable. One of the early Chalkies, John Teggelove (1966–67), considered National Service, particularly the PNG posting, as very positive, productive and beneficial experience. 'Avoiding service in Vietnam, with the associated short-term and long-term tragedy and trauma for many or most who served there, was certainly a good thing,' he said. The unit he belonged to prior to the Papua New Guinea posting left for Vietnam a couple of months after his departure.

Another of that first cohort of Chalkies, Denis O'Rourke, had been in the Artillery before being sent to PNG with Army Education, training at Wacol, near Brisbane. 'Many of the people who went to Vietnam are unwell due to that experience, so I am glad that I didn't go there with 4 Field Regiment,' he said. Nevertheless, 'I would have felt that staying in Australia was a waste of time (unless I was moved about the country).' Russell Jenkin agreed. 'At the time, I did not want to stay in Australia, as that did not make sense after Recruit Training,' he said, 'but in hindsight, I was very fortunate to have been posted to New Guinea in lieu of Vietnam.'

Similarly, Edwinsmith, who had been willing to go to Vietnam, but was plucked from his Artillery unit the night before it was due to ship out, was later not sorry about his reposting. 'For me, missing out on Vietnam, in hindsight, was a very good option,' he said. 'I was spared war action and any possible post-traumatic stress that may have followed as a result of such war service.' Edwinsmith said that most of his time in the Army was an 'exciting, *Boys' Own* adventure,' whereas most of his former Arty colleagues 'have not fared well'. Michael Turnbull also said his time in the RAAEC was at times quite exciting. 'I had considered applying to go to Vietnam when in the Ordnance Corps, but was transferred to Scheyville [as librarian],' Turnbull said. 'Two weeks later my replacement in Ordnance went to Vietnam. Looking back now, many years later, I am very grateful that I did not go.'

Bill Larsen was more blunt about his Nasho experience in PNG: 'Could have done without it, but so much better that the Vietnam alternative.' Phil Adam, who was at Murray Barracks 1969–70 agreed. 'It was a good alternative to Vietnam. There can be no doubt about that. It was worthwhile in the sense that we had a good experience of working in a very different environment and culture both in the army and the PNG culture. Apart from negative views about the issue of conscription and the political cynicism that led to it I found the overall experience of living and working in New Guinea to be both interesting and professionally helpful. I can still tell the story of the Three Little Pigs in Pidgin.'

Another one who thought there would have been 'few positives' about his two years if he'd gone to Vietnam, Tom Derham, a Nasho RAAEC lieutenant who extended his time in the Army and spent 18 months in PNG 1972–73, said he regarded National Service as one of the best experiences of his life and that it helped him grow up as a person. 'I regard myself as being extremely fortunate to not have had to go through a Vietnam experience and to have experienced the terrible stigma carried by these veterans, let alone the ravages of PTSD [Post Traumatic Stress Disorder] and neglect by the Army and Government for so many years,' he said.

While the Chalkies surveyed almost unanimously saw PNG as a preferable alternative to a Vietnam posting, they would all very likely agree with Phil Doecke: 'I'm very, very glad I did not get to go to Vietnam,' he said. 'I deeply respect those who did, however.'

14

Nasho Chalkies in PNG 1966-73: 'Someone else's country'

It seems that when the Army Education scheme was introduced in PNG in 1966, the head of PNG Command, Brigadier Ian Hunter, and senior RAAEC officers in PNG had already assumed that self-government and independence would come sooner rather than later, even though the Australian Government and some PNG leaders themselves at that time were unwilling to set a timeline. The Education scheme was premised on that assumption, and the Chalkies came to be in PNG at a key stage of the country's transition as a nation. From 1966 to 1973, they were at the frontline of upgrading the educational standards of Pacific Islander troops, which was regarded as vital if the Army was to play a meaningful and responsible role in a future independent nation.

Even in the early 60s, when English literacy was the main focus, the need was still for education in the Pacific Islands Regiment both 'to produce good soldiers and to develop citizenship qualities'.[155] The forward-looking 'Report on Education in the Australian Army' in 1963 recommended a higher level of education in the contemporary PIR and 'to superimpose higher education as required on the next generation of soldiers'.[156] When Hunter arrived in 1965, he took this aspect of development seriously, strongly believing that education was 'a vital and integral part of the military training programme'.[157] Encouraged by the Army Minister, Malcom Fraser, and supported by the Deputy Adjutant-General, Brigadier 'Bunny' Austin, from 1966 Hunter initiated the idea of using conscripted teachers to further the education of indigenous soldiers within PNG Command.

Incoming Chalkies in 1971 were told in a memo that 'the major reason for RAAEC staff being present in PNG is *to assist in* the progressive development of the Army within the Territory and the Territory itself.[158] The emphasis in the original emphasises that they were not seen as solely responsible for the soldiers' and the territory's journey to self-government and independence, but to do what they were trained for: teach courses that would contribute to the development of soldiers' knowledge and understanding in prescribed fields of study. Mainly that was through Certificates of Education in English, Maths, Social Studies and Science, as well as the Civics courses aimed at developing the soldiers' understanding of the role of an Army in an independent democratic nation.

Despite other demands on the soldiers' time and the sometimes oppressive Army environment, the often limited resources and occasionally inadequate facilities, the heat and humidity, and even their own short experience as educators, for the most part the Nasho Chalkies beavered away steadily at the task Brigadier Hunter had set for them. The extent of their success doubtless varied from year to year, from location to location, from course to course, and from individual to individual, as it does with any teaching.

'There is no doubt that a scheme that places in an institution like the PIR, forty fully trained teachers each year for seven years, is going to have a lasting impact,' former Chalkie Ian Ogston said. 'The effect of this work of increasing literacy, numeracy and social awareness on this large and stable organization must have had a very positive and perhaps critical effect on the army in PNG. In a country where literacy rates were low, a well-educated professional organization had to be a vital part of society.'[159] Ian Lovell, who spent 14 months at Goldie River in 1967–68, said he believed in what the Chalkies were teaching soldiers about 'how to live their lives within a framework of orderly government'.

Roger Jones, Assistant Director of Army Education in PNG,1967–69, later commented: 'I've never really understood how the Australian Army, which we all know can do some incredibly silly things at times, could undertake such a foresighted, nation-building and essentially altruistic task, but I take my hat off to it.'[160]

Other corps had their own responsibilities in developing an indigenous army for PNG, and although there were racist attitudes and comments in some quarters, those in the RAAEC were fortunate in generally being able to work alongside and under officers and NCOs similarly concerned for the welfare of the troops and the country. Some of those colleagues included a small number of Nashos in other corps, including Infantry (e.g. 2Lt. John Stringfellow, 1966–67; 2Lt. Ian Freeman, 1968–70; 2Lt. Bob Ormston); Signals (e.g. Sig. Trevor Webb, 1969–70; Cpl. Ted Middleton, 1969–70); Psychology (e.g. Sgt. David Sandoe, 1965–66), RAEME (e.g. Corporal Keith Oxenbould, 1967–69), and Medical (e.g. Sgt. Graham Wheeler, 1966–67; Cpl. Greg Leahy, 1969–70; Graeme Johnson's civilian qualifications led to his being posted to PNG 1969–70 as a Hygiene Sergeant at 2PIR).

In 1969, the Army Minister, Phillip Lynch, who had taken over from Fraser, made a spirited defence of the PIR and highlighted the role of education in the development of the Army in PNG. 'The Army in the Territory is putting forth a heavy education effort with a dual purpose – to assist the provision of trained and educated manpower by broadening the soldiers' educational base and to assist in promotion of those characteristics and beliefs which are considered essential to the development of a loyal and disciplined Army in a modern democratic society,' Lynch said. 'To this end, formal education in English, Arithmetic, Science and Social Studies is given; while each soldier attends lectures and participates in group discussions on civics and ethics. Soldiers are encouraged to develop a pride in the history and the unique culture of the Territory, and an understanding of its present institutions and its development towards the goal of a modern self-governing nation.'[161]

For the first time since the inauguration of the scheme, the Army Minister drew public attention to the role of Army Education in this task, and highlighted the role of the Nashos. 'Through the efforts of the Royal Australian Educational Corps, social training and general education are now receiving attention comparable to that given to soldiering. The educational work is being carried out by a team of 60 Australian Army teachers. Their work is most impressive and their work deserves special recognition,' Lynch said. 'It is worth noting that two-thirds of the teachers are National Servicemen who, after basic military training, are primarily concerned with education duties with the Army in New Guinea, concurrently with their own continuation of training.'

In a review of education in the Army two years later, after five cohorts of Chalkies had completed their tours of duty in PNG, R.J. O'Neill, then head of the Strategic and Defence Studies Centre, Australian National University, said 'The extensive program of civil education which the Army runs for its New Guinean [i.e. PI] soldiers indicates a serious approach to Australia's responsibility for leaving to an independent New Guinean government a loyal Army'.[162] O'Neill observed a number of features, including the keenness of the soldiers to learn, the curricula developed by 'experienced civilian teachers', varying levels of soldier interest in civics training, and that 'educational standards throughout the PIR are rising rapidly'. 'Most noticeable,' he said, 'is the insistence on maintaining the principle of the supremacy of the civilian government over the military.'[163]

O'Neill seemed impressed by the quality of the education program, but commented that 'one cannot help but be struck by the unique experience of seeing an army striving hard to talk itself out of a political future'. He wondered, however, whether the program was laying a 'foundation of political consciousness', implying that this could result in the Army taking a more active role in the country's direction if the going became uncertain in the future. He acknowledged that his query was pure speculation, and it echoes the concern of Bill Guest in the Sergeant's Mess at Goldie River in 1954, that education was 'the turning-point in the degree of tranquillity of PIR'[164].

The Chalkies were not radicals, however, and their teaching implicitly or explicitly recognised the responsibility of the Army in an independent PNG. An Army Education newsletter, published midway through the eight-year period in which conscripted teachers were posted to PNG, acknowledged this understanding: 'As 1969 draws to a close, we in PNG Command can look back at an intensive year of educational effort; effort which has brought increasing numbers of Pacific Islands personnel to a higher standard of achievement, and ourselves closer to the day when we can hand over to the PNG Army a nucleus of well-trained and educated men who will be able to support and nourish a young and growing army.'[165]

It's impossible to know the extent to which the Chalkies were able to achieve those noble aims. Good educators always sow seeds, but most Chalkies were not in PNG long enough to know the extent to which their teaching in the Army bore fruit in the long term. As a former Director of Army Education, Major W.H. John, once said, membership of the Educational Corps implies not only professional competence and personal integrity, but 'a faith in ends which are not altogether demonstrable and tangible'.[166]

In discussing why the sometimes-predicted military coup had not occurred in PNG after independence, May and Haley concluded in

2014 that the Defence force had 'played a significant role in maintaining internal security and contributing to national development, as well as securing the country's borders'. [167] There had been 'some deterioration since independence in the capacity and morale of the PNGDF, and several instances of tension between the military and the government', they said, but in the first 40 years, no coup.

May and Haley commented that it 'might be tempting to argue that the concepts of civilian supremacy and military professionalism instilled during the Australian administration and the early years of independence militated against a coup'.[168] The links are problematic, however, and educationally such outcomes are, in Major Johns's words, neither demonstrable nor tangible. Nevertheless, the facts are that over 300 Chalkies made a contribution towards educating a generation of Pacific Islander soldiers in PNG between 1966 and 1973, and those troops subsequently lived through a relatively politically stable period in the country's post-independence history.

In an article about the Chalkies in the *Sydney Morning Herald*, author Mark Dapin asked, 'How was it that, at a time when thousands of Australians were fighting and hundreds were dying in Vietnam, the army could afford to lose up to 40 of its best and brightest – almost two per cent of the average January intake – every year, to a far from urgent nation-building project in PNG?'[169]

They were not necessarily, however, the 'best and brightest'. Arguably the cream of the crop had already been selected ahead of them, for officer training, and only relatively few of those ended up in Army Education. What distinguished all of them from their fellow Nashos was that they were trained teachers, so that when the opportunity arose to educate troops in PNG, they were logically the ones the Army turned to (along with a few others with specialist knowledge). Certainly there was a selection process, which was generally not the case with other Corps, although the criteria used for the RAAEC varied, apart from the basic one of a teacher qualification, in most instances, and perhaps their attitudes to 'non-Europeans'.

For the first cohort, when the scheme had just kicked off, cross-corps transfers, occasionally with seemingly token interviews, were the order of the day, with many of the Nasho teachers drafted within a few days to their new postings in PNG. Later selections were mainly through interview panels, but even then the criteria seem to have been inconsistent and not always on the grounds of teaching ability; cross-corps transfers also still occurred.

As for Dapin's comment about the Army sending conscripted Chalkies to a 'far from urgent nation-building project in PNG', at least the Chalkies were utilising the skills they'd developed as teachers, rather than being posted, often unwillingly, to Vietnam, in other corps. Some teachers did fight in Vietnam – Dapin writes about them in *The Nashos' war*, and at least two died there[170] – but most Chalkies whose views are included in this book don't believe they could have made a better contribution as jungle fighters in that country rather than practising their profession in PNG. It should also be noted that the RAAEC did operate in Vietnam during this period, mostly with full-time ARA officers, although Nasho Sergeants Richard Morgan and Ken Rowe were posted there as Chalkies, and at least one other Nasho teacher ended up in the unit there in a non-teaching appointment.

'On reflection, I suspect the Australian Government decided it needed to do more about our responsibility to prepare TPNG for independence,' said Bruce Nulty, a 22-year-old South Australian high school teacher when he was called up in 1967. 'The Government noticed that there were a number of under-employed teachers in National Service and it was a simple solution to re-deploy them to TPNG. I think we had a positive influence on TPNG natives in the TPNG Army. Furthermore, the Project produced about 300 more Australian citizens who knew more about TPNG culture, which was a positive influence on future relations with the new independent country.'

Social and political commentator, Deni ToKunai, commented that 'there is a danger in Australia and Australians hanging onto the past – of having an imperialist nostalgic perspective of PNG, its towns, and its people', and that this can result in 'no space for the Papua New Guinean'.[171] The Chalkies' reflections reported in this book came some 50 years after their time in Papua New Guinea, and so are subject to the usual vagaries of such memories, and it's likely, as Bob Coppa said, that 'many immediate negatives fade over time and you concentrate on the positives'. In their relatively short time in Papua New Guinea, many Chalkies probably did come to see their temporary home in the ways that Hank Nelson characterised it – as a 'frontier of adventure' and the 'beginning of the exotic'. It was, after all, very different from their native land in its topography, culture and politics, and professionally and personally it provided opportunities and challenges they would never have had back home.

Their response to PNG was of necessity grounded in their professional practice, however, which in turn was undertaken within a military framework in PNG Command, so they were inevitably focussed on their work much of the time, whether it was teaching and administration in Army Education, additional duties such as Orderly Sergeant or Mess Secretary, or extra-curricular activities such as playing or coaching sport for the Army.

Their interactions with Papua New Guineans were therefore strong over the months they spent in the country, arguably not in a paternalistic, neo-colonial manner, but in an encouraging, developmental way appropriate for the members of an Army in an emerging nation.

This is not to romanticise their task or the outcomes – they were neophyte teachers still developing their understanding of teaching and learning, and not always pleased to be there. Although their students were generally keen to learn, they exhibited the same range of abilities that might have been seen in Australian classrooms, and there were sometimes constraints on the extent of their attendance and concentration due to the competition of time and effort from military training.

The Education scheme in PNG between 1966 and 1973 was a product of its time, taking advantage of a process of conscription established for a mainly military purpose, and diverting a very small proportion of the personnel so recruited, for individual and social development. Not all Chalkies who took part in the survey were convinced they made a lasting impact, but there was general agreement that if they had to be in the Army, teaching in PNG at the very least made use of their professional skills. For many, it was a never-to-be-forgotten and sometimes career-changing experience.

***

From the time each annual cohort of Chalkies walked through that curtain of humid air at Jacksons Airport, we immediately knew, as Bev Morgan recognised, that we were in someone else's country. It was if we had gone through the mysterious door in *The Lion, the Witch and the Wardrobe* and discovered our own version of the land of Narnia.

But then we were always in someone else's country. First it was the country of the politicians, with their scheming, spin-doctoring, and backtracking, making this week's decision seem like a considered judgement, when just a fortnight before they'd argued against exactly the same proposition. Good for the nation, they said, and spun the lottery barrel of 'selective National Service'. When the barrel stopped spinning, they picked out birthdates with a pronged fork – our birthdates – when most of us were quite happy just where we were, thank you very much, and on the cusp of our teaching careers. Nevertheless, there were some who were happy to be called up, and a few even volunteered.

Soon we were in another country – recruit training. Consigned in buses to hot, dry training barracks in the bush, we were like a mob of sheep at their first shearing – huddled together, wondering what was coming next. Mostly ignorant NCOs snapped at our heels, harried us, rounded us up, trained us to jump to their whistle. Some recruits were channelled off to officer training. Despite the constraints and harassment, a few enjoyed their initial Army experience.

When the trainers thought we'd mastered the course, they drove us out, now marching in impeccably straight lines, three abreast, deeper into the country of the Army. We trained some more – in infantry, artillery, ordnance, medical, until through often mysterious ways and means we came out of the crush and were diverted into yet another country – Army Education. We recognised the topography of this country, because its paths and highways took us back to the classroom, where we'd been before the lottery finger of National Service picked most of us out.

Lest familiarity breed contempt, however, the Army soon picked us up again and deposited us in Papua New Guinea. We looked around and quickly realised that this time we really were in someone else's country, not just a metaphorical one. The Army spread us across five bases, each with its own personal and professional demands.

We were 20 years old or thereabouts at the time, and what does a 20-year-old know? Everything and nothing. We put those two things together and learned what it was like to live in someone else's country, and tried to help PNG soldiers prepare for the time when they'd have to shoulder more responsibility for the future of their nation. We developed and taught courses we thought were aligned with their interests and abilities, we coached their sporting teams and played sport with and against them, we went on civic action patrols, and generally tried to understand 'where they were coming from' in the relatively short time available to us. Sometimes we tried to be real soldiers by doing orderly duty and other military tasks, and a few of us signed on again at the end of our compulsory term. Occasionally we escaped by car or motorbike, or on a DC3 to the other side of the country, and tried not to raise the flag outside the Brigadier's house upside down.

When we'd finished living, teaching and learning in someone else's country, we went back to our own country, and tried to take up the lives we'd left behind; a small number found new lives for themselves; and a few went back to PNG. Having to adapt to those other 'countries' – conscription, the Army, the Educational Corps, PNG, return to civilian life – affected us in various ways.

Whether that period was perceived as good, bad, mixed or indifferent, almost 50 years later the experience of National Service and Papua New Guinea evoked strong reminiscences, often in considerable detail, from the Chalkies whose recollections have been recounted in these pages. It seems Graham Leader was right: two years isn't a long time in your life, but at age 20 it can be significant.

Appendices

1. National Servicemen posted to PNG with RAAEC 1966–73

A list compiled by ex-Chalkie Terry Edwinsmith of those believed to have been National Servicemen who served with the Royal Australian Army Educational Corps in Papua New Guinea between 1966 and 1973.

Adam, Phillip J.
Aitchison, Roger R.
Alexander, Colin
Allington, Philip J.
Arnold, Barry K.
Artomonow, Alex

Bailey, William F.
Bailey, Ross
Barton, Ken F.
Bassett, Ray
Bates, Russell
Bates, Jim
Beer, Ross M.
Bennetts, Max
Bensley, Wayne R.
Benson, Don A.
Beveridge, Stephen.J.
Blackburn, Peter
Blinkhorn, Steve F.
Boddington, Richard
Bodiski, Guy
Bodlay, Zoltan J.
Bowen, Ian M.
Bowman, Laurie
Bowrey, Ian K.

Boxal, Bruce G.
Boyd, Andrew
Boyle, Mick
Bremner, Ken A.
Brook, Peter A.
Bryant, Keith A.
Buffier, Greg
Burgess, Steve
Butcher, Robert N.

Calder, Alan W.
Calnan, John C.
Campbell, Ted
Carnes, Graham
Cassidy, Rod
Chard, Peter R.
Cizauskas, Vlad
Clark, Ross A.
Clarke, Terry
Colwell, Ian
Connell, Dennis J.
Connolly, Jim
Cook, William
Coppa, Robert A.
Cordingley, Frank S.
Corrie, Neville

Coward, Dan
Cumming, Douglas A
Curtis, Ian

Dalziel, Andrew
Daniel, Robert
Dark, Wayne
Dark, John
Darmody, Peter W.
Davidson, Jim E.
Davies, Brian R.
Day, Alan G.
Deane, Ray J.
Derham, Tom
Devlin, Peter J.
Dickson, Stuart A.
Diery, Ed
Dillon, Matt
Doecke, Philip
Dohring, Kerry B.
Donnan, Chris
Duff, Rob A.
Dunn, Warren
Durrant, John
Dymock, Darryl R.

Edgerton, Graeme
Edwinsmith, Terry

Farr, Greg
Fennell, John F.
Fifer, Geoff
Fletcher, Rob T.
Forbes, Martin
Ford, John E.
Foreman, Brian
Forsyth, Peter S.
Foster, Robert J.
Fragomeni, John
Garrard, J.W
Garvey, Bernie J.
Gerrish, Ron A.
Gershiedle, Glenn

Gibson, Neil J.
Gibson, John R.
Glenister, Ian
Gough, Murray
Grigg, Roger H.

Haid, Anthony J.
Hain, John
Haines, Brian
Hall, Glenn
Hall, John
Hall, Tom
Hannaford, Ken L.
Hansen, Des F.
Harris, John K.
Harris, Brian
Harris, David
Harris, Bruce L.
Harris, Warwick
Hartshorn, Bruce
Hassett, Gordon
Headland, Anthony J.
Herlihy, John
Hickson, Terry C.
Hietbrink, Hans
Hilder, Graham
Hill, Steve
Hill, Gordon
Hodder, Ian W.
Hole, Arthur
Holmes, Brian
Honeyman, Brenton
Hornsby, David
Horton, Kev
Howard, Roger W.
Howman, Leo M.
Humphrey, John
Humphries, Robert
Hunter, Norm W.
Hurrell, Grahame

Imison, Phil C.
Inglis, Ron

Isenberg, Norman
Ison, Warren
Ivey, Greg J.
Iwanowitsch, Wolf

Jach, Zeno
Jeffkins, Richard
Jenkin, Russell T.
Jenkins, Denis
Jenner, Morris
Johnson, Paul B.
Johnson, Tony
Jones, John P.

Kee, Kevin N.
Keegan, Gerry
Kilian, Peter
Kiss, Zsigmund
Kitzelman, Robert
Knight, Richard G.

Large, Robert
Larsen, William
Larsen, Richard J.
Leader, Graham
Leahy, Greg
Lean, Greg
Lee, Michael
Lee, Robert E.
Lindsay, Graham
Livermore, Alan Wm.
Lovell, Robert J.
Lovell, Ian
Lynch, Ron

Macauley, Ed
MacKay, K. Ian
Manchester, Peter
Mangano, Edward
Mark, Graham
Marshall, Anthony
Martin, John A.
Mason, Robert J.

Mason, Peter T.
Mason, Terry T.
Mathieson, Bruce
McCarthy, R.B.
McCauley, Ed
McCluskey, Ian W.
McDonald, Jim
McEwen, Rory J.
McGuin, Dennis P.
McKillop, Michael J.
McLouglin, Kevin
McPhee, John
Meadows, David
Meyer, John G.
Middleton, Ted
Miller, Barney
Miller, Graeme
Milligan, Mick
Minns, Ian
Mobbs, Laurie
Moore, Gordon
Moore, John
Morcom, Ken W.
Morgan, Richard
Morris, John
Morriss, Russell S.
Morrissey, Brian P.
Mount, Ken E.
Mousamas, Arthur G.
Muller, Robert B.
Mulligan, Mick R.
Murphy, Graeme E.
Murphy, Greg T.
Murray, Jim

Nagorcka, Malcolm
Neal, Daryl
Neeson, Bernard C.
Newton, Ray A.
Nichol, Ray M.
Noack, Ziggy
Nolan, Brendan

Nolan, Frank
Nulty, Bruce R.
Nunn, Barry L.

O'Rourke, Denis J.
Ogston, Ian
Olson, Gary
O'Meara, Tom
O'Reilly, Geoff T.

Parker, Philip P.
Percival, Alan
Peters, Geoff J.
Phillips, David
Piper, Graham I.
Pollock, David J.
Porteous, Peter
Poulton, Chris J.
Powell, Greg
Powell, David J.
Pryke, Robert
Pyle, Jim M.

Quanchi, A. Max
Quinn, Martin

Radford, Reg
Rae, John R.
Rathbone, Doug
Ray, Greg A.
Remenyi, Andrew
Retallick, John
Richter, Bruce D.
Ridgeway, Kerry
Riley, Denis
Robertson, Barry J.
Robertson, Boyd M.
Roedder, Heinz
Rogers, Tony
Rogers, Rodger
Rogers, Greg
Rothe, Kym F.
Rowe, Les A.

Rowe, Ken J.
Roxburgh, David J.
Roxby, Steve
Russo, Frank

Schmidt, Gunter
Schroder, Peter M.
Scott, Robert F.
Scott, Don
Screen, Garry W.
Sears, George
Semple, Jim
Shackleford, Peter
Shea , Phil
Sheahan, Gaven P.
Sibson, Stephen
Slater, William
Sloane, Alwyn M.
Smith, Kevin J.
Smith, Greg H.
Smith, David
Smithard, John A.
Snowden, Russell J.
Speekman, John
Spiteri, Joe M.
Stapleton, Roger
Stewart, Darryl C.
Stewart, Ken
Stone, Viv
Stosic, Bernd
Strachan, Bob
Suna, Peter J.
Sweeney, John G.
Symons, Col. J.

Tanner, Nigel S.
Taylor, Peter
Taylor, Ian
Taylor, Paul R.
Teggelove, John A.
Thompson, David
Thomson, Alex J.
Thomson, Graham

Thorley, Michael
Todd, John I.
Travers, Trevor C.
Tully, Gus
Turnbull, Mike
Turner, Barry
Tymoc, Peter

Uil, Tom
Upwood, Frank H.

van Dalfsen, Jan
van Pelt, David

Wadley, Ken
Wallace, Wayne
Waller, Roger F.
Walsh, Wayne
Walsh, Ken
Ware, Les
Weedon, Barry
Weedon, John
Wedgwood, Peter F.
Wellman, Brian
Wells, Jim T.
Werder, Keith F.
Whalan, Sid C.
White, Barry
Wilbers, Rod W.
Wilkinson, Hugh
Winkel, Dan
Winsley, Geoff R.
Wishart, John
Wittwer, Randell L.
Wood, Ron
Worthington, John

Yates, Ross
Young, Barry W.
Young, Gary

2. Responses to 2015 survey of ex-Chalkies – Profile

No. of ex-Chalkies on database at time of survey: 180 (Mailout courtesy Terry Edwinsmith)
No. of responses: 73 = 40%

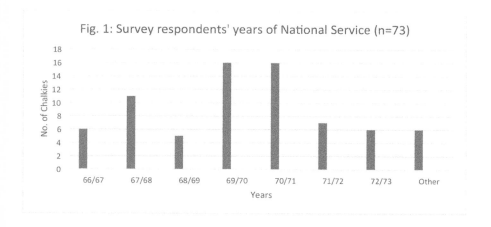

Fig. 1: Survey respondents' years of National Service (n=73)

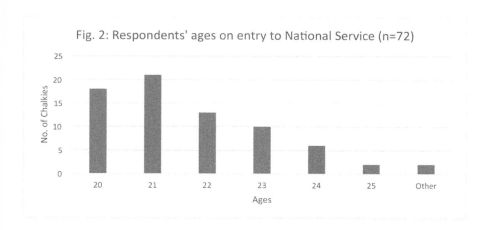

Fig. 2: Respondents' ages on entry to National Service (n=72)

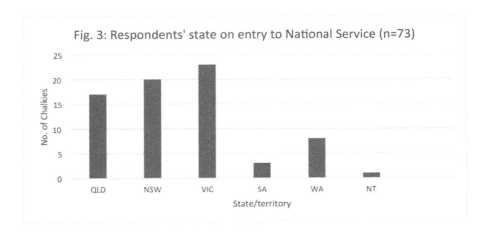

Fig. 3: Respondents' state on entry to National Service (n=73)

Fig. 4: Respondents' recruit training location (n=72)

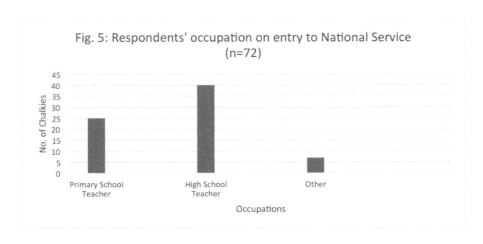

Fig. 5: Respondents' occupation on entry to National Service (n=72)

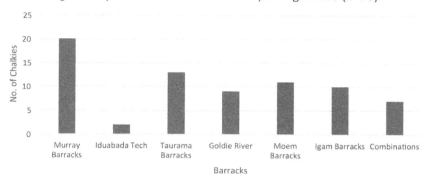

Fig. 6: Respondents' National Service postings TPNG (n=70)

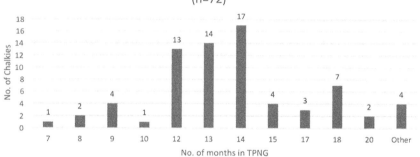

Fig. 7: No. months National Service respondents spent in TPNG (n=72)

Bibliography

Armstrong, D.J. (1972). 'An examination of the effects of ethnic contact upon the attitudes of some Australians in Papua New Guinea'. Unpublished MA thesis, University of Queensland.

Bean, C.E.W. (1942). *Official history of Australia in the war of 1914–18*, vol. 6. Sydney: Angus and Robertson.

Dapin, M. (2014). *The Nashos war*. Melbourne: Viking.

Dapin, M. 'The Graduates', *Good Weekend, Sydney Morning Herald*, 15 February 2014, 26–29.

Doran, S. (Ed.). (2006). *Australia and Papua New Guinea 1966–1969*, Canberra: Department of Foreign Affairs and Trade.

Dymock, D. (1995). *A sweet use of adversity: The Australian Army Education Service in World War II and its impact on Australian adult education*. Armidale: UNE Press/Canberra: AAAE.

Dymock, D. (1997). '"Non Military Enjoyment": Adult Education for Australian Troops abroad in World War One', *Studies in the Education of Adults*, 29 (1), 11–24.

Dyson, M. (2005). 'Australian teacher education: Although reviewed to the eyeball is there evidence of significant change and where to now?' *Australian Journal of Teacher Education*, 30 (1), 37–54.

Forward, R. (1968). 'Conscription 1964–1968', in R. Forward and B. Reece (Eds.), *Conscription in Australia*. Brisbane: University of Queensland Press.

Forward R. & Reece, B. (Eds.), *Conscription in Australia*, University of Queensland Press.

Gould, E.C. (1970). 'Adult education in the Australian Army', in D. Whitelock (Ed.), *Adult education in Australia*. Sydney: Pergamon Press.

Granter, N.E.W. (1970). *Yesterday and today*, Port Moresby: South Pacific Post.

Griffin J., Nelson, H. & Firth, S. (1979). *Papua New Guinea: A political history*. Richmond, Victoria: Heinemann.

Ham, P. (2008). *Vietnam: The Australian war*. Sydney: Harper Collins.

Hasluck, P. (1976). *A time for building: Australian administration in Papua and New Guinea, 1951–1963*. Melbourne University Press.

Hastings, P. (Ed.). (1971). *Papua New Guinea: Prospero's other island*. Sydney: Angus & Robertson.

Hope, A.D. (1977). *Collected poems 1930–1970*. Sydney: Angus & Robertson.

Langdon, R. (1971). 'A short history', in P Hastings (Ed.), *Papua New Guinea: Prospero's other island*, Sydney: Angus & Robertson.

Langford, S. (1997). 'The national service scheme, 1964–72', Appendix in P. Edwards, *A nation at war: Australian politics, society and diplomacy during the Vietnam War. 1965–1975*. The official history of Australia's involvement in Southeast Asian conflicts 1948–1975, vol. vi. Sydney: Allen & Unwin.

Lipscomb, A., Murray, J. & McKinnon, R. (1998). *Papua New Guinea* (6th ed.). Lonely Planet.

Lloyd, S., Jeffrey, M. & Hearn, J. (Eds.). (2001). *Taim bilong misis bilong armi: memories of wives of Australian servicemen in Papua New Guinea 1951–1975*. Canberra: Pandanus Books, Research School of Pacific and Asian Studies, Australian National University.

May, R. & Haley, N. (2014). The military in Papua New Guinea: A 'culture of instability' but no coup. *Security Challenges*, 10, (2), 53–70.

Nelson, H. (2008). 'Lives told: Australians in Papua and New Guinea', Brij. V. Lal and Vicki Luker (Eds.), *Telling Pacific lives: Prisms of process*, Chapter 18, Canberra: ANU Press.

Nelson, H. (1982). *Taim bilong masta: the Australian involvement with Papua New Guinea*. Sydney: Australian Broadcasting Commission.

O'Neill, R.J. (1971). *The Army in Papua-New Guinea*, Canberra: Australian National University Press.

Ogston, I. (2003). *Chalkies: Conscript teachers in Papua New Guinea 1970–71*. Brisbane: Self-published.

Ogston, I. (2004). *Armi wantoks: Conscript teachers in Papua New Guinea 1966–1973*. Brisbane: Self-published.

Phillips, K. (2013), 'Rear Vision', Radio National, 2 July 2013, 9.30 am, www.abc.net.au/radionational/programs/rearvision/4792034.

Sinclair, J. (1990). *To find a path: The life and times of the Pacific Islands Regiment*, vol. 1 – Yesterday's Heroes 1885 to 1950. Brisbane: Boolarong Publications.

Sinclair, J. (1990). *To find a path: The life and times of the Pacific Islands Regiment*, vol. 2 – Keeping the peace 1950 to 1975. Bathurst: Crawford House Press.

Sugiyama, M. (2002). 'The world conception of Japanese social science', Tani E. Barlow (Ed.), *New Asian Marxisms*, Duke University Press, 2002.

Twomey, C. (2011). '"Nasho": How a nation responded', *Your memento*, issue 1, Canberra: National Archives of Australia.

Tyquin, M. (n.d.). *The contribution of the Australian Army and the Pacific Islands Regiment to nation building in Papua New Guinea*, Pacific Islands Regiment, www.army.gov.au/Our-history/Primary-Materials/Unit-Histories-and-Formations/Pacific-Islands-Regiment.

Ville, S. & Siminski, P. (2011). *A fair and equitable method of recruitment? Conscription by ballot into the Australian Army during the Vietnam War*. Department of Economics, University of Wollongong, Working Paper 05–11. http://ro.uow.edu.au/commwkpapers/233.

Whitelock, D. (Ed.) (1971). *Adult education in Australia*. Sydney: Pergamon Press,

Whitlam, E.G. (1985). *The Whitlam Government 1972–1975*, Melbourne: Viking.

Wolfers, E.P. (1971). 'Political development', in P Hastings (Ed.), *Papua New Guinea: Prospero's other island*. Sydney: Angus & Robertson.

Woolford, D. (1976). *Papua New Guinea: Initiation and independence*. Brisbane: University of Queensland Press.

Notes

Throughout the book, quotes taken from the 73 Chalkies' responses to the online survey are attributed in the text (unless otherwise requested), but not cited in the Notes.

Chapter 1

1 Quoted in 'No alternative to call-up, says Minister', *Canberra Times*, 17 November 1964, p. 10.

2 Troy, 2000, p. 718, cited in ABS, 4102.0 – Australian Social Trends, www.abs. gov.au/ausstats/abs@.nsf/2f762f95845417aeca25706c00834efa/e0a8b4f57a46da-56ca2570ec007853c9!OpenDocument p. 5.

3 Quoted in 'It's simply a matter of balance', *Canberra Times*, 17 November 1964, p. 13.

4 K.S. Inglis, 'The great conscription row', *Canberra Times*, 21 November 1964, p. 2.

5 Ibid.

6 Quoted in 'How long dare we wait for recruits?', *Canberra Times*, 22 August 1964, p. 2.

7 'Old battles', *Canberra Times*, 24 November 1964, p. 1.

8 Quoted in 'Minister defends call-up', *Canberra Times*, 28 November 1964, p. 4.

9 Quoted in 'No alternative to call-up, says Minister', *Canberra Times*, 17 November 1964, p. 10.

10 'Conscripts must not serve abroad – Calwell', *Canberra Times*, 13 November 1964, p. 1.

11 'Australia's defence review still leaves some gaps', *Canberra Times*, 13 November 1964, p. 2.

12 'Will not disrupt industry', *Canberra Times*, 17 November 1964, p. 15.

13 *Sydney Morning Herald*, 12 November 1964, p. 9.

14 'Conscripts must not serve abroad – Calwell', op. cit.

Chapter 2

15 C. Twomey, '"Nasho": How a nation responded,' *Your memento*, Issue 1, January 2011, National Archives of Australia.

16 Quoted in R. Forward, 'Conscription 1964–1968' in R. Forward and B. Reece (Eds.), *Conscription in Australia*, University of Queensland Press, 1968, p. 135.

17 'The birthday ballot – National Service', Australia and the Vietnam War, Department of Veterans' Affairs, http://vietnam-war.commemoration.gov.au/conscription/birthday-ballot.php

18 M. Dapin, *The Nashos' war*, Viking, 2014, p. 57.

19 R. Boddington, 'Memories of a Chalkie', PNG Nashos website, http://www.nashospng.com/memories-of-a-chalkie

20 Simon Ville & Peter Siminski, 'A Fair and Equitable Method of Recruitment? Conscription by ballot into the Australian Army during the Vietnam War', Department of Economics, University of Wollongong, Working Paper 05–11, 2011, p. 3. http://ro.uow.edu.au/commwkpapers

21 M. Dapin, *The Nashos' war*, Viking, 2014, p. 53.

22 Ville & Siminski, loc. cit.

23 Dapin, loc. cit.

Chapter 3

24 Ronald Ryan, found guilty of murdering a prison officer, was the last person to be legally executed in Australia.

25 I recall there was a female officer in Administration, but I don't recall seeing one in any other role at Singleton.

26 Boddington, loc. cit.

27 A.D. Hope, 'Australia', *Collected poems 1930–1970*.

28 Quoted in R. Forward, 'Conscription 1964–1968', in R. Forward and B. Reece (Eds.), *Conscription in Australia*, University of Queensland Press, 1968, p. 123.

29 I. Ogston, 'Singleton Summer 1970', PNG Nashos website, www.nashospng.com/singleton-summer-1970

30 Quoted in Forward, loc. cit.

31 Quoted in Forward, Ibid.

32 Quoted in Dapin, op. cit., p. 186.

33 Ogston, loc. cit.

Chapter 4

34 S. Black, 'Homage to the men who helped turn the tide', *Daily Telegraph*, 22 October, 2012, online; http://www.theaustralian.com.au/news/homage-to-the-men-who-helped-turn-the-tide/story-e6frg6n6-1226500264685

35 R. Langdon, 'A short history', in P Hastings (Ed.), *Papua New Guinea: Prospero's other island*, Sydney: Angus & Robertson, 1971, p. 49.

36 H. Nelson, 'Lives told: Australians in Papua and New Guinea', Telling Pacific lives: Prisms of process, Brij V. Lal and Vicki Luker (Eds.), Chapter 18, 2008, ANU Press.

37 J. Sinclair, *To find a path*, vol. I, Brisbane: Boolarong Press, 1990, p. 284.

38 Ibid.

39 Langdon, op. cit., p. 55.

40 'Australia in New Guinea to stay: PM', *Sydney Morning Herald*, 25 April 1957, p. 1.

41 Sinclair, op. cit. p. 45.

42 'Menzies changes mind on New Guinea', *Sydney Morning Herald*, 26 June 1960, p. 34.

43 P. Hasluck, *A time for building*, MUP, 1976, p. 398.

44 Sinclair, op. cit., p. 95.

45 Hasluck, op. cit., p. 369.

46 'Report to Parliament on New Guinea', *Sydney Morning Herald*, 22 August 1962, p. 6.

47 Quoted in Sinclair, op. cit., p. 96.

48 Quoted in 'The border situation, May–June 1969: Government reaction and public opinion', in Doran S. (ed.), *Australia and Papua New Guinea 1966–1969*, 2006, Department of Foreign Affairs and Trade, Canberra, p. 780.

49 Quoted in Sinclair, op. cit., p. 107.

Chapter 5

50 C.E.W. Bean, *Official history of Australia in the war of 1914–18*, vol. 6, Sydney: Angus and Robertson, 1942, p. 1062.

51 'War History of the Australian Army Education Service, 1939–1945', AWM 54, item 492/4/34, p. 2.

52 'Tuition for soldiers', *Sydney Morning Herald*, 2 January 1941, p. 9.

53 W.C. Groves, 'Report on Army Education – 8MD', 27 October, 1941, AWM 54, item 52/2/3.

54 *RAAEC Newsletter*, vol. 8, 1 December 1960, p. 13.

55 'Front line reports', *Army Education Service Newsletter*, December, 1943, p. 6.

56 Quoted in Sinclair, op. cit., p. 53.

57 Quoted in Sinclair, op. cit., pp. 53–4.

58 *AAEC Newsletter*, 6 (2), 1958, p. 6.

59 *AAEC Newsletter*, 6 (4), 1958, p. 11.

60 Interview H. Dachs with S. Crane, 25 June 2005, Transcript, p. 16, RAAEC Archives, Box 46, Item 6177-1980.

61 *South Pacific Post*, Port Moresby, 9 March 1962.

62 'Annual Report 1961 – Papua and New Guinea', *RAAEC Newsletter*, 9 (2), 1962, p. 9.

63 'Report on Education in the Australian Army', Department of the Army, 10 September 1963, p. 44.

64 P. Hasluck, 'The Present Policies and Objectives', address at the Summer School of the Council of Adult Education, *The Future in Papua and New Guinea*, Melbourne, 6–10 January 1964, p. 10.

65 E.P. Wolfers, 'Political development', in P Hastings (ed), *Papua New Guinea: Prospero's other island*, 1971, p. 149.

66 Interview H. Dachs with S. Crane, op. cit. p. 8.

67 *RAAEC Newsletter*, 11 (6), 1966, p. 1.

68 G. Kearney, 'Address to Queensland Chalkies', Nashos (online), www.nashospng.com/address-to-queensland-chalkies-by-professor-george-kearney-18102008

69 M. Ashton, 'Foreword', in I Ogston (2004) *Armi wantoks: Conscript teachers in Papua New Guinea 1966–1973*, p. lvi, self-published.

70 *RAAEC Newsletter*, 11 (7), 1966, p. 35.

71 E.C. Gould, 'Adult education in the Australian Army', in D. Whitelock (ed.), *Adult education in Australia*, 1970, Sydney: Pergamon Press, p. 205.

72 Quoted in 'Military thinking reaches its turning point', *The Age*, 11 December 1969, p. 5.

73 Ibid.

74 'Military thinking reaches its turning point', *The Age*, 11 February 1969, p. 5.

Chapter 6

75 W.J. Lucas, 'Two years', *RAAEC Newsletter*, 11 (9), 1967, p. 7.

76 Ibid, p. 8.

77 Boddington, loc. cit.

Chapter 7

78 Nelson, loc. cit.

79 J.V.S. Freeman, 'Brief for NS Educ Instrs posted to PNG Cmd', 21 August 1971, p. 1, www.nashospng.com/instructions-to-all-new-raaec-instructors, courtesy of John Hain.

80 D. Woolford, *Papua New Guinea: Initiation and independence*, University of Queensland Pres, 1976, p. 4.

81 'Latin America since the mid-20th century', *Encyclopaedia Britannica*, www.britannica.com/place/Latin-America/Latin-America-since-the-mid-20th-century

82 M Sugiyama 'The World Conception of Japanese Social Science', Tani E. Barlow (ed.), *New Asian Marxisms*, Duke University Press, 2002, p. 225.

83 Quoted in 'The United Nations resolution on PNG, 1966', in Doran S. (ed.), op. cit., p. 257.

84 'The United Nations resolution on PNG, 1966', in Doran S. (ed.), op. cit., p. 256.

85 Ibid.

86 'The Army's task in the Territory of Papua and New Guinea as seen by Commander PNG Command as at 11 July 67', The Chief of the General Staff's Briefing at AHQ Canberra, 18 July 1967, NAA: A6846, Papua New Guinea Command: The Army's task in the Territory of Papua and New Guinea.

87 Tom Ellis was also at times District Commissioner for Western Highlands, Head of the Department of District Administration, and a member of the PNG House of Assembly.

88 Kearney, loc. cit.

89 Quoted in 'The Territory of Papua New Guinea', *Australian Journal of Politics & History*, 1967, 13 (2), p. 276.

90 Memorandum, Hay to Department of Territories, 'Select Committee on Constitutional Development', 1 April, 1967, in Doran S. (ed.), op. cit., p. 306.

91 'The United Nations visiting mission, 1968', in Doran op. cit., p. 446.

92 Ibid., p. 447.

93 Quoted in 'The United Nations visiting mission, 1968', in Doran op. cit., p. 447.

94 D. Woolford, op. cit., pp. 26–7.

95 'Pacific Islands regiment: ongoing debate over its size and role', in Doran op. cit., p. 521.

96 'Pacific Islands regiment: ongoing debate over its size and role', in Doran op. cit., p. 522.

97 Quoted in 'Territories: changes to the department and portfolio', in Doran, op. cit., p. 451.

98 Quoted in C.E. McDonald, 'Transition arrangements for Papua and New Guinea', in Doran, op. cit., p. 693.

99 C.E. McDonald, 'Transition arrangements for Papua and New Guinea', in Doran, op. cit., p. 693.

100 C.E. McDonald, 'Transition arrangements for Papua and New Guinea', in Doran, op. cit., p. 709.

101 'Military thinking reaches its turning point', *The Age*, 11 February 1969, p. 5.

102 'Draft submission', Barnes to Cabinet', in Doran, op. cit. p. 765.

103 The White Australia Policy was the common name for the Immigration Restriction Act (1901) which sought to keep people of non-European descent from settling in Australia, particularly through an infamous 'Dictation Test' applied unilaterally and discriminately by government immigration officers. Although the Dictation Test was abolished in 1958, signalling the end of the White Australia Policy, the legacy of the Act took some time to dissipate, and the Australian Labor Party did not expunge the policy from its platform until 1965. As an apparent sign of Australians' more liberal attitude, in a 1967 Referendum an overwhelming majority voted for full constitutional rights for Aborigines.

104 Woolford, op. cit., p. 70.

105 Ibid, p. 75.

106 Ibid., p. 81.

107 'ADAE and HQ PNG Comd Educ Sect', *RAAEC Newsletter*, 15 (3), November 1971, p. 41.

108 'Murray Barracks', *RAAEC Newsletter*, 15 (3), November 1971, p. 42.

109 'Lae Area', *RAAEC Newsletter*, 15 (3), November 1971, p. 42.

110 'PNG Training Depot Educ Sect', *RAAEC Newsletter*, 15 (3), November 1971, p. 42.

111 Sgts R.H. Bassett, G.E. Leader, & W.R. Wallace, 'Some thoughts on teaching the PI soldier', *RAAEC Newsletter*, 15 (2), August 1971, p. 16.

112 The practice of having 'haus-bois' (and 'meris') to do domestic work was long-established in TPNG, although some regarded it as another example of the colonial mentality.

113 Sgts R. Strachan & J. McPhee, 'An education for an education sergeant in PNG' OR 'Some first impressions', *RAAEC Newsletter*, 15 (3), November 1971, pp. 23–4.

114 '1 PIR', RAAEC Newsletter, 15 (3) November 1971, p. 59.

115 E.P. Wolfers, op. cit., p. 166.

Chapter 8

116 'Military thinking reaches its turning point', *The Age*, 11 February 1969, p. 5.

117 Freeman, op. cit., p. 2.

118 Bassett, Leader, & Wallace, loc. cit.

119 'Papua and New Guinea', *RAAEC Newsletter*, 11 (9), October 1967, p. 36.

120 'That other Army', *RAAEC Newsletter*, 11 (9), October 1967, p. 35.

121 The slightly clunky epidiascope, or opaque projector, would display any object placed under its lens, including pages of books, as distinct from an overhead projector, which would display on a screen in enlarged form only text and line drawings that had first been transferred to a square of transparent plastic.

122 'Educ Sect, PNG Trg Dep', *RAAEC Newsletter*, 15 (2), August 1971, p. 42.

123 A. Sandery, 'Pacific Islanders join the Army and go to school', *RAAEC Newsletter*, 11(7), p. 18.

124 Strachan & McPhee, op. cit., p. 25.

125 R.F. Scott, 'Agriculture in 2 PIR', *RAAEC Newsletter*, 15 (2), August 1971, p. 27.

126 '2 PIR', *RAAEC Newsletter*, 15 (1), April 1971, p. 38.

127 Vanimo Surf Lodge, www.theperfectwave.com.au/surf-trips/remote-pacific/papua-new-guinea/vanimo-surf-lodge-png

Chapter 9

128 L. Horton, 'Life as an Army wife in Papua New Guinea 1970-71', PNG Nashos website, www.nashospng.com/life-as-an-army-wife-in-papua-new-guinea-in-1970-71

129 Lipscomb, A. et al. (1998). *Papua New Guinea* (6th ed.). Lonely Planet. p. 189.

130 P.J. Semmens, 'Exercise Luk Luk Nabaut', *RAAEC Newsletter*, 17(1), 1973, p. 43.

Chapter 10

131 M. Tyquin, 'The contribution of the Australian Army and the Pacific Islands Regiment to nation building in Papua New Guinea', n.d., Pacific Islands Regiment, www.army.gov.au/Our-history/Primary-Materials/Unit-Histories-and-Formations/Pacific-Islands-Regiment

132 *Canberra Times*, 23 January 1969, quoted in R.J. May, 'Government and the military in Papua New Guinea', in R.J. May & V Selochan (eds.) *The military and democracy in Asia and the Pacific*, ANU ePress, 2004, Chapter 10, p. 2.

133 Bob Wurth, 'Cameron tapes: Governor General Paul Hasluck blocked Prime Minister John Gorton from sending in the troops in Rabaul in 1970', Books and essays by Bob Wurth on the Asia/Pacific Region, http://www.bobwurth.com/essay5

134 Email, H. Howard to S. Beveridge, 'Re: Rabaul, the Mautangans and 1 PIR', 27 November, 2015.

135 'Papua/New Guinea – possible domestic violence at Rabaul', Minute by Defence Committee, Canberra, 2 September 1969, in Doran, op. cit. p. 903.

136 D. Winkel, 'Dan's TPNG adventure tours', PNG Nashos website, www.nashospng.com/dans-tpng-adventure-tours

137 Ibid.

Chapter 11
138 Freeman, op. cit., p. 2.

139 Horton, loc. cit.

140 Ibid.

Chapter 12
141 Woolford, op. cit. p. 69.

142 *The Canberra Times*, Wednesday 6 December 1972, p. 14.

143 'PNG Defence Force Education Section', *RAAEC Newsletter*, 17(2), 1973, p. 41.

144 M. Forbes, 'The last PNG National Chalkie sergeant?' PNG Nashos website, http://www.nashospng.com/the-last-png-national-service-chalkie-sergeant/

145 'PNG Defence Force Education Section', *RAAEC Newsletter*, 17(2), 1973, p. 41.

146 Australian War Memorial, 'Minister for Defence visits Papua New Guinea', www.awm.gov.au/collection/F04742/

147 'Editorial', *RAAEC Newsletter*, 1973, 17 (2), pp. 1–2.

148 'Papua New Guinea', *RAAEC Newsletter*, 18 (1), 1974, pp. 17–18.

149 Woolford, op. cit., p. 232.

150 '1 PIR', *RAAEC Newsletter*, 14 (2), August 1970, p. 50.

151 Boddington, loc. cit.

152 Ogston, *Armi wantoks: Conscript teachers in Papua New Guinea 1966–1973*, op. cit. p. 22.

Chapter 13
153 'Murray Barracks', *RAAEC Newsletter*, 15 (3), November 1971, p. 42.

154 Dennis J Armstrong, 'An examination of the effects of ethnic contact upon the attitudes of some Australians in Papua New Guinea'. Unpublished MA thesis, University of Queensland, 1972.

Chapter 14
155 'Papua and New Guinea', *RAAEC Newsletter*, 9 (1), March 1962, p. 36.

156 'Report on Education in the Australian Army', Department of the Army, 10 September 1963, p. 43.

157 HQ PNG Command, 'The Army's task in the Territory of Papua and New Guinea as seen by Commander PNG Command as at 11 July 67', The Chief of the General Staff's Briefing at AHQ Canberra, 18 July 1967, NAA: A6846.

158 Freeman, op. cit., p. 4.

159 Ogston, *Armi wantoks: Conscript teachers in Papua New Guinea 1966–1973*, op. cit. p. 53.

160 R. Jones, 'Letter from Lt. Col. Roger Jones (ret.) for Reunion 2012', PNG Nashos website, www.nashospng.com/letter-from-roger-jones-regarding-re-union-2012

161 P. Lynch, 1969, Extract from: 'Newspaper article from the 'Townsville Herald' August 1969', PNG Nashos website, www.nashospng.com/newspaper-article-from-the-townsville-herald-august-1969.

162 R.J. O'Neill, *The Army in Papua-New Guinea*, Canberra: Australian National University Press, 1971, p. 15.

163 Ibid., p. 17.

164 Quoted in Sinclair op. cit., pp. 53–4.

165 'PNG', *RAAEC Newsletter*, 13 (3), December 1969, p. 40.

166 *RAAEC Newsletter*, vol. 8, 1 December 1960, p. 13.

167 R. May & N. Haley, 'The military in Papua New Guinea: A "culture of instability" but no coup.' *Security Challenge*s, 2014, 10, vol. 2, p. 68.

168 Ibid.

169 M. Dapin, 'The Graduates', *Good Weekend, Sydney Morning Herald*, 15 February 2014, p. 29.

170 Errol J. Bailey, 23, of Kurri Kurri, NSW, was a teacher when he was called up in February 1967. He died at 24 US Evacuation Hospital, Long Binh, of wounds received in Bien Hoa Province on 13 May 1968; David Patterson, 25, of Adelaide SA, a teacher, was called up on 2 February 1967 and graduated as a 2nd Lieutenant from the Officer Training Unit at Scheyville. On completion of his National Service he re-enlisted in February 1969 and volunteered for Vietnam with 3RAR where he was shot dead during an enemy contact on 20 March 1971 in Phuoc Tuy. Source: National Service Honour Roll, www.nashoaustralia.org.au/honour%20roll.htm

171 D. ToKunai, 'Australia's imperialist nostalgia', *The Garamut*, https://garamut.wordpress.com/2008/09/11/australias-imperialist-nostalgia-papua-new-guinea/

Index

112, 157, 167
Hill, Steven 14, 32, 87, 106, 112–13, 117, 124, 132, 161, 165
Ho Chi Minh 6
Hodder, Ian 62, 117, 122, 131–2
Holt, Harold 58, 72, 80, 84
Hope, A.D. 23, 26
Horton, Kev 93, 137
Horton, Lindy 111, 137
House of Assembly 48, 85, 87, 96, 104–5, 149
Howard, Hori 126–8
Hughes, Billy 5
Humphrey, John 65, 69, 91, 109, 132, 144, 156, 170
Humphrey, Marg 144–5
Hunter, Ian Murray 49, 54, 57–9, 70, 73–6, 86–7, 89, 99, 125, 134, 175–6
Hunter, Norm 32, 82, 121, 155, 163
Hurrell, Grahame 158

Iduabada Technical College 73, 100, 105, 122, 143, 164
Igam Barracks 48–9, 99, 104, 112–13, 123, 132–3, 163–4, 166
Indonesia/n 3, 6, 13, 46–8, 74, 108, 117
Infantry Corps 63, 65, 68–9, 98, 140, 161, 177
Inglis, Ron 14, 29, 32, 35, 38, 49, 92–3, 106, 112, 123, 156, 165
Isenberg, Norm 121
Ison, Warren 19, 33, 149, 156
Ivey, Greg 32, 88, 106, 108, 123, 165, 169
Iwanowitsch, Wolf 104, 166

Japan, Japanese 5, 9, 37, 40–3, 51–2, 81, 113, 130
Jenkin, Russell 26, 35–6, 68, 80, 83, 125, 169, 173
Jenkins, Denis 16, 121, 164

John, W.H. 51, 178–9
Johnson, Graeme 177
Johnstone, Tony 134
Joint Services College (JSC), *see* Military Cadet School
Jones, J.H. 43
Jones, Roger 176

Kapooka (1RTB) 24, 27, 29–30, 32–3, 35, 37–8, 49, 60, 64, 69, 77, 91–2
Kearney, George 57, 75–6
Keating, Paul 40, 42
Keegan, Gerry 121
Kokoda Track 40, 42, 66, 82, 103, 130, 143, 165
Korean War 5

Lae 42, 48–9, 65, 73, 93, 95, 99–100, 104–5, 113, 115, 120–1, 123, 135, 141, 144, 149–50, 165–6
Lange, Colonel (Ron) 138
Larkin, G.F. 54
Larsen, Bill 66, 134, 139–40, 153, 173
Larsen, Jill 139–40, 145
Leader, Graham 8, 29–30, 93, 100, 140–1, 164, 183
Leader, Merlyn 140–1
League of Nations 41
Leahy, Greg 177
Lee, Michael 35, 158
Legislative Council 44, 46
Leunig, Michael 8
Lindsay, Graham 18, 30, 64, 77–8, 110, 156, 166
Lovell, Ian 13, 81, 158, 170, 176
Lucas, W.J. 64
Lynch, Phillip 177

McIlwraith, Thomas 40
Mackay, Ian 37, 126, 128, 158
McKay, J.D. 123

Lightning Source UK Ltd.
Milton Keynes UK
UKHW011950060319
338617UK00001B/88/P